Rethinking Vietnam

Can Vietnam's history and ideology explain its position internationally? To what extent is Vietnam engaged in a process of reform? To what extent is Vietnam's social structure changing?

Rethinking Vietnam is a uniquely comprehensive overview of a fascinating and rapidly changing country, dealing with the politics, economics, society and foreign policy of Vietnam from the *doi moi* reforms of market socialism in 1986 to the present day. Drawing on fieldwork and analysis by an international team of specialists, this book covers all apsects of contemporary Vietnam including recent history, the political economy, the reform process, education, health, labour market, foreign direct investment and foreign policy. The contributors show how the blurring of old and new pressures and traditions within Vietnam requires a more complex analysis of the country than might initially be assumed.

Broad in sweep and rich in empirical detail, *Rethinking Vietnam* will engage students and scholars of Southeast Asia who are interested in understanding all levels of society within this complex and intriguing country.

Duncan McCargo is Professor of Southeast Asian Politics at the University of Leeds.

Rethinking Southeast Asia
Edited by Duncan McCargo
University of Leeds, UK

Southeast Asia is a dynamic and rapidly changing region which continues to defy prediction and challenge formulaic understandings. This series will publish cutting-edge work on the region, providing a venue for books that are readable, topical, interdisciplinary and critical on conventional views. It aims to communicate the energy, contestations and ambiguities that make Southeast Asia both consistently fascinating and sometimes potentially disturbing.

This series comprises two strands:

Rethinking Southeast Asia aims to address the needs of students and teachers, and the titles will be published in both hardback and paperback.

Rethinking Vietnam
Duncan McCargo

RoutledgeCurzon Research on Southeast Asia is a forum for innovative new research intended for a specialist readership, and the titles will be available in hardback only. Titles include:

1. **Politics and the Press in Thailand**
   Media machinations
   Duncan McCargo

2. **Democracy and National Identity in Thailand**
   Michael Kelly Connors

3. **The Politics of NGOs in Indonesia**
   Developing democracy and managing a movement
   Bob S. Hadiwinata

4. **Military and Democracy in Indonesia**
   Jun Honna

5. **Changing Political Economy of Vietnam**
   The case of Ho Chi Minh City
   Martin Gainsborough

6. **Living at the Edge of Thai Society**
   The Karen in the highlands of Northern Thailand
   Claudio O. Delang

Rethinking Vietnam

Edited by Duncan McCargo

RoutledgeCurzon
Taylor & Francis Group

LONDON AND NEW YORK

First published 2004
by RoutledgeCurzon
11 New Fetter Lane, London EC4P 4EE

Simultaneously published in the USA and Canada
by RoutledgeCurzon
29 West 35th Street, New York, NY 10001

RoutledgeCurzon is an imprint of the Taylor & Francis Group

Typeset in Baskerville by
HWA Text and Data Management, Tunbridge Wells
Printed and bound in Great Britain by
The Cromwell Press, Trowbridge, Wiltshire

British Library Cataloguing in Publication Data
A catalogue record for this book is available from the British Library

Library of Congress Cataloging in Publication Data
Rethinking Vietnam / edited by Duncan McCargo.
     p.   cm.
Includes bibliographical references and index.
  1. Vietnam. I. McCargo, Duncan.
   DS556.3.R48 2004
   959.704′4–dc22   2003021152

ISBN 0–415–31621–9 (hbk)
ISBN 0–415–33585–X (pbk)

Contents

Illustrations

Figures

Tables

Contributors

Marie-Eve Blanc is a postdoctoral fellow in the Département d´Histoire and Centre d´Études de l´Asie de l´Est (CETASE), Université de Montréal. She gained her PhD from the Université de Provence with a thesis on associative practices in Vietnam. Email marie-eve.blanc@umontreal.ca.

Gerard Clarke is a senior lecturer in the Centre for Development Studies, University of Wales, Swansea. Author of *The Politics of NGOs in South-East Asia: Participation and Protest in the Philippines* (Routledge 1998), he has also worked extensively as a development consultant in the region. Email g.clarke@swansea.ac.uk.

Chris Dixon is professor of development studies at London Metropolitan University. He has researched and published widely on social, economic and political issues in Vietnam and Southeast Asia. Email cdixon@lgu.ac.uk.

Doan Hue Dung gained her PhD from the University of Nottingham in 2000, with a thesis entitled 'Foreign-trained academics and the development of Vietnamese higher education'. She is currently dean of the Faculty of Foreign Languages and deputy director of the Center for Foreign Studies, Nong Lam University, Ho Chi Minh City. Email doanhuedung@hcm.vnn.vn.

Jörn Dosch is a senior lecturer in the Department of East Asian Studies, University of Leeds. His main research interests lie in the politics and international relations of Southeast Asia, and he is co-author of *New Global Politics of the Asia Pacific* (Routledge, forthcoming). Email j.dosch@leeds.ac.uk.

Nick Freeman is a freelance economic consultant based in Ho Chi Minh City. He is also an associate senior fellow at the Institute of Southeast Asian Studies, Singapore. Email njfreeman@fastmessaging.com.

Martin Gainsborough is a lecturer in Southeast Asian politics at the School of Oriental and African Studies, University of London. The author of *Changing Political Economy of Vietnam: A Case Study of Ho Chi Minh City* (Routledge 2003), he has considerable experience of Vietnam-related research and consultancy. Email mginuk@supanet.com.

Ari Kokko is a professor at the European Institute of Japanese Studies, Stockholm School of Economics. He has published widely on economic issues in the Asia-Pacific region, and has served as a consultant on numerous Vietnam-related projects. Email ari.kokko@hhs.se.

Jonathan London is currently completing his doctorate in sociology at the University of Wisconsin-Madison, entitled 'Social policy, inequality and the transformation of the socialist state: the fiscal sociology of education and health policy in Vietnam, 1986–2000'. Email london@ssc.wisc.edu.

Duncan McCargo is professor of Southeast Asian politics at the University of Leeds. His recent books include *Reforming Thai Politics* (edited, NIAS 2002) and *Media and Politics in Pacific Asia* (Routledge 2003). Email d.j.mccargo@leeds.ac.uk.

Curt Nestor is currently completing his PhD on Vietnamese FDI at the University of Goteburg, Sweden, where he is a lecturer in economic geography. Email curt.nestor@geography.gu.se.

Phuong An Nguyen recently completed her PhD at the University of Hull, with a thesis on social attitudes of young people in Vietnam. Email anphuong@hotmail.com.

Sophie Quinn-Judge's School of Oriental and African Studies PhD thesis has been published as *Ho Chi Minh: The Missing Years* (Hurst 2003). Email sophie_qj@yahoo.com.

Ta Minh Tuan is a researcher at the Centre of Euro-American Studies, Institute of International Relations, Hanoi. He recently completed a doctorate on Vietnamese foreign policy at the Polish Academy of Sciences in Warsaw. Email taminhtuan@yahoo.com.

Tran Thi Thu Trang is a doctoral student at the Institute of Social Studies, The Hague, where she is working on agricultural change in Vietnam. Email ttff@antenna.nl.

Claudia Zingerli recently completed a PhD in development studies at the University of East Anglia. She is currently a research fellow at the Swiss Federal Institute of Technology, Chair of Forest Policy and Forest Economics. Email zingerli@fowi.ethz.ch.

Preface and acknowledgements

This volume is closely linked with a panel, also entitled 'Rethinking Vietnam', which I convened at the European Southeast Asian Studies (EUROSEAS) conference held in London on 6–7 September 2001. Yet the resulting book is by no means a thinly disguised collection of conference papers: only four of the chapters now presented here substantially resemble papers given in London. The remaining chapters have been extensively revised, totally rewritten, combined with other papers to create co-authored book contributions, or commissioned from new authors to fill important gaps in the volume. I must thank all the panellists and contributors for their co-operation and forbearance during this highly interventionist editorial process.

Many edited books start life as a conference panel: but my EUROSEAS panel started life as an idea for an edited book. Dissatisfied with existing introductory books on recent developments in Vietnam, I sought to assemble a team of people who could create the sort of book that students, academics, journalists, analysts and investors would most like: a strategic overview of key questions and issues affecting Vietnam, informed by some of the very best first-hand research, but presented in an accessible way.

I am very grateful for everyone who helped make the original panel possible, especially conference organisers Anne Booth and Mike Hitchcock, ably supported by Pauline Khng; the British Academy Committee for Southeast Asian Studies, for generously funding the participation of Tran Thi Thu Trang; and the Ford Foundation, for generously funding the participation of Doan Hue Dung and Ngyuen Thi My. In the event, it proved impossible to include contributions from all conference participants in the resulting volume. I should like to thank the following for their invaluable participation in the panel, and for useful contributions to the lively discussions that informed the process of paper revision: Pietro Masina, Martha Morrow, Nguyen Do Anh Tuan, Nguyen Thi My and Irene Norlund. Our EUROSEAS panel was dedicated to the memory of the late Professor Ralph Smith of the School of Oriental and African Studies, whose presence was sadly missed.

I must also express my thanks to all those who have helped shape the present volume. Martin Gainsborough has been much more than simply a contributor, but also a constant source of advice, not to mention a provider of comments on various draft chapters. Ricardo Blaug and Ngoc Nguyen provided helpful input on particular chapters, while two anonymous readers offered extremely useful suggestions concerning the final structure of the book – virtually all of which I have adopted. Chris Dixon and Ari Kokko kindly provided substantial and important additional chapters at a late stage of the project, with amazing promptness. Chunyao Yi made a number of invaluable contributions to the final phase of manuscript preparation. My own involvement with Vietnam has been supported over the years by several past and present colleagues at the University of Leeds, notably Jackie Findlay, Laura Barjonas, John Macklin and Louise McCarthy.

Duncan McCargo
Leeds, August 2003

Abbreviations

ADB	Asian Development Bank
AFTA	ASEAN Free Trade Area
AIA	ASEAN Investment Area
AICO	ASEAN Industrial Co-operation
AIDS	acquired immune deficiency syndrome
AMM	ASEAN Ministerial Meeting
APEC	Asia Pacific Economic Co-operation Forum
ARF	ASEAN Regional Forum
ASEAN	Association of Southeast Asian Nations
ASEM	Asia–Europe Meeting
BoP	balance of payments
BTA	Bilateral Trade Agreement
CBOs	community-based organisations
CCP	Chinese Communist Party
CEPHAD	Centre of Public Health and Development
CHCs	commune health centres
CIEM	Central Institute for Economic Management
CPI	consumer price index
CPRGS	Comprehensive Poverty Reduction and Growth Strategy
CTBT	Comprehensive Test Ban Treaty
DfID	Department for International Development (UK)
DRV	Democratic Republic of Vietnam
EPI	Expanded Programme of Immunisation
ERF	Enterprise Restructuring Fund
ESAF	Enhanced Structural Adjustment Facility
EU	European Union
EUROSEAS	European Association for Southeast Asian Studies
FCP	French Communist Party
FDI	Foreign Direct Investment
f.o.b.	free on board
FRW	Fund for Redundant Workers
FY	financial year
GDP	gross domestic product

GMS	Greater Mekong Sub-Region
GNP	gross national product
HDI	human development index
HEPR	hunger eradication and poverty reduction
HIV	human immunodeficiency virus
ICP	Indochinese Communist Party
IMF	International Monetary Fund
IPNs	International Production Networks
IT	information technology
MARD	Ministry of Agriculture and Rural Development
MBA	Master of Business Administration
metro.	metropolitan
MoET	Ministry of Education and Training
MoH	Ministry of Health
MoLISA	Ministry of Labour, Invalids and Social Affairs
MPI	Ministry of Planning and Investment
NAC	National AIDS Committee
Natexco	Nam Dinh Textile Company
NATO	North Atlantic Treaty Organisation
NAVs	net asset values
NERC	National Enterprise Restructuring Committee
NGOs	non-government organisations
NICs	newly industrialised countries
NPLs	non-performing loans
NSCERD	National Steering Committee for Enterprise Reform and Development
ODA	overseas development aid
OECD	Organisation for Economic Co-operation and Development
OTC	over the counter
PCF	French Communist Party
PCL	People's Council
PCT	People's Committee
PFP	Policy Framework Paper
PIN	Public Information Notice
PLWHA	people living with HIV/AIDS
PRC	People's Republic of China
PRGF	poverty reduction and growth facility
SAC	structural adjustment credit
SBV	State Bank of Vietnam
SEANWFZ	Southeast Asian Nuclear Weapons-Free Zone
SMEs	small and medium-sized enterprises
SOEs	state-owned enterprises
SRV	Socialist Republic of Vietnam
STIs	sexually transmitted infections
UK	United Kingdom

UN	United Nations
UNCTAD	United Nations Conference on Trade and Development
UNDP	United Nations Development Programme
UNESCO	United Nations Educational, Scientific and Cultural Organisation
UNICEF	United Nations Children's Fund
US	United States (of America)
USA	United States of America
USSR	Union of Soviet Socialist Republics
VAT	value-added tax
VCCA	Vietnam Coffee and Cocoa Association
VCP	Vietnamese Communist Party
VET	*Vietnam Economic Times*
Vinacafé	Vietnam National Coffee Corporation
Vintex	Vietnam National Textile and Garment Corporation
VIR	*Vietnam Investment Review*
VND	Vietnam Dong
VNGO	Vietnamese non-governmental organisation
VNLSS	Viet Nam Living Standards Survey
VUSTA	Vietnamese Union of Scientists and Technicians Associations
VWP	Vietnam Workers Party
WHO	World Health Organisation

Vietnam country profile

Country name: *Conventional long form*: Socialist Republic of
                      Vietnam
                      Conventional short form: Vietnam
                      Local short form: Viet Nam
                      Abbreviation: SRV
                      Local long form: Cong Hoa Xa Hoi Chu
                      Nghia Viet Nam

Independence: 2 September 1945

Reunification: 2 July 1976

Capital: Hanoi 2,543,700 (metro. area), 1,396,500
                      (city proper)

Major cities: Ho Chi Minh City (Saigon),
                      5,894,100 (metro. area), 3,415,300
                      (city proper); Haiphong, 581,600;
                      Da Nang, 452,700; Hué 271,900;
                      Nha Trang, 70,100; Qui Nho'n, 199,700

Currency: Vietnam dong (VND)

Terrain: Low, flat delta in south and north; central
                      highlands; hilly, mountainous in far north
                      and northwest

Highest point: Ngoc Linh 3,143 m

Lowest point: South China Sea 0 m

Land boundaries: *Total*: 4,639 km *Border countries*: Cambodia
                      1,228 km, China 1,281 km, Laos 2,130 km

Total area: 329,560 sq km (slightly larger than New
                      Mexico)

Land use: *Arable land*: 17%
                      Permanent crops: 5%
                      Other: 78% (1998 est.)

Natural resources: Phosphates, coal, manganese, bauxite,
                      chromate, offshore oil and gas deposits,
                      forests, hydropower

Population: 81,098,416 (July 2002 est.)

Population growth rate: 1.43% p.a. (2002 est.)

Population density: 205 persons per sq km (1991)

Natural hazards: Occasional typhoons (May to January) with
                      extensive flooding, especially in the
                      Mekong River delta

Sources: CIA (2002) *The World Factbook 2002*, Washington, DC: CIA; *Atlapedia Countries*, Latimer Clarke Corporation, available online at http://www.atlapedia. com/online/countries/vietnam.htm; *Almanacs: Countries of the World*, available online at http://www.infoplease.com/ipa/A0108144.html.

1 Introduction

Duncan McCargo

As every Southeast Asianist knows, Vietnam is a country, not a war. Yet the legacy of ideological and military conflict that has shaped Vietnam has long impeded dispassionate discussion of Vietnamese society. Writers on Vietnam typically bring with them considerable intellectual baggage. Much work on Vietnam derives – to use a phrase coined by Herbert Phillips in another context – from a 'scholarship of admiration' (Phillips 1979: 449). Yet this widespread enthusiasm is a mixed blessing for critical analysis. Commentators and academics who admire the achievements of Vietnam, notably the remarkable achievement of successively defeating both the French and the Americans, have tended to write in broadly positive terms about the country's performance in a wide range of areas. In particular, Vietnam's record in the basic education and health sectors, combined with its relatively low socio-economic inequalities, has attracted considerable plaudits. Many of those plaudits have come from writers on the left, especially the European left, who saw in those statistical indicators further evidence that the nationalist struggle with the United States of America had been a just cause. For them, Vietnam was the socialist society that worked. For some American scholars, those same achievements vindicated their own previous opposition to United States (US) involvement in the Indochina conflict. For these writers, Vietnam's success would be determined by the degree to which the country could defend the socialist ideals underlying the revolutionary struggle.

The 1986 introduction of *doi moi*, a programme of economic reform and renovation, introduced a new form of admiration for Vietnam, especially when the early years of reform produced striking benefits in ameliorating the shortcomings of a centralised state structure. Vietnam acquired a new set of admirers: neo-liberals who saw the country as a laboratory for the introduction of a very different set of economic principles, and international investors who saw Vietnam as a country ripe for entrepreneurial activities, a sizeable domestic market, and an important regional player in the wider Indochinese and Southeast Asian economies. The mood of this period was captured in Thai prime minister Chatichai Choonavan's call for the battlefields to be turned into marketplaces. Implicit here was a quiet triumphalism on the part of conservative analysts, for whom Vietnam's adoption of free market principles was a belated vindication of the Indochina conflict: Vietnam might have dealt the United States a temporary military setback, but the forces of capitalism were now defeating Vietnamese communism on the basis of the inexorable logic of the market. The demise of the Berlin Wall and the collapse of Soviet bloc communism at the end of the 1980s served to reinforce this view, according to which the sooner Vietnam embraced Western market principles, the more successful the country would become. Linked to this argument was a wide range of policy changes urged upon Vietnam by international institutions such as the World Bank and the International Monetary Fund, including reducing the size of the state sector and deregulating large swathes of economic activity. Behind these pressures lay hopes that sooner or later economic liberalisation would be followed by political change, including a loosening of the Vietnamese Communist Party's (VCP's) hitherto firmly monopolistic grip on power. This was the heyday of the 'third wave' of democratisation: just as once the Americans had feared that the countries in Southeast Asia would fall to communism like a set of dominoes, now many in the West hoped that the region would similarly succumb to democracy (McCargo 2001: 145–6). For observers with this perspective, the measure of Vietnam's success would be the degree to which the country 'opened up', to embrace Western economic, social and political values.

Yet many scholars working on post-*doi moi* Vietnam continued to harbour considerable admiration for the tenacity and independence of the regime, preferring to believe that Vietnam might be able to strike the optimal balance between retaining a distinctive identity and political order, whilst making the requisite concessions to the demands of the global market place. For these scholars, Vietnam's success or failure will ultimately be determined by the degree to which Vietnam can convincingly perform a tricky balancing act, negotiating between a range of competing pressures and interests. Perhaps the majority of social science researchers now working on Vietnam – including many Vietnamese scholars themselves – fall somewhere within this camp, undertaking case-specific, sectoral and overview studies in the hope of elucidating analytically this complex negotiation process.

Broadly speaking, then, those working on contemporary Vietnam can be divided into three main groups: admirers of the revolution, still looking for socialism to work; advocates of capitalist change, confidently expecting socialism to fail; and critical sympathisers, looking for mechanisms by which Vietnam can negotiate a distinctive socio-economic and political order within a complex domestic and international environment. The aim of this volume is to 'rethink' Vietnam by moving beyond the scholarship of admiration, asking awkward questions about Vietnam's politics, economy, society and international relations – and not shirking from inconvenient or incomplete answers. Many of the contributors to this volume have recently completed doctoral theses on Vietnam; others are well-established academics with a longstanding interest in the country; some are Vietnamese, but most are not.

Rethinking Vietnamese politics

Chris Dixon's chapter is the real introduction to this book, raising issues and flagging up debates that are returned to throughout the volume. His central question concerns the nature of state-society relations in Vietnam: how far is the state dominant, and how far has society been able to secure any substantive autonomy? Dixon is convinced that there are no easy answers to these questions: simple alternative typologies, such as those suggested by Kerkvliet (2001b), actually mask much larger debates. Dixon argues that there is far more continuity between pre-reform and post-reform Vietnam than is generally assumed: Vietnam never was a monolithic one-party state, but always permitted considerable divergence of views and of regional practices, along with well-established mechanisms for consulting the masses. He sees the VCP as generally 'absorbing' rather than 'repressing' dissent. This longstanding tendency was reinforced by political changes after 1986, including strengthening the role of the National Assembly – membership of which was refreshed with a new influx of members – after 1992. The National Assembly flexed its muscles in 1998 by rejecting land reform measures proposed by the VCP. By 1994, clear factional divisions were evident in the VCP leadership, partly reflecting a greater climate of openness and popular anxieties about the reform process. Dixon cautions against a simple division into conservative and reformist cadres, arguing that positions and groupings are rarely fixed, and typically vary from one issue to another. The late 1980s saw a backlash against dissenting voices; yet this was followed by a further period of liberalisation, which saw the growth of political activity outside the direct control of the state. Even official publications were full of critical discussions about the failure of key policies and programmes. Despite persistent discrimination against the domestic private sector, a new business elite was now emerging, leading to a blurring of old boundaries between the state and private sectors.

Out in the provinces, significant environmental movements began to emerge in places, as did rural protests over issues such as corruption and land rights. Demonstrations became a relatively common occurrence (Ngo Vinh Long 2002: 459–60); the state typically reacted by combining tough action to quell protests with attempts to address core local grievances. An unspoken pact appeared to operate, under which a certain degree of dissent would be tolerated within the context of shared efforts to develop the economy, and state intervention to address striking inequities. Yet this pact is predicated on the basis that the VCP's monopoly on power will not be challenged. Accordingly, there has been no overt challenge to the Party itself: civil society groups tacitly support greater democratisation of the existing order, rather than any dismantling or overthrow of that order. Within the broad framework of what Dixon (like many others) terms the 'party-state', a wide range of formal and informal political activity is thriving. The party-state has gradually 'softened' since 1986, despite intermittent reversions to clampdown mode. Dixon therefore suggests that the Vietnamese regime might best be described as 'soft authoritarian-corporatist', informed by growing levels of dialogue between the party-state and wider society. An alternative description could be 'participatory-authoritarian', holding out the promise of a very gradual increase in pluralism.

In her chapter, Sophie Quinn-Judge offers an historical explanation that rather neatly supports Dixon's analysis. Reviewing the history of the VCP, she argues that the Party (and its precursors, the ICP and the VWP) was never the monolithic entity that many observers have assumed. Rather, the VCP has long done a superb job of concealing its internal wranglings, projecting the misleading image of a highly disciplined body, unified beneath the overarching leadership of Ho Chi Minh. Quinn-Judge suggests that the VCP has always actually been a coalition of competing interests. A close analysis of recent memoirs and new documentary evidence reveals the extent to which the early history of the party was characterised by intense ideological debates, in which Ho Chi Minh's views by no means held universal sway.

In fact, Quinn-Judge argues that it was only at the beginning of the 1950s that Ho Chi Minh established his current dominant position in party historiography. Ho had no formal party position during the 1930s; at the end of the Pacific War he faced substantial challenges from a rival faction, culminating in open resistance to his authority by 1948. Only after receiving endorsement from Mao and Stalin was Ho able to consolidate his hold over the Party, yet factional divides over issues such as land reform and revisionism persisted right through the 1960s. Quinn-Judge argues that these old factions have now become partly institutionalised in two broad 'wings' of the VCP, one pro-openness and reform, the other intent on preserving the communist order. Yet she notes that the full picture is more complex, an interlocking matrix of regional clans over-ridden by ideological disagreements. This internal complexity has been compounded by Vietnam's small size: far more than the Russians or the Chinese, the VCP needed to retain a pragmatic, flexible international stance reflecting its multiple strands of opinion.

In a chapter that perfectly straddles the troublesome divide between politics and the economy, Martin Gainsborough concentrates on one central question: what is meant by 'reform' in the Vietnamese context? He links this to the related issue of whether reform has been slowing in Vietnam since the second half of the 1990s. By reform, he refers primarily to key structural changes, building upon the wholesale marketisation that commenced in 1986. These changes include administrative reform, trade reform, state enterprise reform and banking reform, all of which are shaped by principles of decentralisation and a scaled-down state. By focusing on four important claims made about reform, Gainsborough is able to plot their progress during the 1990s. These claims are that reform is export-oriented, stresses the private sector, supports reducing the state sector, and involves tightening credit to state-owned enterprises.

In brief, he finds that Vietnam's reforms fail to meet all four of these criteria. These failures reflect the existence of pervasive bureaucratic and financial interests among sections of the party-state, dedicated to resisting changes of this kind; they also reflect a residual ideological aversion to the free market and to global capitalism. If reform has slowed, this could reflect an apparent trend towards 're-centralisation', perhaps reflecting conscious or unconscious alarm among Vietnam's elite that decentralisation may have gone too far. Gainsborough argues that the Vietnamese state has a highly developed capacity for reinventing itself, breathed centralising life into areas where reform has lost the initiative. Overall, Gainsborough presents a picture of a strong party-state reluctant to relinquish control, and unwilling to address core issues such as curtailing credit to state enterprises.

Claudia Zingerli takes the debate out into communes in the Northern mountain region – the site of her doctoral research – where she examines how far Decree 29 has been implemented. This 1998 Decree called for the promotion of 'grassroots democracy' in local areas, an example of the decentralisation viewed with scepticism by Gainsborough. Vietnam has a long history of democratic centralism – typically associated with top-down power structures. Zingerli argues that this tradition makes the Vietnamese leadership very nervous about broadening political participation, or allowing autonomous civil society groups to emerge. Thus the decree calling for strengthening of grassroots participation was often implemented simply as another party-state directive by local bureaucrats and cadres. At the same time, there was considerable ambiguity in such decrees, allowing for flexibility of interpretation by local authorities. Zingerli argues that socialist ideology was alive and well in the mountain communes, sustained by regular dialogue between local cadres and villagers. Nevertheless, many cadres held paternalistic views, seeing local people as lacking the necessary education and understanding to implement important policies. 'Lack of knowledge' on the part of villagers was sometimes a bureaucratic code for foot-dragging or active resistance by local people in the face of unpopular edicts.

In practice, the grassroots democracy decree was not implemented uniformly. In one community studied by Zingerli, residents did enjoy a degree of self-determination, and had been able to continue with customary practices to support their livelihoods; yet in another community, national policies completely overrode local concerns. Zingerli's findings support Dixon's view of a very heterogeneous state apparatus, applying policies with varying degrees of consistency in different places and during different periods of time. She notes that by strengthening local autonomy, the Vietnamese state has created greater scope for popular participation – yet also greater scope for the arbitrary use and abuse of power by local bureaucrats. Despite her scepticism about the implementation of Decree 29, Zingerli arrives at the cautiously optimistic conclusion that there may be 'a trend towards more discursive politics in Vietnam'.

Rethinking Vietnam's economy

During the initial years of *doi moi*, Vietnam enjoyed remarkable levels of economic growth: the end of collectivised agriculture gave a substantial boost to the rural economy, while an influx of foreign investment coupled with liberalisation of private sector economic activity brought considerable benefits. By the second half of the 1990s, however, the economy was slowing, partly influenced by wider regional problems after the 1997 Asian crisis, but primarily because of domestic factors. Ari Kokko picks up the argument where Martin Gainsborough left off, asking how far that slowdown reflected a decline in Vietnam's commitment to the reform process, and also the extent to which the downturn reflected structural problems rather than temporary setbacks. His answers focus on three key areas: trade policy, state-owned enterprise (SOE) reform, and the position of the private sector.

On trade policy, Kokko paints a fairly positive picture. Vietnam's 2001 Bilateral

Trade Agreement with the United States was a major landmark in the direction of eventual World Trade Organisation (WTO) accession, and there is plenty of evidence that Vietnamese exports have been enjoying a sustainable recovery in recent years. This reflects the outward orientation of private sector Vietnamese firms and of multinational corporations with operations in Vietnam. Substantial overseas development aid disbursements and private cash remittances (often transferred by overseas Vietnamese to relatives and business partners in the country) have helped boost Vietnam's balance of payments. State enterprise reform is another matter entirely. Like Gainsborough, Kokko insists that the lack of progress here is undeniable; most SOEs are loss-making and have continued to enjoy preferential access to credit, while the bulk of 'equitisations' to date have not affected the largest and most troublesome state enterprises. Kokko notes that the private sector remains underdeveloped, faced with various forms of discrimination and limited access to credit. At the same time, he is more positive than Gainsborough in highlighting certain areas where private sector reform has proceeded quite rapidly. He praises the 1999 Enterprise Law, which has led to the registration of numerous new small and medium-sized enterprises (SMEs). Kokko also singles out support from international donors for private sector capacity-building – notably Japan's 'Miyazawa plan', which has provided substantial funding to nurture SME development. Ultimately he suggests that SOE's reform might be tacitly bypassed: 'future strategies should focus on the development of the private sector while accepting more gradual reform of the SOE sector'. He also expresses concern that Vietnam needs a better welfare and 'safety net' infrastructure to protect its citizens from the uncertainties of the market, and to reduce both urban and rural poverty.

Ari Kokko's concluding remarks set the scene perfectly for Gerard Clarke's chapter on the social aspects of SOE reform. Drawing upon consultancy work undertaken in the Nam Dinh 'textile town' and in the coffee-growing region of the Central Highlands, Clarke focuses on two major SOEs: Natexco and Vinacafé. He argues that most existing work on SOEs has focused on economic questions, rather than the underlying social issues. He discusses in some detail the paternalistic relations between SOEs and their workforces, relations that are based upon rights and responsibilities enshrined in legislation such as the 1994 Labour Code. Since SOEs are an important constituency of support for the Vietnamese Communist Party and related mass organisations, reducing employment in the sector would have a direct impact on vested political interests. In practice, much of the retrenchment in the sector has affected female contract labourers rather than permanent male employees. The government has been considering extending the range of welfare benefits available to retrenched SOE workers, thus creating a dilemma for the donor community. On the one hand, donors are tempted to fund such benefits to help achieve the long-term goal of reducing Vietnam's state sector. Yet on the other hand, state sector employees are already a privileged social group; there is a much stronger case for deploying donor funding to reduce poverty levels – and to boost welfare provision for the truly disadvantaged and marginalised in Vietnamese society. Such groups, however, lack political clout and are of much less concern to party cadres at both national and local level. Despite the government's ambitious plan to reduce the size of the SOE sector substantially by 2005, Clarke seems dubious that the target for the 3,000 remaining SOEs to employ only 1.2 million workers will be realised. The explanation for this probable failure is that the associated social and political costs are simply too high.

Tran Thi Thu Trang takes us to the northern mountain province of Hoa Binh, where she conducted her doctoral research in two Muong villages. Turning from large-scale SOE activities to village-level agriculture, she examines the rural transformation experienced by two communities, when collectivisation gave way to a more entrepreneurial mode of agriculture after 1986. She notes that despite the failures of co-operative farming, the state was not weak at the village level; party cadres were close to the problems, needs and concerns of the villagers. Yet when new economic opportunities arose – such as the chance to plant lucrative new crops – it was often former veterans and party cadres who were the first to know, and the first to reap the benefits. Access to information became the key factor underlying successful agricultural diversification. In effect, the villages were divided into two classes of people: those 'in the know' and those deprived of the information needed to make informed economic choices. Televisions in the village had been appropriated by party cadres for private use, while newspapers were similarly available only to cadres. In effect, cadres had been able to assume privileged economic positions inside their villages on the basis of their access to information, leading to a rise in socio-economic inequalities within the communes Tran studied. Her detailed snapshot of rural life in post-*doi moi* Vietnam demonstrates that the process of agricultural diversification is a highly complex one, with considerable social and political ramifications. It also offers us a different view of the same region studied by Zingerli, casting doubt on the extent to which ideas of grassroots democracy have really made any impact.

Rethinking Vietnamese society

Jonathan London's chapter opens this section with a review of Vietnam's education and health policies in the *doi moi* era. London sets out to challenge standard, idealised views of Vietnam's achievements in these areas. Whilst noting successes in terms of positive educational and public health outcomes, he draws on his doctoral fieldwork in the central province of Quang Dam to demonstrate the extent to which access to health and education has become crucially related to the ability to pay. Like Clarke and Tran, he discovers evidence of growing and persistent social inequalities. London uncovers a burgeoning informal sector of moonlighting teachers and health workers – 'extra study' classes for examination preparation, taught by government teachers after hours, and doctors who expect the families of sickly patients to stuff cash-filled envelopes into the pockets of their white coats. The blurred distinction between the state and the private sector mentioned in earlier chapters is here graphically illustrated. Attempts to ameliorate the introduction of medical fees and prescription charges through exemptions have largely failed, partly since formal fees constitute only a small proportion of the real costs of healthcare. The jury is still out on the government's extensive hunger eradication and poverty reduction scheme. While the state continues to meet a very basic level of social needs, increasingly users need to pay for post-primary education and healthcare services. London's chapter demonstrates just how far the continuing use of socialist rhetoric by the Vietnamese state fails to reflect realities on the ground.

Doan Hue Dung offers a similarly critical view of Vietnamese education, returning to the theme of reform. How can a system subject to such a high degree of central control be effectively reformed? Doan notes the extent to which decision-making is bound up in exceptionally bureaucratic processes that stifle innovation and change. There is little scope for localisation of either school curricula or hiring practices. Using her own doctoral research on foreign-trained university lecturers in Vietnam, she demonstrates how the current system fails to match skilled personnel with appropriate posts. In theory a centralised structure has the advantage of imposing tightly controlled academic standards, yet in reality grade inflation is the norm in Vietnamese classrooms, and the faking of educational certificates is common practice. In other words, Vietnam's education system suffers from most of the negative consequences of centralisation, with few of the associated benefits in terms of quality assurance. At the same time, commercialisation – in the form of more private educational institutions – is lowering rather than raising standards. Neither the state nor the market seems to be effective in 'disciplining' the education system or curbing its tendencies towards inefficiency and low-level corruption. Doan portrays a hybrid Vietnam, caught between two different problematic directions, and so completely failing to create an effective education system. This Vietnam is characterised primarily by considerable inequalities. Doan does not advocate wholesale decentralisation as a catch-all solution, but suggests that selective decentralisation carried out with subtlety and sensitivity might reap considerable dividends for Vietnam's education system.

Marie-Eve Blanc addresses an important question raised by Chris Dixon: does Vietnam really have an autonomous civil society, or is associational life firmly subordinated to Doan Hue Dung's omnipresent centralising state? She takes the example of organisations that have emerged from the early 1990s onwards to combat the human immunodeficiency virus/acquired immune deficiency syndrome (HIV/AIDS) epidemic. Some of these groups have been founded by well-connected elite actors, including medical doctors and academics with good ties to the party-state. Others are grassroots organisations, often led by people themselves living with HIV, working with drug addicts, slum-dwellers and street children. HIV/AIDS is a particularly difficult issue for a Vietnamese society, which has sought to demonise 'social evils' such as sexual promiscuity and drug taking by constructing them as negative consequences of 'opening up' and Westernisation. Yet this aversion to such issues on the part of the Vietnamese bureaucracy creates a social space into which other actors can move – especially since aid donors have been very interested in funding work of this kind.

Blanc comes to a number of interesting conclusions. One is that the HIV/AIDS issue reveals considerable differences in the quality of associational life in the South of Vietnam, especially Ho Chi Minh City. Drawing on support from religious bodies and overseas Vietnamese communities, non-governmental organisations (NGOs) and community-based organisations (CBOs) have tapped into a longstanding stream of more independent voluntary activity that has persisted in the South. She relates this tradition to the relative autonomy enjoyed by Vietnamese villages in earlier centuries. Overall, Vietnamese society is characterised by very considerable diversity, with a discernibly more 'democratic' and partici-patory ethos in the South. Yet CBOs working on HIV/AIDS continue to work largely unrecognised by the state, and have not been very successful in 'main-streaming' the problems of deprived and marginalised groups. So long as these organisations do not form activist networks and agitate for policy changes, they may be tolerated; but if they become too overtly 'political' in orientation, their position will be much more difficult. However, Blanc is optimistic that some form of civil society is really emerging in contemporary Vietnam, supporting the view expressed by Dixon. Yet in seeing this tendency as demonstrating the emergence of new social classes, she goes beyond Dixon's position.

Phuong An Nguyen discusses an important segment of Vietnamese society: young graduates in Hanoi. Though not a representative sample of youth in Vietnam as a whole, these graduates reflect the changing values of a country in economic and social flux. Whereas prior to *doi moi*, 'success' was often defined in terms of making a contribution to such national goals as reunification and the building of socialism, after 1986 more individualist notions of success were popularised, often focusing on educational attainment and securing good economic status. For many young urban Vietnamese, becoming well-off through employment in the private sector became an important life goal. Nguyen quotes from interviews with young Hanoians conducted for her doctoral research, illustrating how some of her subjects boasted of their high incomes and educational attainments. She examines how the shortcomings of Vietnam's overcentralised higher education system mean that young people are increasingly interested in overseas study, or take evening classes in specialist subjects such as English and information technology, in order to improve their skills and employability. At the same time, young people are also deeply concerned about achieving successful relationships, including marriage. Overall, the concept of success has been 'privatised' in today's Vietnam – and the aspirational gender gap has greatly diminished – yet residual elements of socialist ideology can be seen in the desire expressed by many young people to contribute to the well-being of the country. Nguyen's study again illustrates the enormous diversity of contemporary Vietnamese society, and the grave difficulties of general-ising about life in such a large, populous, unequal and heterogeneous country.

Rethinking Vietnam's external relations

Since the onset of *doi moi*, Vietnam has stepped out of the shadow of the former Soviet Union to engage with a much wider range of states, international organisa-tions and companies, and foreign investors. Yet this 'opening up' has often been a troubled process for a country dominated for much of its history by more powerful states. For all its official rhetoric about integration into the world community and global economy, Vietnam's leadership has often hesitated to make concessions that could amount to a surrender of state control. When Vietnam emerged relatively lightly from the Asian economic crisis of 1997–8, some domestic commentators saw this as a vindication of the country's cautious approach to embracing the forces of international capitalism.

In their chapter exploring debates about foreign direct investment (FDI) in Vietnam, Nick Freeman and Curt Nestor find that even assessing the level of investment is a contentious business, mired in statistical ambiguities, opacities and omissions. Drawing on Nestor's doctoral research, they compare a range of competing definitions of FDI, highlighting the differences between approved investments, and investments that have actually been disbursed. Clearly, Vietnamese government statistics have tended to emphasise approval-based data, which forms the basis of a much more positive picture. Yet the problem is compounded by the fact that foreign investors frequently overvalue their investment contributions in kind (for items such as machinery), whilst contributions made by Vietnamese partners (domestic equity share) are often included in the government's FDI figures. In other words, 'real' foreign direct investment in Vietnam might be substantially lower than some people have assumed. It could follow that Vietnam's substantive integration into the global economy may also be smaller than is popularly believed. Yet it might also be the case that international estimates of FDI levels underreport the real position, in which case figures for Vietnam's international debt may also be underreported. If Vietnam has higher debt levels than is popularly assumed, then the country is more integrated into the global economy – and more vulnerable to global market fluctuations – than is generally appreciated. The critical questions raised in the chapter about FDI data highlight serious concerns about the difficulty of making accurate and informed assessments of the Vietnamese economy more generally.

In the second half of the chapter, drawing upon Freeman's work, the authors argue that the reasons for fluctuating investor sentiment in Vietnam are complex. To a large extent, the excessive enthusiasm of the early 1990s reflected naivety and short-sightedness on the part of investors themselves, many of whom rushed into a new market anticipating easy profits. Investment came in waves, starting with oil and gas, then hospitality and financial services, followed by manufacturing – particularly labour-intensive manufacturing such as garment factories. The subsequent scaling back of investment from the mid-1990s often simply reflected a more realistic appraisal of business opportunities; in some cases, there were simply too many investors in Vietnam chasing too little business (for example, 10 new car factories were proposed in 1995, at a time when only 4,000 cars were sold annually in the whole country). Yet slow progress in creating a sound business environment undoubtedly contributed to the decline in FDI levels.

On the foreign policy front, Jörn Dosch and Ta Minh Tuan examine the way in which Vietnam's international relations have changed in the post-*doi moi* era. Based on the guiding principles of diversification and multilateralisation, Vietnam normalised diplomatic relations with an astonishing range of countries. In a short space of time, Vietnam moved from a stance of relative isolation to one of active engagement with a wide range of bilateral ties and multilateral organisations. After the problematic 1979 invasion and occupation of Cambodia, which blighted Vietnam's relations with much of the world during the 1980s, the emphasis was now on settling all disputes by negotiation.[1] Ideology was now marginalised, whereas previously it had formed the core of Vietnamese foreign policy: pragmatism prevailed. Vietnam was particularly anxious to find ways of countering Chinese economic and strategic dominance in the region, and this helps explain Vietnamese enthusiasm for building stronger ties with other Southeast Asian countries – best seen in the decision to join the Association of Southeast Asian Nations (ASEAN). Another crucial juncture was the normalisation of relations with the United States.

Within ASEAN, Vietnam has acted as an informal leader for the 'new entrants' of the 1990s (the others were Burma, Cambodia and Laos). Yet the ASEAN summits held in Hanoi in 2001 lacked clear focus; Vietnam seemed to prefer ASEAN to adopt a lower profile, and was uneasy with recent moves towards ideas of 'flexible engagement', 'constructive intervention' or 'enhanced interaction', which would permit member states to comment critically on developments inside other states. Vietnam was attached to an older model of ASEAN, the so-called 'ASEAN way', based upon principles of consensus and non-interference – a much more comfortable model for a one-party state. Yet Vietnam also sought to use ASEAN membership as a means of pressing its claim for admission to other multi-lateral bodies such as the WTO, laying itself open to charges of crude pragmatism. In its relations with the rest of the world, Vietnam (like many other states) often wanted things both ways: the benefits of foreign investment without the constraints of playing by international economic rules, or the benefits of ASEAN membership without the pressure to conform to regional norms of behaviour. In a way, this duality resembles other aspects of Vietnam's post-*doi moi* order: Vietnam has persistently sought to take advantage of opportunities presented by globalisation and economic liberalisation, whilst avoiding the associated social and political costs.

The central questions: a provisional list

This volume seeks to address a series of central questions, the answers to which would enable a systematic 'rethinking' of contemporary Vietnam. The chapters included are contributions to a continuing debate – none purports to contain definitive or final answers.

Among the political questions raised here are the following:

- How far does Vietnam have a civil society, autonomous from the state?
- How far is Vietnam engaged in a process of reform, what does reform mean, and is reform slowing?
- How far is the VCP a unified force?
- How far do people at the grassroots have the ability to participate in decision-making?

Economic questions include:

- How far is the economy engaged in a process of liberalisation?
- How far is the private sector expanding and developing?
- How far is the state sector contracting, and with what consequences?
- How far has agricultural diversification proved successful?

Social questions include:

- How far is Vietnam's social structure changing?
- How far are new socio-economic groups and classes emerging?
- How far are community organisations able to assume roles formerly taken by the state?
- How far are education and health services meeting basic social needs?
- How far is social equity being preserved?

Questions concerning Vietnam's external relations include:

- How far is the economy really opening up to trade and foreign investment?
- Why is foreign investment apparently declining?
- How far are history and ideology still salient in explaining Vietnam's position on the international stage?
- How far is Vietnam committed to promoting Asian regionalism?
- How far is Vietnam's 'multilateral' foreign policy now purely pragmatic?

The original London panel that gave birth to this volume took place just days before the tumultuous events of 11 September 2001, yet (as Dosch and Ta Minh Tuan point out), these events had relatively little impact in Vietnam. To a large extent, change and reform in Vietnam is a process driven by domestic forces, despite the significance of wider global economic and political trends. Only by engaging in a close study of developments inside the country – ideally through extended fieldwork – can scholars hope to create the basis of solid new thinking about the answers to the questions listed above.

Note

1 Vietnam has long insisted that the intervention – which brought to an end the murderous Pol Pot regime – was justified on humanitarian grounds. Many Western academics sympathise with the view, whilst remaining sceptical about Vietnam's real motives for the invasion. More than 20 years after the event, this remains a difficult topic for Vietnamese scholars to debate openly and frankly.

Part I
Politics

Political facts about Vietnam

Government type:	Communist state
Administrative divisions:	58 provinces and 3 municipalities
Constitution:	15 April 1992
Legal system:	Based on communist legal theory and French civil law system
Suffrage:	18 years of age; universal
Political party:	Dang Cong San Viet Nam [Communist Party of Vietnam (VCP)], General Secretary Nong Duc Manh (since April 2001)
Executive branch:	*Head of state:* President Tran Duc Luong (since 24 September 1997)
	Elections: president elected by the national Assembly from among its members for a five-year term; prime minister appointed by the president from among the members of the National Assembly; deputy prime ministers appointed by the prime minister
	Head of government: Prime Minister Phan Van Khai (since 25 September 1997)
	Cabinet: Cabinet appointed by the President on the proposal of the prime minister and ratification of the National Assembly
Legislative branch:	Unicameral National Assembly or Quoc-Hoi (498 seats; members elected by popular vote to serve five-year terms)
Judicial branch:	Supreme People's Court (chief justice is elected for a five-year term by the National Assembly on the recommendation of the president)
Military branch:	People's Army of Vietnam (includes Ground Forces, People's Navy Command, Air and Air Defense Force, Coast Guard)
Military expenditures:	$650 million (financial year 1998)
Military expenditures as % of GDP:	2.5% (financial year 1998)

Sources: CIA (2002) *The World Factbook 2002*, Washington, DC: CIA; *Atlapedia Countries*, Latimer Clarke Corporation, available online at http://www.atlapedia.com/online/countries/vietnam.htm; *Almanacs: Countries of the World*, available online at http://www.infoplease.com/ipa/A0108144.html.

2 State, party and political change in Vietnam

Chris Dixon

This chapter examines the nature of the relationship between the Vietnamese state and society. The starting point is Kerkvliet's (2001a; 2001b) excellent review of studies of Vietnam's political system and state–society relations, which he synthesises into three main interpretations. These he terms: the 'dominating state', which stresses the core role of the Vietnamese Communist Party (VCP) plus other official organisations and institutions, suggesting that other groups and societal activities have little or no influence in the political system, or over policy; 'mobilisation corporatism', which emphasises the role of organisations dominated by the state in mobilising support for state programmes; and 'dialogue', which stresses the limits to the state's authority, and the ways that the state and its policies can be influenced outside formal channels. In the case of 'dialogue', policies appear to be the result of forms of indirect negotiation between the central party-state, more localised administrators and functionaries, and the target groups. Kerkvliet (2001b) demonstrates that in most studies there is a dominant interpretation, but in many cases it is accompanied by one or both of the others. He illustrates this even more clearly by applying the three interpretations to four areas where the relationship between the state and society has been problematic: government institutions and processes; mass media; agricultural collectives; and corruption. This revealed that:

> Each area has considerable evidence of the 'dominating state' interpretation ... There is also evidence for the 'mobilizational corporatist' interpretation ... But individuals, groups and social forces outside of official channels can also affect the political system. This is what the 'dialogue' interpretation is pointing out.
>
> (Kerkvliet 2001b: 268–9)

A central tenet of this chapter is that Kerkvliet's (2001a; 2001b) groupings broadly encapsulate the main interpretations of the Vietnamese situation. However, behind them lie very different conceptualisations of the Vietnamese state, the role it has played in the whole reform process, and its contribution to Vietnam's rapid economic growth since around 1990. The view of the Vietnamese state as a highly unified entity, an 'old fashioned socialist regime' dominated by the VCP, which takes swift action to stifle dissent within its structure and agencies, is deeply embedded in official American views and seems to permeate such agencies as the United Nations Development Programme (UNDP) (Koh 2001a: 533–4). Womack (1992: 180) depicted Vietnam as a 'vast and co-ordinated party state'. While, few, if any, recent commentators would fully subscribe to these views (Koh 2001a: 533), they still colour studies that depict the relations between state and society in strongly authoritarian or 'dominating' terms.

Many studies see the Vietnamese political system and state structures as changed almost beyond recognition since the beginning of the reform process (Fforde and Goldstone 1995: 100). Such authors generally subscribe to the view that a unified authoritarian or 'neo-Stalinist' state characterised the pre-reform period (see, for example, Fforde and de Vylder 1996; Schraner 2001: 23). As a result of reforms, the Vietnamese state has become much less unified and authoritarian, and has been depicted as multifaceted, multisegmented and multilayered, featuring significant local power structures and inconsistencies (Heng 2001; Koh 2001b: 291).

It is argued here that changes since the beginning of the reform period have principally involved the bolstering of long-established features and tendencies. In addition, change has taken place extremely unevenly in extent, depth and direction. Thus, the nature of the state and its interaction with society can appear very different, depending on when a given study was carried out, and on what part of the system it focused. In other words, diverse interpretations of Vietnam's state–society relations largely reflect commentators 'touching' the system in different places, to different extents and at different times. This is reinforced by marked ideological differences between commentators – something perhaps inevitable in studies of Vietnam – and the extent to which observers carry intellectual 'baggage' from Western perspectives on centrally planned economies and economic transitions as a whole. It is argued that only against this background can the relative significance of Kerkvliet's three interpretations (2001a; 2001b) be understood.

Against the above background, this chapter examines the changing form of the Vietnamese state, its relation to society and the nature and extent of activities that could be recognised as civil society. The material is arranged under three broad headings: the pre-reform situation; reform and the party-state; party, state and civil society.

The pre-reform situation

Prior to the *doi moi* reforms, the Vietnamese system was already significantly more diverse than the regimes of either the Soviet bloc or China. While in cultural, ethnic and linguistic terms Vietnam exhibits considerable homogeneity, there are deep social and political divisions that have a long history (Pike 2000: 277). Under the French there were three 'Vietnams'; and between 1954 and 1976 two Vietnams, with their own sets of elites and politics at all levels. In the North there was frequent change of policy, implemented through complex hierarchies which tended to operate at all levels with high degrees of autonomy, both functional and adminis-trative (Dang Phong and Beresford 1998). The result was that even before reunification, the party-state system operated in a far from uniform manner. This was reinforced by significant regional diversification of the central planning system, local administrative autonomy and control over production and resources (Beresford and McFarlane 1995; Mallon 1993: 205; Thrift and Forbes 1985). Under these conditions, there was considerable scope to evade inconvenient regulations, or to negotiate over their enforcement, sometimes by playing one part of the bureaucracy or party off against another (Hardy 2001: 187, 195). The latter approach was facilitated by the frequency of disputes and divisions within the vast bureaucratic system (Heng 2001: 228). Under these conditions considerable formal – and more especially informal – political activity took place within and around the party system. This is well illustrated by the negotiation of the household registration system (see Hardy 2001) and the informal processes of resource allocation that operated within the bureaucracy (see Rondinelli and Litvack 1999: 7–8). These activities seem analogous to strategies for coping with life under the party-state system identified by Miller in Eastern Europe (1992: 1), but in Vietnam they were taking place under a much less centralised system and closely linked to a deep-seated tradition of informal political activity (Pike 2000).

While decision-making was very clearly 'top-down', the Vietnamese version of 'democratic centralism' involved running proposed decisions past lower levels of the party-state system, and wider 'consultation' and 'testing of the water' through various mass organisations. To a degree, the final form and implementation of many policies in the pre-reform period were negotiated at the local level through a process of action and reaction (Koh 2001b: 281). In some cases policies were initiated from below, with the party-state following the lead of the people (Koh, 2001b: 285). There appears to have been a reluctance on the part of the central party-state to impose policies in the face of major opposition.[1] This partly reflects wartime needs to maintain broad popular support and maximise political participation (Turley 1980: 182–8). Under such conditions, people seemed broadly willing to accept unpalatable policies. However, this willingness appears to have been part of a relationship between party-state and society based on clear mutual obligations and expectations. It is possible that this relationship – which developed in the North during the long period of struggle – also has much deeper roots in Vietnamese culture (Pike 2000: 270–3).

By the late 1970s there were increasing signs of discontent and non-compliance with central directives. This has to be seen in the context of substantial policy failures and reversals, particularly with respect to the South, the cost and difficulties of national integration, economic stagnation, and declining external threats. The party-state was not fulfilling its promise of improved conditions, and its legitimacy – based on revolutionary credentials and victory over the forces of Western imperialism – was beginning to wear thin (see discussion in Fforde and Goldstone 1995: 100–15). This situation did not result in the emergence of any consistent, broad-based opposition movements which might have challenged the party-state system (Beresford 1987, 1989, 1993: 218; Kerkvliet and Porter 1995: 26; Kolko 1997; Vo Nhan Tri 1992; Vu Tuan Anh 1995). However, increasing signs of divisions of opinion and dissent appeared within the key policy-making bodies of the party over foreign policy, development strategies, planning failures and economic stagnation (Tan Teng Lang 1985). Koh (2001a: 535) concluded that after 1975, very clear pluralistic tendencies emerged in the VCP 'under an umbrella of authoritarianism'. Yet these tendencies built on long-standing divisions of interest within the Central Committee and the Politburo. For much of the pre-reform period, this included pro-Beijing and pro-Moscow groupings (Thai Quang Trung 1985). More significantly, in order for the Central Committee to represent the diversity in Vietnamese society, membership quotas were allocated for such groups as the trade unions, women and the military (Koh 2001a: 537).

In the immediate pre-reform period, the outward *form* of the Vietnamese state perhaps conforms to Kerkvliet's 'dominating state' category. However, in practice authoritarianism was 'softened' by the operation and weaknesses of the system, the extent to which power was localised, inputs into policy by local administrators and elements of wider society, limited direct control over production and the relationship that had developed between people and party-state. In general, the Vietnamese party-state system appears to have attempted to absorb dissent rather than merely repress it (Fforde and Goldstone 1995: 116). This suggests a 'soft', diffused and highly qualified form of domination, particularly compared to that which developed in South Korea and Taiwan (Fforde and Goldstone 1995: 116) and, perhaps even more, the East European states. As Schraner (2001: 23) has stressed, by the mid-1970s the Vietnamese system had diverged significantly from a 'neo-Stalinist' order, yet this remains a persistent image, implicitly informing much writing on Vietnam.

Reform and the party-state

The implementation of economic reforms in Vietnam appears to have been a highly pragmatic and considered response to serious economic problems that had emerged by the late 1970s and concerns over the related loss of popular support and political legitimacy (Vo Nhan Tri 1992; Kolko 1997). Yet reforms were not driven by state failure: they were formulated and implemented by a system still functioning effectively. Despite the problems of the pre-reform period, in many respects the Vietnamese party-state bureaucracy was effective in policy formulation and implementation (Forsyth 1997: 257–8; Mol and Frijns 1997; Kelly *et al.* 2001; UNDP 2001). The reform process, particularly in its early stages, was essentially 'top-down'. However, the overall approach has been a gradualist one, characterised – as earlier – by considerable testing and negotiating of measures. Local adminis-trations continued to play a major role as the interface between society and the party-state. The local role was enhanced by the way reforms reduced central control and bolstered local initiatives, control over resources and ability to generate and retain surplus funds (Litvack 1999: 63–7; Watts 1998; World Bank 1994, 1996). Further power and scope for economic activity accrued to local administration through the reform of state-owned enterprises (SOEs); in 1999 43.9 per cent of state industrial capacity was locally controlled (General Statistical Office 2002; Probert and Young 1995: 501). The state sector has continued to be favoured:

sectors of the economy remain heavily protected, state sector preserves (St John 1997; Scholtes 1998). In consequence, economic expansion has been heavily concentrated in the state sector and related joint ventures with foreign capital (Griffin 1998: 43–4, 55; Nguyen Tuan Dung 1996: 77–9).

To a degree, economic reforms and related changes created a vacuum, into which local administrations and subsections of the central functional system could expand. This was reinforced by changes in the membership of the National Assembly. Thus as reforms progressed, a coalition of provincial interests and technocrats became increasingly influential, central to the implementation of reforms, yet also major beneficiaries of the process (Fforde and Goldstone 1995: 103). This produced a marked development of localised economic and political structures, closely linked to the development of new alliances and forms of economic activity. As a result, clusters of the new economy grew up around local administrations and subsections of the central state structure. In many cases, administrators and functionaries supplement their official income with a second – and frequently larger – unofficial one. In some cases official duties may well be neglected, though the unofficial income may be a direct result of the official position held. Activities range from consultancy for foreign firms on how to deal with the system, through setting up businesses and channelling work to them, to accepting bribes (Koh 2001b: 283–4). Thus, many administrators and functionaries who have become actors in the new economy are outwardly supporters of existing state institutions, while at the same time taking advantage of them by trying to achieve private gaols at the expense of official ones.

Overall, much of the new economy in Vietnam is controlled by elements of the party-state system. Thus, lower echelons of the state, such as local governments in the provinces, parts of the army,[2] People's Committees, SOEs and other elements of the party and bureaucracy, 'are emerging as a form of new business elite' (Forsyth 1997: 245, 257). Much of the new economy that remains within the state sector could be considered as private, market-oriented activity (Fforde 2001a, 2001b). There is significant blurring of the boundaries of the state, and the potential for considerable conflict between national and public goals on the one hand, and local and private goals on the other. These issues have come to the fore since the early 1990s, through increasingly open debates over the consequences of economic reforms.

Until the end of 1993, the party-state system generally managed to maintain a unified external front over reform. This is not to suggest that either individual measures or the programme as a whole have been universally supported. Indeed, diversity of opinion and outright opposition at all levels of the system have been features of the reform process since its inception, building on the pluralist tendencies of the pre-reform period. However, much of the opposition was 'behind the scenes', or even clandestine. Quan Xuan Dinh (2000: 377) has commented on officials engaging in 'guerrilla activity', making use of the reduced central control to 'ambush' developments, sometimes by simply making new regulations unworkable. From January 1994 divisions begin to appear, coming very firmly into the open at the Eighth Party Congress of the VCP in 1986 (Quan Xuan Dinh 2000: 366–7).

At high levels in the system there were deep-seated concerns over increasing unemployment, trade union and popular discontent, and the compromising of socialist principles (Quan Xuan Dinh 2000: 327). To a degree, the more open debates reflected the economic success of the reforms. The immediate economic crisis that confronted the party during the mid-1980s had been overcome and the dissenters could more openly voice their concerns. Expressing dissent was made more feasible by the liberalisation of the media; and the resonance with popular concerns over the direction and consequences of reform.

While attention has inevitably focused on the conflict between 'reformers' and 'conservatives', the situation is much more complex. Within the Central Committee it is possible to see a series of competing groups including 'reformers, conservatives, the balancers (the in-betweens), opportunists and individuals in the economic ministries' (Koh 2001a: 537). However, this is complicated by the representation of sectors, such as the military, trade unions and women, regional divisions and the various ministries and departments. These groupings are further and variously reinforced, cut across and divided by the proliferation of the new economic and localised interests outlined above. Many of these interests either have direct representation in decision-making and policy formulation, or have sufficient influence for their concerns to count. Hence the Central Committee comprises a matrix, in which there are no fixed groups (Koh 2001a: 537–8). To a degree, this situation is mirrored throughout the party-state. Many individuals and groupings adopt positions on reform based on particular measures, rather than the process as a whole.

The economic reforms have had a significant impact on the party-state structure. In general, tendencies that were evident in the pre-reform period have been intensified. Most importantly, the party-state has become less unified, with a marked development of localised economic and political structures and a proliferation of interests that have direct or indirect inputs into policy formulation and implementation.

Party, state and civil society

The Sixth Party Congress – which set *doi moi* in motion – saw substantial changes in the Politburo, the Central Committee and its secretariat. Most of the surviving founders of the party had now retired and there was a reduction in the number of central party, state officials and military members. These were replaced by lower-level and provincial officials. Other reforms were aimed at renovating the party organisation and elements of the governing structure, notably the National Assembly, relaxing controls over the media and promoting more open comment and discussion.

While the key areas of the media remained state controlled, there was increasing freedom, under which it expanded, diversified, and became more critical. However, this has been an extremely uneven process, with repeated partial clampdowns and reversals (Thomas 2001: 313; Unger 1991). Thus, the basis of media freedom remains precarious, with 'broadly defined national security legislation continuing to offer a virtual carte blanche for political crackdowns' (Heng 2001: 219). Despite this, the media has played a major role in political change, particularly with respect to increasing the responsiveness of the party-state to protest and public concern.

The 1992 Constitution redefined the relationship between party and state, giving state institutions greater autonomy and making the party subject to the rule of law. Heng (2001: 219) sees this as beginning to foster a political environment where citizens can hold the leadership legally accountable, so strengthening the basis of civil society. Perhaps more significantly, the 1992 Constitution increased the decision-making power of the National Assembly (Dang Phong and Beresford 1998: 89–96, 104; Fforde and Goldstone 1995: 109, 111; Tonneson 1993: 41). This was reinforced by increasing the number of candidates for Assembly seats, loosening party controls over their selection, promoting more open debate, lengthening sessions and changing the character of elections (Thayer 1992: 120–2).

While 1992 elections were not democratic in any Western sense, there was greater choice of candidates and the process was by no means fully party-managed (Fforde and Goldstone 1995: 109). The result was a rejuvenated Assembly; 74 per cent of those returned were new members, who were generally better educated and younger than those they replaced and more likely to be full-time politicians (Tonneson 1993: 41). These developments were furthered by the 1997 elections and the 1998 grassroots democracy campaign, which saw increased formal representation of local interests, more open debate and greater conflict within the system. This is particularly well illustrated by the 1998 refusal of the National Assembly to approve changes to the 1993 land legislation agreed by the Central Committee. While opposition to the measure centred on concerns over the exploitation of farmers, some observers see the move by the Assembly as reflecting local party interests, which would have been adversely affected by the land reform measures (Keenan 1998).

Overall, political reforms engendered increased comment on policy and the VCP through the media, within the party structures and, perhaps most significantly, outside. During 1988–9, concern over the level of dissent resulted in attempts by the conservative elements to re-impose central control, which were most apparent at the Seventh Plenum of the VCP Central Committee held in August 1989. While this was followed by new censorship regulations and the closure of a number of publications that had appeared since 1987, these measures had only a limited and short-term impact (Thayer 1992: 118, 128–9). More significantly, attempts were also made to suppress extra-party organisations and replace them with bodies under party control. While there was nothing new in the latter approach, from 1989 to 1990 efforts to establish new and more varied mass organisations – and to revamp existing ones – became a much more significant and consistent part of central policy (Yeonsik Jeong 1997). Considerable effort went into maximising membership, keeping close relations with the leadership of the VCP and increasing 'the sense of participation by leading interest groups to believe that they are closely connected to the state and their voices are sincerely heard' (Yeonsik Jeong 1997: 167). This suggests a significant shift in the direction of 'state corporatism' (Yeonsik Jeong 1997), or Kerkvliet's (2001b) 'mobilising corporatism'. However, within this context, the system was becoming more responsive and open (Quan Xuan Dinh 2000: 369, 378–9). In addition, the changes within the party-state system facilitated – and were to some extent linked to – the emergence of political activity which might be regarded as outside direct state control, constituting elements of conventionally defined civil society.

As already seen, economic reforms rapidly led to the emergence of a new economic elite that lay principally within, or was closely allied to, the party-state system. This seriously limited the extent to which this elite could form the basis of an 'economic civil society', conventionally expected to reside in the domestic private sector. However, while the private sector involves a large number of enterprises and people, activities have generally remained limited in scale. Although since 1992 the private sector has enjoyed the same legal status as state activities, in practice foreign and state activities continue to be favoured. Discrimination against the private sector, linked to serious operating difficulties, has been widely reported (Kokko and Sjöholm 2000: 270–1; Scholtes 1998). In addition, the sector is highly fragmented, lacking significant organisations or voices. There is little to suggest the emergence of an autonomous business group that is able or willing to challenge the party-state. Indeed, for many the central issue is to have their views heard and incorporated into policy within the existing party-state framework (Dixon and Kilgour 2002: 612).

It may well be, as Forsyth (1997: 255) has suggested, that the party-state is reluctant to increase support for the private industrial sector precisely because the development of an autonomous business elite might challenge its power. In addition, a stronger private sector would threaten the vested interests of SOEs. As a result, within the private sector many feel that they are excluded from full participation in the new economy, either through policy choices, or by what some see as corruption (Forsyth 1997: 255). Some consider that the state is neither listening to, nor responding to, activities that are beyond its control. Some businesses have reacted by attempting simply to 'disengage' from the state, and to operate partially or fully beyond its reach. Thus, a significant proportion of the private sector may be considered 'informal', operating outside state control and regulation, and outside the tax system (Koh 2001a: 543). In 1995 the informal sector's share of gross domestic product was estimated in an official study at 33.9 per cent (Nguyen Van Chinh 2001: 8).

The *doi moi* period has seen increased public participation in environmental initiatives and protests, sometimes helped by international organisations such as UNDP or the World Wildlife Fund and by support from prominent national figures (Beresford and Fraser 1992: 3; Kilgour 2000: 380–9). A small number of Vietnamese environmental non-governmental organisations have emerged, notably 'Eco Eco' (Nguyen Van Troung 1992; Jamison and Baark 1995: 281). These remain largely urban-based and supported, even where their issue focus is rural. Most protests remain localised; single-issue and grassroots organisations still have limited scope to campaign politically. Effecting policy changes requires the support of more powerful elements and, increasingly, the media. In a few cases, environmental issues have been linked in popular protest and media coverage with corruption or unjust allocation of natural resources. This has resulted in some significant policy changes, for example over open-cast mining in Halong Bay (see Bach Tan Sinh 1995).

Local corruption, often involving land rights, has been central to a number of major rural protests, notably in Thai Binh (1997), Nam Dinh (2000) and Gia Lai, Dac Lac and Kon Tum (February 2001). The last of these, although sparked by religious repression, also centred on corruption and access to land. The central state appears to have been deeply concerned over the scale and intensity of the protests; since September 2000 a number of ministerial delegations have visited provinces to resolve long-standing disputes (Koh 2001a: 548). In general, the centre has attempted to 'manage' protests. Alongside arrests and police activity, the centre has usually taken the part of the people against local administrators and officials, large numbers of whom have been 'disciplined' (Thomas 2001: 324). Such an approach reinforces the image of a party-state system responsive to significant protests by parts of society.

Some protests suggest continued adherence to socialist values and resentment over the impact of liberalisation. These positions are often reflected in disputes by trade unionists, who expect the state to protect the interests of the workers from those of capital – reflecting 'pre-reform' ideas of state–society relations. These ideas, like adherence to some form of socialist ideology, seem much stronger amongst the older generation of Vietnamese (Kilgour 2000: 304–6, 309–12). However, other commentators have detected in some protests the emergence of class interests opposed to the state and its policies. Forsyth (1997: 257, 259–60) cites evidence for what might be termed 'working-class' and 'middle-class' positions; with media support, these interests have formed brief alliances. Such a view resonates with developments in Eastern Europe, but evidence for significant class formation in Vietnam remains scant.[3] Gainsborough (2002) reviews the various elements that might be expected to form the middle class. He concludes that the critical groups are the new business elite and the professional state employees. However, these overlapping groups remain very closely tied to the party-state system.

By the early 1990s, a wide variety of extra-state activity, public commentary, and even criticism of the party-state had become acceptable, or at least tolerated – so long as the supremacy of the VCP was not questioned (Wain 1990).[4] There appeared to be an unspoken compromise between party-state and people: in return for growth, a degree of social equity and reasonable governance, the population would accept the continuing conduct of politics according to the rules of the party-state, suitably adjusted to meet the requirements of the new economic order (Fforde and Goldstone 1995: 100).

Those who are opposed to the present regime or its policies appear to lack the unity, organisation or strength required to challenge the party-state or significantly to alter its policies through sustained political campaigns. However, the party-state has become extremely sensitive to protest and pressure, wishing to be seen to respond – yet limiting those responses to the existing framework. The VCP has repeatedly stressed since 1986 that moves toward a pluralist political system will not be tolerated (Yeonsik Jeong 1997: 153–4). This does not preclude changes in policies, or, where necessary, adjustments to the party-state structure and operation. Change has continued to take place in response to the reactions of the people and elements within the party-state. As has been outlined, this frequently involves various forms of 'negotiation', as well as using established formal and informal channels. Where new positions, interests or movements have emerged, the party-state has attempted to absorb and control them, an approach backed by varying degrees of coercion.

While there are dissident groupings, some with international connections, who wish to see the establishment of a pluralist party system, it is difficult to establish how extensive they are. The party-state is so sensitive on this issue that little media coverage or clear information is available. A combination of censorship, fear of repression, and a long tradition of clandestine politics (Pike 2000: 273–6), makes any meaningful assessment impossible. Significant numbers of people may favour dismantling the VCP; yet most visible demands appear to be for greater representation and responsiveness, broadly within the existing framework. The emergence of civil society does not seem to be challenging the party-state system in the direction of Western-style democracy, but rather supporting, at least *tacitly*, official moves towards greater party-state democratisation. This could, of course, reflect self-preservation rather than true aspirations. However, Pike (2000: 277) has argued that Vietnamese culture is not receptive to electoral systems that produce winners and losers, or the virtues of a civil society that operates independently of the party-state system.

Despite Vietnam's very substantial political changes since the mid-1980s, compared with economic reforms they 'were given much less prominence by outside observers and writers' (Thayer 1992: 113; Turley 1993b). Indeed they were often completely ignored, or seen as a 'natural' consequence of economic change, rather than the result of active political reforms. Many Western political scientists adopted the view that only changes in the direction of democracy could be considered political reform (Tonneson 1993: 15), a stance that obscures the political realities of the Vietnamese system. A contrary view advocated treating:

> ... the Vietnamese political system as a normal one in which objectives and understanding of the issues by leading personalities, competition for leadership positions, advocacy of particular goals of social and state institutions, hierarchical processes and expressions of interest by various social groups, all have a role to play.
>
> (Dang Phong and Beresford 1998: 11)

While these authors may overstate their case, there is considerable merit in an approach that recognises the full range of formal and informal political activity that has come to operate under the broad auspices of the party-state.

The limited emergence of civil society – as conventionally defined – has been accompanied by a very considerable increase in formal and informal political activities within, or closely connected to, the party-state system. Indeed, the system appears to have become increasingly – and more openly – pluralistic. In many instances, activities could be interpreted as autonomous interactions with parts of the state, despite those involved remaining formally within the state. This is perhaps most significant with respect to the new business elite that has emerged within or closely allied to the state sector. The activities of this group could be interpreted as the beginning of the unchallenged takeover of elements of the state by business, a process that has developed to a much greater extent in parts of Eastern Europe (see, for example, European Bank for Reconstruction and Development, 2000). More contentiously, the new business elite might be regarded as some form of civil society, as Wank (1995) has argued with respect to the People's Republic of China. There are real conceptual problems here for analysis that assumes clear separation of state and society. Overall, attempts to apply a conventional conceptualisation of civil society to Vietnam often hinder a nuanced understanding of empirical realities.

Conclusion

As has been outlined in this chapter, a combination of economic reform, political reform and related changes has altered the Vietnamese state and its interaction with society. However, while new elements have emerged, essentially the changes built on the forms and tendencies that were present at the beginning of the reform period. In this light, how can the form of the contemporary Vietnamese state and its relations with society be most effectively depicted?

Since the beginning of the reform period, the Vietnamese state has significantly softened. However, the retreat from authoritarianism has taken place unevenly; the state has retained very considerable power to clamp down, certainly in the short run. This is demonstrated in occasional, abrupt, often apparently arbitrary, and sometimes extreme, manifestations of authoritarian rule. Such measures have been most frequently directed at corrupt officials, the media, local administration and the informal economy. These actions serve as reminders of the state's power, and as warnings to those engaged in non-sanctioned activities. While some measures, particularly those directed against corruption, do appease popular and media-based concerns, they can also be interpreted as signs of weakness and even desperation over the loss of central control. They reflect the slow and uncertain progress being made through the rule of law, regulation and administrative reform in shifting power back to the centre and away from the provinces (Thaveeporn Vasavakul 1996: 43; 1999). However, in the absence of a major and credible threat, sustained broad-based repression of the Vietnamese people seems difficult to envisage. Any such repression seems unlikely given the history of relations between people and state, and the varied interests represented in the central system. In addition, there are serious doubts over the extent to which the military, given its structure and substantial economic interests, would be able or willing to implement such a policy (Fforde and Goldstone 1995: 116).

With the above in mind, 'soft authoritarian-corporarist' is a broad label that reflects a long-standing position of the Vietnam central state in its approach to society, one that has been substantially reinforced since the late 1980s. Within this, an increasing amount of dialogue is taking place among subsections of the party-state and society. This is generally informed by a gradualist, incrementalist and cautious approach based on 'testing out' policies, coupled with a reluctance to go substantially against the views of the people – or rather, the perceived views of the people. Thus, to a considerable extent Kerkvliet's 'dialogue' interpretation can be subsumed into a broader 'authoritarian–corporatist' view. However, within the party-state there has also been significant reform and democratisation. This has substantially increased the scope and importance of political activity, suggesting that a label such as 'participatory–authoritarian' might also be appropriate. In other words, the dominant tendencies have become corporatist and participatory, under a form of authoritarianism that continues to soften.

Clearly, the Vietnamese system is characterised by some substantial contradictions; in some areas, there are signs of dysfunctionality. However, it would be dangerous to suggest that these issues can only be addressed by moves towards some form of Western-style multiparty democratic system. The party-state is well aware of its own internal problems and contradictions, and may well prove capable of containing or resolving them (Communist Party of Vietnam 2001: 23–4, 125, 141). One realistic likely prospect involves the continuation of gradual pluralisation and democratisation within the existing system. That is, as Gainsborough (2002: 707) has suggested, political change coming from within the institutions of the state rather than through the 'assertive rise of civil society'. This could follow the lines suggested by Ljunggren (1993: 29–30), with the emergence of a variation on the Asian developmental state.[5] Vietnam might yet adopt a less authoritarian, less centralised and more responsive version of the Singaporean single-party system.

Notes

1 In some instances, the state was willing and able to attempt the imposition of policies in an extreme manner. This was most notably the case during the collectivisation drive of the mid-1950s and in the early stages of the reunification.
2 The army has emerged as a major business force, particularly in construction, and, since 2000 in telecommunications.
3 While the emergence of individuals with middle-class lifestyles is clear in the major urban centres, income differentials remain low, and over 75 per cent of Vietnamese are rural residents.
4 During 1999, criticism of the VCP was the official reason for the expulsion of General Tran and the arrest of writer and geophysicist Nguyen Thanh Giang.
5 See also Pike (1994) and Watts (1998: 463).

3 Rethinking the history of the Vietnamese Communist Party

Sophie Quinn-Judge

The Vietnam Workers Party (VWP)[1] pulled off a remarkable feat during the years of the Vietnam War. The party presented a united, if not monolithic, façade to the outside world. This public unity only occasionally cracked enough to allow Western intelligence experts to speculate on rivalries among the top leadership. The belief in the Vietnamese leadership's unity grew more firm in the years after 1975, as what had earlier been thought of as the Party's pro-Chinese wing united with the 'pro-Soviet' faction to oppose Chinese policy in Indochina and combat the Khmer Rouge. From 1954 until 1990, there were only two major crises which resulted in expulsions from the Politburo: the correction of the errors of Land Reform in late 1956, and the break with China, which led to Hoang Van Hoan's demotion in 1976.[2]

The persona of Ho Chi Minh has been a key to the public image of the Vietnamese Party. He came to symbolise the ardent nationalism of the Vietnamese communists, who were exhorted to emulate his simple, self-denying lifestyle. In the West both left- and right-wing commentators accepted the idea that Ho was the supreme leader of his Party, in the image of Mao Zedong or Kim Il Sung. The current Vietnamese leadership has clung to this image of Ho, as a way of legitimising its current monopoly on power. From the time of the Party's founding congress in 1930 until the Tet offensive of 1968, he has been pictured, not only as the personification of virtue, but as the ultimate arbiter of all disagreements. The demonisation of Ho by the right wing of the overseas Vietnamese community in America is the mirror image of this phenomenon.

During the 1990s, however, new light has been shed on the Party's history by several unauthorised memoirs from veterans of the Revolution (Bui Tin, Vu Thu Hien and Nguyen Van Tran), as well as by political debates in Hanoi (in particular over the 1963 Ninth Plenum and its aftermath in the 1967 Anti-Party affair). Fresh archival sources in Russia, France, China and Eastern Europe are adding to our knowledge base. From such sources we can begin to see that Ho Chi Minh's power was not so unquestioned as has been assumed, and that major factional differences have split the Vietnamese communists through much of their history. It would not be an exaggeration, in my view, to say that the Party has always been a coalition, which has survived by practising the art of compromise in conditions of duress. In some periods, however, the compromise at the top seems to have been cosmetic: in 1967 it concealed the imprisonment of a group of the members of one faction.

Ho Chi Minh himself did much to foster the spirit of collective leadership, by complying with Party decisions with which he was not in agreement. At the same time, though, he can be identified as a proponent of an inclusive style of leadership, which put greater emphasis on national unity than on class struggle. From his early career as a trainer of Vietnamese revolutionaries in Guangzhou and Siam, to his wartime leadership of the Viet Minh, he advocated a nationalist coalition which had its ideological roots in Lenin's 1920 Theses on National and Colonial Questions.[3] But his policies and leadership were strongly contested from 1929 onwards by more radical proletarian communists, as I will discuss below. Although some historians have maintained that Ho enjoyed a 'cult of personality' during the 1940s and 1950s, it is very difficult to defend this idea by any of the usual definitions, which take as their basis Stalin's god-like status *and* absolute dominance of the political process in the Union of Socialist Soviet Republics (USSR).[4]

The newly available evidence on basic issues of Vietnamese communist history makes this an ideal time to begin a rethink of the Communist Party's history. We are now far enough from the end of the Cold War, with a new generation of researchers bringing fresh perspectives to the task, to undertake this project in a meaningful fashion. This chapter will discuss a few approaches to this question, and propose one possible framework for understanding the Party's origins. It is the product not only of my own research, but of considerable cross-fertilisation from other scholars. In addition to evaluating the significance of new documentary sources, we need to examine the Party's own historiography, which is surprisingly rich in debate. Although official Party history does not always tell us the truth, it does reveal what issues have most preoccupied the leadership. Another aspect of this exercise should be the re-examination of the traditional categories which Western analysts have employed to make sense of the Party's internal debates: such classifications as internationalist and nationalist party factions; pro-Soviet and pro-Chinese factions; Western-oriented or Chinese-oriented Party groups; or the idea of a north–south divide. To prevent a knee-jerk revisionism, one should avoid the temptation to see every new memoir coming from Vietnam as the truth at last revealed. Memoirists, no matter how well-meaning, have their own blind spots and in a highly secretive society such as Vietnam's, they often rely on hearsay more than they would like to admit. The same caution should be applied to the spate of new biographies which have been produced in Vietnam in the 1990s – the quality is very uneven, in my experience. Another challenge is to retain a feeling for the times in which the first group of party leaders functioned, when Marxism was the ideology of a young, disenfranchised intellectual elite. Yet writing the Party's history of the Cold War era requires 'the detachment which comes from following, not reflecting a historical epoch' as John Lewis Gaddis puts it (Gaddis 1997: 282). One should remember, too, that we are starting from a very small base of provable data. Vietnamese communist history is not unlike the field of paleontology – every newly discovered set of bones adds so much to the knowledge base that the landscape for researchers is totally changed.

Historiography

One of the things which distinguishes the VCP from its neighbouring party in China is that it has never published a *Resolution on Certain Questions of Party History*, such as was adopted by the Chinese communists in 1945, and again in 1981. The 1945 resolution, passed in preparation for the Chinese Communist Party's (CCP) Seventh Congress, bestowed 'the formal approval of the Central Committee on the Maoist version of party history ...'; 'this would terminate once and for all the endless debate over who was right and who was wrong', writes Raymond Wylie (Wylie 1980: 263). While the Vietnamese communists would publish many textbooks and summaries of their Party's history from 1960 onwards, which show subtle changes over time, there is to the best of my knowledge no single moment at which one individual or group has been able to impose their reading of the past or to rewrite history, as Stalin did in his 1938 *History of the CPSU.* Instead, contentious issues, such as the replacement of Ho Chi Minh's February 1930 Party Programme the following October, have been smoothed over in official histories or avoided altogether. In many instances, the only reason one knows that an issue is contentious is that a new version or twist to a particular episode has been added at a later date.

With a few exceptions, it is only recently that students of Vietnamese communism have begun to look at what the Party's writing of its own history reveals. Christoph Giebel points out that 'no systematic attempt has ... been undertaken to shed light on the "workings" of Vietnamese historiography in constructing these images that seek to explain the nature, "the origins", and the trajectory of Vietnamese communism' (Giebel 1996: 9). As he points out, Vietnamese historiography is neither static nor monolithic. Historical writing has been 'employed by competing interests within the revolution' and 'the history of the Vietnamese Revolution continues to be contested and reshaped' (Giebel 1996: 9–10). A number of historical debates have taken place in the Communist Party's own journals. One of these, described by Georges Boudarel, concerned the nature of the August Revolution (Boudarel 1980: 143). It came to a head in 1963 and was clearly also a discussion of the strategy to be followed to reunify the country. This debate revealed a wide range of opinion on the place of armed violence in the revolution, as opposed to political struggle. Another debate, delineated by Giebel, concerns the claim first put forth by Tran Van Giau, that a communist trade union, led by Ton Duc Thang, existed in Saigon as early as 1925 (Giebel 1996: 232–45).

New documentary evidence

Christoph Giebel's research on the origins of the official biography of Ton Duc Thang reveals the tenacity of stories which achieve credibility simply by circulating for a number of years. The claim that Thang took part in the 1919 Black Sea Mutiny in the French fleet, first given official sanction in 1947, Giebel shows to be extremely unlikely, given the lack of evidence that Thang ever served on board ship. The same sort of process, the transmutation of anecdote or propaganda into 'historical fact', has been at work in the biography of Ho Chi Minh. In fact, much of the history of the early communist movement has been distorted by such 'facts'.

In part this situation is the result of the propaganda war which was fought over Vietnam, with French and other intelligence organisations attempting to diminish the prestige of Ho Chi Minh, while the Vietnamese communists worked to build his image as a national icon.

One of the most deeply rooted clichés about Vietnamese nationalism is that Ho Chi Minh split with his more respectable 'reformist nationalist' colleagues when he joined the French Communist Party (FCP) in 1920. In an account which first seems to have come from the Trotskyist journalist Ho Huu Tuong, Ho is portrayed as a simple messenger for the Paris-based Group of Vietnamese Patriots, whose best-known members in 1920 were the scholar Phan Chu Trinh and the lawyer Phan Van Truong (Dang Huu Thu 1993: 29). A thorough reading of the documents available in the French Overseas Archives, however, forces a change of view. First of all, the French police and Ministry of Colonies reports kept on Ho Chi Minh during his stay in Paris show that he behaved as the social and intellectual companion of his two elders, certainly as more than an errand boy.[5] Although he could not yet write fluently in French and relied on Phan Van Truong to write the petition which he presented to the delegations to the Paris Peace Conference in 1919, he seems to have played a major role in its formulation. The French files show that he had been consulting Korean nationalists in both America and France on their strategy for demanding independence from Japan, before submitting the Vietnamese petition in June. Secondly, these documents show that both Phan Chu Trinh and Phan Van Truong were considered by the *Sûreté* to be dangerous nationalists, and that both remained in touch with Ho until his 1923 departure from Paris. Truong himself seems to have become a communist and remained an active collaborator of Ho Chi Minh.[6] And the reformist Phan Chu Trinh is shown to have encouraged Ho to take his Marxist ideas back to Vietnam to test them out.[7] But the idea that there had been a clean break between reformist bourgeois nationalists and violent revolutionaries as early as 1920 is one to which writers of both left and right have clung.

Another legend which has become fixed in the Western literature on Ho Chi Minh is the story that he betrayed Phan Boi Chau to the French police in Shanghai, as he was attempting to consolidate his hold over the group of Vietnamese revolutionaries exiled in southern China (for example, Turner 1975: 8–9; McAlister 1971: 76). This version of events originates in the memoirs of Hoang Van Chi and has done much to establish the image of Ho Chi Minh as a manipulative and callous leader (Hoang Van Chi 1964: 18). Again, from the French reports of Ho's years in Canton, based on a prolific informer in his circle of exiles, one learns that the French were getting all the information they needed on Phan Boi Chau's movements from their own spies. Moreover, Ho had not had much difficulty in winning the exiles over to his group, including one nationalist, Nguyen Hai Than, who later became his bitter rival.[8]

The communist literature on these early years has its own distortions and lacunae. One of these is the failure to mention the influence of Chinese organisations within Vietnam on the early revolutionary movement: indeed, the whole idea of Chinese influence on Vietnam's revolution became a taboo topic in the late 1970s. By early 1927, however, the French Foreign Ministry was receiving reports about an Indochinese branch of the CCP's Nanyang (Southern Seas) Provisional Committee, which was known as the Cochinchine-Cambodge branch.[9] In 1927 Hoa-kieu in Cochinchina were involved in sending young Vietnamese to Canton for training, under the auspices of the proto-communist Association of Revolutionary Vietnamese Youth, usually known as Thanh Nien or Youth. The usual story of the VCP's origins lays all the emphasis on the training programmes in Canton, led by Ho Chi Minh from 1925 to the spring of 1927. By 1928–9, however, the Chinese left's influence within Vietnam may have become a significant factor in the VCP's development. During those years, with the Comintern presence in China greatly reduced, communist policy was more likely to have filtered to Vietnam via different CCP organisations than to have come in the form of orders from Moscow.[10]

Although from mid-1928 until the autumn of 1929, Ho Chi Minh was working in Siam, he kept his presence there a closely-guarded secret. When the Comintern's Far Eastern Bureau in Shanghai was instructed in 1929 to recruit Southeast Asian youth for an anti-imperialist congress in Berlin, the European personnel, newly arrived from Moscow, said that they had no contacts with indigenous revolutionary youth organisations in Indochina or other countries of the region. 'The only possibility is to work through the Chinese organisations there …', the correspondent wrote to Berlin.[11]

This issue of Chinese influence becomes important when an open split in Thanh Nien occurs in the spring of 1929. By June of that year the Tonkin Regional Committee of Thanh Nien had transformed itself into a communist party, the Dong Duong Cong San Dang or Indochinese Communist Party (ICP), and had begun to send members to the other parts of Vietnam to recruit adherents. This group had already shown itself to be in the avant-garde of the revolutionary movement, when in September 1928 they had begun a drive to 'proletarianise' themselves, that is to send their mainly middle-class members to work in mines, plantations and factories. When one of their leaders, Ngo Gia Tu, came to Saigon in mid-1929, he concentrated his organising on the Saigon proletariat, unlike the southern branch of Thanh Nien, which had strong roots in several rural areas as well as the beginnings of a trade union movement in Saigon.[12] The hostility between this new communist group and the Thanh Nien Central Committee, then based in Hong Kong, has been portrayed in official Vietnamese accounts as a passing phenomenon. But evidence from the Comintern's files in Moscow shows that even after Nguyen Ai Quoc returned from Siam to Hong Kong at the end of 1929, and organised a unifying congress in February 1930 to create what was then named the Vietnamese Communist Party, the northern party faction demonstrated 'separatist tendencies' and some of its members refused to accept the Comintern's instructions.[13]

When one examines the leadership of this ICP faction, one finds a remarkable continuity between this group and the core of leftist leaders who organised the Land Reform Campaign from 1952 to 1956. Among them were Le Van Luong (Nguyen Cong Mieu) and Hoang Quoc Viet, who lived together in Saigon in late

1929, along with Ngo Gia Tu (Hoang Quoc Viet 1965: 155). Truong Chinh (Dang Xuan Khu), party leader from 1941 to 1956, and briefly in 1986, worked with one of his schoolmates from Nam Dinh in 1929 to produce the ICP labour union's newpaper, *Lao Dong (Labour).*[14] This schoolmate was Nguyen Duc Canh, one of the leaders of the ICP faction. It is Canh who is credited with organising the first trade union, the Tong Cong Hoi Bac Ky (The Northern General Trade Union), in mid-1929 (*Nhung Nguoi Cong San* 1976: 96). Of the leaders of this group who went to Canton for training in the 1920s, almost all were there after Ho Chi Minh's departure. Thus they had no personal ties to Ho, either by geographical region or as his students.[15]

Vietnamese communist history does not accentuate this continuity within the Party's left wing, or the differences which this group had with Ho Chi Minh in 1929–30. The Party's early history remains centred on Ho Chi Minh's work of nurturing and unifying the communist movement, even though the essential correctness of the ICP's proletarianisation and speed in forming a communist party is also proclaimed. This is an example of the compromise process which has served to keep the VCP united, but which also creates a strangely blurred and confusing history.

Until 1950–1 it was not clear, in my view, that Ho Chi Minh's image would be the one around which the Vietnamese communists organised their history. After all, from his June 1931 arrest until 1940–1, when Ho linked up with Party members in southern China, he played no role in the Party's structures. During the united front of World War II, when Ho pulled the ICP into the Viet Minh coalition, as the Comintern's official representative he once again became a dominant force. But his relationship with the ICP, by then under the leadership of Truong Chinh and a small group of northerners, remains something of a puzzle. Part of the puzzle is why so little Viet Minh organising was carried out within Vietnam until late 1944.[16] By the end of the war, there appear to have been two major clans within the Party. One group was composed of the communists grouped around Ho Chi Minh, who formed the backbone of the Viet Minh: Vo Nguyen Giap, Pham Van Dong and Hoang Van Hoan. Dong and Hoan had both been trainees in Ho's Canton school for revolutionaries in 1926. Giap, in addition to being one of the most forceful proponents of a United Democratic Front in pre-war Hanoi, was the brother-in-law of one of Ho's closest collaborators and one-time wife, Nguyen Thi Minh Khai. All three were from Central Vietnam. The other clan was made up of the northern ICP leaders, a number of whom had been in prison together in Son La during World War II. This leadership group included Truong Chinh, Hoang Quoc Viet, Le Duc Tho, Tran Quoc Hoan and Tran Huy Lieu. Le Van Luong emerged from 15 years on Con Son prison island in 1945 to join this group.[17] His long-term prison mate, Ton Duc Thang, seems to have been one southerner who was associated with this clan.

In the uneasy days after the August Revolution, when the communist-controlled Viet Minh worked to gain the public trust, Ho Chi Minh's decision to disband the ICP, making it a 'Marxist study group', gave the ICP leadership a less visible role. The decision was apparently taken to placate the Chinese Guo Ming Dan generals whose troops had occupied northern Vietnam to oversee the ceasefire. But it would be a cause of dissension between Ho Chi Minh and the ICP leadership in coming years. After more than a year of tense negotiations with the Chinese and French to gain recognition of Vietnam's independence, not to mention appeals for US support, in December 1946 the Viet Minh were forced to evacuate Hanoi and start a new phase of warfare in the maquis. Even before the evacuation from Hanoi, criticism of Ho's conciliatory policies began to be heard from Truong Chinh himself. In his September 1946 essay, 'The August Revolution', he singled out 'lack of firmness in the repression of counter-revolutionary elements' as one of the weaknesses of the uprising which brought the Viet Minh to power. He also emphasised the need to move quickly to the anti-feudal task of agrarian reform, and even to the construction of socialism (Truong Chinh 1963: 39–41, 59). This was in effect a call to increase class warfare, at a time when Ho was working to develop a nationalist consensus to support the aims of his government.

By the autumn of 1947, the deepening Cold War in Europe, intensified by the creation of the Cominform, brought new tensions to the surface among the Vietnamese communists. They were in total isolation, fighting without recognition or financial support from the Soviet Union or the French communists, and must have feared for their survival. The Chinese communists' victory was not yet in sight.

Here we return to the issue of Ton Duc Thang and his inflated official biography. At what must have been a hastily held meeting to celebrate the Russian October Revolution, the underground ICP introduced a new proletarian hero and father figure, Ton Duc Thang. At that November meeting in Vo Nhai, Le Van Luong informed the leadership that Ton Duc Thang had been a seaman in the French fleet which mutinied in the Black Sea in 1919. Over time, as Christoph Giebel explains it, this story came to represent 'one of the clearest and earliest manifestations of the Vietnamese spirit of revolutionary internationalism'.[18] He sees its 'chief addressees' as the USSR and the FCP (Giebel 1996: 102). However, as the story was first introduced in a secretive ICP meeting, I would contend that it was initially intended for internal consumption, as a challenge to Ho Chi Minh. Ho's strategy of conciliation with France had failed; his erstwhile allies, the Americans, had refused any concrete support, and the new Vietnamese state was in a very exposed position. Was this emphasis on Ton Duc Thang's longstanding revolutionary connections an attempt to create a new figurehead for the Vietnamese revolution, an impeccably proletarian one, who possessed the added prestige of having served 15 years in prison? In comparison, Ho Chi Minh's background was that of a bourgeois revolutionary nationalist. He had spent most of his career outside of Vietnam. In 1945 he had, moreover, co-operated with the Americans, who were now assuming the status of number one enemy of the communist bloc. Although theoretically Ho was head of the whole apparatus of Party and state at this time, there is little sign that he was actually involved in day-to-day decision-making within the Party. In fact, Vo Nguyen Giap writes in his memoirs that Ho was unwell in 1947, and by late October of that year was sent out of danger to a Dao village in the mountains (Vo Nguyen Giap 1995: 183).

By 1948, open currents of resistance to Ho's leadership within the Party had made themselves felt. Recently discovered documents from communist party archives in Prague give an idea of the depth of hostility which some Vietnamese communists felt towards Ho. Tran Ngoc Danh, the Democratic Republic of Vietnam (DRV) representative in France (and younger brother of Tran Phu, the Party's first official leader) was one of those who tried to persuade the Russians that Ho was an unworthy leader. In 1949 he abruptly closed the Paris representative office and fled to Prague (Hoang Van Hoan 1988: 252–3). From there, he sent at least two letters to Moscow. In one of these he expresses the Party's opposition to its own dissolution:

> After the Cominform's criticism, I am at present in total disagreement with the opportunist and nationalist line followed by my party since its official dissolution. This dissolution, which goes against the will expressed several times by our comrades, could not have been carried out without the energetic intervention of comrade Ho Chi Minh, at present President of the DRV.[19]

In another letter, of 10 January 1950 addressed to 'Comrade Iudin', Danh wrote that the ICP was dominated by its 'nationalist, petty-bourgeois element'; which 'lacked faith in the revolutionary force of the proletariat'. 'The decisive, divisive element is the personality of Ho Chi Minh', he emphasised.[20]

An additional element of disunity within communist ranks may have been confusion over the role of the CCP within southern Vietnam, where as we have seen, it had had a presence since the late 1920s. French military intelligence captured a document dated August 1949, from the 'Mytho sector', which said that an agreement between the central committees of the two parties had been reached, making the Chinese sections within Vietnam directly answerable to the ICP. If the Chinese and Vietnamese members of a section were equal in number, the section could be divided into two cells, placed under the command of the province committee, the directive stated.[21] The fact that there was still a question about the affiliation of Chinese communists within Vietnam in 1949 shows that attempts to solve this question in 1930 had not been effective.

In 1950, when Ho finally got to Moscow in Mao Zedong's entourage to make his case for support, the letters received from Tran Ngoc Danh, who himself had been trained in Moscow, must have made the Russians leery. I would argue that it was lack of support from within his own party, and perhaps criticism from the FCP, as much as any fixed view which Stalin held about Ho's policies, which made Ho's position in Moscow so difficult at this juncture. As Khrushchev's memoirs describe it, Stalin gave Ho a very cold reception. When Ho was granted an audience with Stalin, he came with a magazine carrying one of the Russian leader's articles, which he asked Stalin to sign. Stalin agreed, but according to Khrushchev, he later had it removed from Ho's hotel room (Khrushchev 1990: 155). This strange story seems to show, not only how conditional Stalin's endorsement was, but just how insecure Ho felt in his control over his party. It appears to have been Mao Zedong who persuaded the Russians to endorse Ho's leadership, by pointing out that Ho's united front strategy had helped to preserve the ICP.[22] The price of this assistance for Vietnam was that for much of the 1950s the Vietnamese communists became ideological apprentices of the CCP, in particular in the implementation of land reform.

Ho Chi Minh's first official biography, now believed to be his autobiography, appeared in a handwritten Chinese version in 1948. A version was published in Paris in 1949, with the author named as Tran Ngoc Danh, 'assemblyman from Cantho' (Tran Ngoc Danh 1949). Danh, a Central Committee member, would in 1950 be expelled from the Party for 'provoking internal dissension in the ranks of the Party', as well as for having 'distanced the Party from other parties'.[23] The publication of this hagiographic account of Ho's early political activity with Danh's by-line must have been a way of quashing rumours of a split among the Vietnamese communists. The book, in an expanded version, would later appear as *Glimpses of Chairman Ho's Life* (*Nhung Mau Chuyen ve Doi Hoat Dong cua Ho Chu Tich*). Seen in a vacuum, this little volume appears to be a routine work from a communist propaganda machine. It extols Ho's simplicity and makes much of his early experiences as a worker – first as a sailor and then as a labourer in London, where he is said to have shovelled snow and worked as a pastry cook. It confirmed that Ho Chi Minh and the young man who presented the Vietnamese demands to the Paris Peace Conference in 1919, Nguyen Ai Quoc, were one and the same.

Seen as an answer to an assault on Ho's leadership, however, the book becomes not only a skilful piece of propaganda, but also a timely effort at political self-preservation. It would, in the end, provide the unifying image of the origins of the Vietnamese independence movement. This picture emphasised the nationalist character of Vietnamese communism, in addition to the proletarian internationalist vision represented by Ton Duc Thang's embellished biography.

In 1951, when the re-baptised party, now the Dang Lao Dong Viet Nam (Vietnam Workers Party), resurfaced at the Second Party Congress, the Party endorsed Ho Chi Minh's role as 'the soul of the Vietnamese revolution and the Vietnamese resistance', but reserved for Truong Chinh, the VWP's First Secretary, the place of 'builder and commander' of the revolution.[24] From then on, the Vietnamese Party has preserved the principle of collective leadership and Ho Chi Minh's place as its father figure has been secure. But he seems never to have regained the personal authority which he had enjoyed in 1945, certainly not enough to enable him to mould the Party's history or ideology single-handedly.

The group, which had its base in the Viet Minh, with which the VCP has been identified in the West, has often been on the defensive against the proponents of radical class struggle – in particular during the Land Reform and the campaigns against 'Revisionism' in 1963–4 and again in 1967–8. Most of the communists identified with the Viet Minh, such as Giap and Dong, saw their power bases restricted to the executive branch (the government, as opposed to the Party). Truong Chinh, in contrast, who was dropped from his post as First Secretary during the criticism of the Land Reform campaign, retained his place in the Politburo and Secretariat, and built up a power base as Chairman of the Standing Committee of the National Assembly. He also remained a powerful ideologist, as head of the

Nguyen Ai Quoc School for training party cadres. Le Van Luong, who as head of the Party Rectification campaign from 1952–6 was responsible for purging many middle-class Party members, was dropped from the Politburo during the correction of errors of land reform. But he was apparently playing an important political role again by 1970, the year following Ho's death, when he reported at the Twentieth Party Plenum on relations with socialist countries.[25] Le Duc Tho, about whose early political career very little information is available, developed into perhaps the most powerful leader in Vietnam during the 1960s, as head of the Party Organization Commission. His two periods of imprisonment, first on Con Son island in the early 1930s, and later in Son La from 1939 to 1943, may have helped him to cement political ties which later served to consolidate his power in the communist party. In an open letter to the National Assembly in 1981, the well-known publicist Nguyen Khac Vien accused Tho's Organization Commission of encroaching on the powers of the government, at all levels.[26] Tran Quoc Hoan, the Minister of the Interior from 1951 to 1980, Tho's fellow prisoner at Son La, played the role of enforcer, according to the memoirs of Vu Thu Hien (Vu Thu Hien 1997).

Le Duan's power base and exact role in the leadership have yet to be elucidated, but it now seems clear that he teamed up with Tho and Truong Chinh during the anti-revisionism campaigns, to promote the goal of liberating the South. As a promoter of economic liberalisation after 1978, however, he later appears to have come into opposition to the policy of rapid socialisation of the South.[27] It may be the case that the Party, which was suddenly confronted with the task of running the wartorn and divided nation in 1975, was less united than appeared at the moment of victory. The decision to move to rapid unification in 1976, followed by the campaign to socialise the southern economy in 1977–8, are two aspects of a policy which from the evidence was championed by Truong Chinh in his role as ideologist. While this policy was also influenced by external events – worsening relations with China and Cambodia, as well as the threat of resistance from émigré Vietnamese – by 1982, as the Fifth Party Congress was approaching, Nguyen Khac Vien would criticise the Party leadership for its 'leap forward mentality' (Paul Quinn-Judge 1982). At the March Congress that year, Le Duc Tho admitted that 'the internal debate was fostering factions within the Party apparatus' (Thai Quang Trung 1985: 83). But it would not be until 1986, when Mikhail Gorbachev's moves to promote restructuring in the USSR helped to legitimise new policies in Vietnam, that the reform process known as *doi moi* (literally, new change) would be approved – after many false starts – in the early 1980s.

The Vietnamese communist leadership retained its façade of unity by adhering to the Bolshevik discipline instilled in the Soviet party under Lenin and Stalin – once the collective will had been made known, dissenters had no right to create factions or make open criticism of the Party. But by 1967 this collective discipline seems to have been cemented by fear, as the revelations of those imprisoned in the 1967 'Anti-Party Affair' make clear.[28] Today, thanks to the tenacity of a few old Party veterans such as Hoang Minh Chinh and Tran Do, and the memoirs of Vu Thu Hien, the intra-Party conflicts of the 1950s and 1960s are better known.

However, the act of revealing the contents of internal Party documents to non-Party members can still result in prison sentences on grounds of 'distributing state secrets' (*tan phat bi mat cua nha nuoc*). This was the charge against three individuals arrested in 1996 during the lead-up to the Eighth Party Congress, when a 22-page document by Vo Van Kiet, advocating intensified economic and legal reform, as well as greater democracy, was circulating among Party cadres and made its way to France.[29]

The earlier party factions have to a certain extent been institutionalised: now the government technocrats and economists associated with Vo Van Kiet and Phan Van Khai represent the forces more open to the West and reform, while the army has increasingly come to represent the party wing intent on preserving the state-run economy and orthodox communist power (Thayer 2001: 21). Neither group has retained much prestige in the eyes of the population, which tends to view the Party's infighting as a distraction from the more serious challenges facing the country. What is surprising today is that there is still a Party faction which views 'peaceful evolution attempts by hostile forces' as one of the major dangers to Vietnam's future (*Draft Political Report,* VCP, Ninth Party Congress). The Party has found a way of retaining an image of moderation, however, by selecting a new General Secretary who is rumoured to be Ho Chi Minh's son. Chosen in April 2001, Nong Duc Manh has been accorded something of Ho Chi Minh's aura of rectitude by means of these rumours, which he neither confirms nor denies (see Abuza 2002: 142–3).

Conclusion

This framework for rethinking the history of Vietnamese communism can undoubtedly be improved upon. But in one basic way I believe it will stand up: that is the necessity to view Party history as the history of groups and not just one unilinear progression. In my view the main distinguishing factor of these groups has been their interpretation of what it meant to be a communist. Regional clans have been very strong elements in Party history, but in the end ideology has cut across geographical boundaries. We should keep in mind, in particular, that in the southern part of Vietnam, there were several different sources of leftist revolutionary thinking, which led to the development of early communist groups.

A final point which we should keep in mind is the fact that the Vietnamese communists were far more dependent on external circumstances than were, for example, the Chinese. They lived in a small country with a long open coastline, which had been thoroughly taken over by the French colonial administration, and which in the later stages of the independence wars was wide open to American airpower. The upshot was that they could not afford to be eternally pro-Chinese or pro-Russian, or to go their own way like Albania. Vietnam had to steer a course which at any particular juncture offered the most support against powerful enemies.

Notes

1 Known as the Indochinese Communist Party (ICP) from October 1930 to its formal dissolution in November 1945; then as the Vietnam Workers Party from 1951 until 1976; and finally as the Vietnamese Communist Party (VCP) from 1976 until the present.

2 In early 1990 Tran Xuan Bach, a former secretary to Le Duc Tho, was dropped from the Politburo at a Party plenum, on the grounds that he had exposed differences within the Politburo to the public.

3 These theses advocated a two-stage path to socialism in colonial countries. During the first phase, the bourgeois democratic revolution, the communists would have to work with nationalist revolutionary groups to achieve independence and carry out agrarian reform to end feudalism. There was no clear demarcation in these theses to define when the second phase, the construction of socialism, would start.

4 Duiker (2000: 572) speaks of Ho's 'cult of personality', but does not use the phrase to denote absolute power.

5 Centre d'Archives d'Outre-Mer (hereafter CAOM), SPCE boxes 364 and 365.

6 CAOM, SPCE 365, Note de la Préfecture de Police, 18 February 1923; Note de l'Agent de Villier, 4 April 1923.

7 A Vietnamese translation of the letter written in Chinese characters, sent by Phan Chu Trinh to Nguyen Ai Quoc from Marseilles, 18 February 1922, is in the Ho Chi Minh Museum in Ho Chi Minh City. It is published in French translation in Gaspard (1992: 181–7).

8 CAOM, SPCE 365 includes several references to Nguyen Hai Than's early co-operation with HCM, for example, annexe à note Noel, no. 213, 1 October, 26 and 27 September 1925.

9 CAOM, SLOTFOM III, 116, report from 'le Conseiller d'Etat, Directeur des Affaires Politiques', Paris, February 1927.

10 See Sophie Quinn-Judge 2003, chapters 3, 4 and 5 for a fuller exposition of this idea.

11 RGASPI, 542 (Anti-Imperialist League), 1, 96, p.2, letter of May 1929 signed 'M'.

12 See the biography of Ngo Gia Tu in *Nhung Nguoi Cong San* (1976: 30). This underlines the fact that he developed three main revolutionary bases: in the Ba Son factory, in Phu Rieng Plantation, and in Vinh Kim Village in My Tho. This was the native village of Ton Duc Thang's wife.

13 RGASPI, 495, 154, 569, p.52, unsigned letter written after 4 April 1931, from Far Eastern Bureau to ICP; also 495, 32, 95, p.23, Joseph Ducroux letter of 15 April 1931 to FEB.

14 Ban Nghien Cuu Lich Su Dang, *Nhung Su Kien Lich Su Dang Bo Ha Noi* (1982: 33).

15 A number of ICP leaders had studied together at the College du Protectorat, the Buoi School, in the suburbs of Hanoi. These included Ngo Gia Tu, Nguyen Phong Sac, Do Ngoc Du, Trinh Dinh Cuu, Nguyen Van Cu, Do Huy Liem and Le Van Luong.

16 Marr (1995: 184–94) provides a number of valuable sources on this issue.

17 Le Van Luong's brother, the writer Nguyen Cong Hoan, claims that Le Duc Tho, after his release from Poulo Condore (Con Son prison island) recruited him for party membership during the Popular Front era. See Zinoman (2001: 287).

18 Giebel (1996: 14). Giebel stresses that he received only one eyewitness account of this meeting, from Thang's adjutant Duong Van Phuc.

19 Goscha (2000: 678–9), citing Archives of Czech CP CC, collection 100/3, vol. 207.

20 Goscha (2000: 680), citing document 89357/425, letter received 14 April 1950 in Moscow, Archives of the CP of the USSR.

21 Archives of Service Historique de l'Armée de Terre, Vincennes, 10H 3978, Dossier: Parti Communiste Indochinois, 1951; FTEO, FFVS, Secteur de Mytho, no. 3050/

CZ-S, traduction de document recupéré a Go Cong; no. 6, Comité du Parti au Nam Bo, 13 August 1949.

22 Paper by Yang Kuisong, 'Mao Zedong and the War in Indochina'.

23 Central Committee document dated 23 November 1950.

24 Cited in Thai Quang Trung (1985: 20), from *Nhan Dan*, 25 March 1951.

25 RGANI, Collection 89, inventory 54, document 8; 'Report of Central Committee Secretary of VWP Hoang Anh of the Twentieth Plenum, December 1970 – January 1971. Soviet and Vietnamese records diverge on the numbering of this plenum, which Vietnamese sources describe as the Nineteenth Plenum.

26 Paul Quinn-Judge (1982: 14), citing Nguyen Khac Vien's letter dated 21 June 1981.

27 For a discussion of disagreements over economic reform in the 1970s and 1980s, see Dang Phong and Beresford (1998: 61–71).

28 For a comprehensive view of this campaign and relevant source materials, see Stowe (1997). Also 'Thu ngo cua cong dan Hoang Minh Chinh' (An open letter from Citizen Hoang Minh Chinh), *Dien Dan (Forum)*, no. 23/01 October 1993; Nguyen Van Tran (1995: 326–9).

29 'Dang sau hai tai lieu "mat", mot cuoc dau tranh gay gat' ('Behind Two Secret Documents : A Nasty Struggle'), *Dien Dan (Forum)*, no. 48/ 01, 1996.

4 Key issues in the political economy of post-*doi moi* Vietnam

Martin Gainsborough

In the first half of the 1990s – after 1992, but before 1996 – Vietnam was surrounded by an air of collective euphoria on the part of foreign businesspeople, analysts and academics. The achievement of a trade surplus and a debt agreement with the Paris Club in 1992, France's President Mitterrand's visit in 1993, and normalisation of relations with the US in 1995, all contributed to a new mood of hope. Vietnam was declared the 'Next Asian Tiger'. Foreign investment poured in, economic growth rates soared, and for a period Vietnam could do no wrong; yet this mood did not last long. By 1996, unhappy foreign investors were swapping tales of double-crossing joint venture partners, infuriating red tape, and crippling levels of corruption. Economic growth and foreign investment approvals began to slow in 1996, well before the effects of the Asian financial crisis began to be felt in 1998–9.[1] The run-up to the Eighth Communist Party Congress in June 1996 provided an obvious occasion for rethinking. Susan Boyd, then Australian ambassador to Vietnam, spoke of the Eighth Party Congress as having given the 'forces of control a renewed mandate', suggesting that foreign businesses and others were 'suffering increased harrassment' as a result (Boyd 1997: 142). The change in sentiment was also reflected in popular writings about the country. *Shadows and Wind*, a 1998 book by a former Agence France Presse Hanoi correspondent, epitomises the new 'cynical' view of Vietnam (Templer 1998). It provides a sharp contrast with the more ebullient *Chasing the Tigers*, a book published just two years earlier by another journalist with chapter headings such as 'Asia's Youngest Tiger Roars' and 'Vietnam Awakes' (Hiebert 1996).

How can this changed mood be explained? A common interpretation would be to suggest that the early corporate pioneers simply got it wrong. In their thirst for business profits they closed their eyes to the difficulties, painting a picture of Vietnam which was wildly divorced from reality. As unrealistic expectations were dashed, their accounts inevitably changed. However, it was not so much Vietnam that had changed, but rather the perceptions of observers. This apparently plausible line of argument leaves unanswered the question of how to characterise Vietnam's post-*doi moi* political economy, which is the main task of this chapter.

Another often-heard interpretation is that the reform process actually slowed. This is evident in writing which began to emerge in the second half of the 1990s, chastising Vietnam for its lack of progress on reforms, and calling for a '*doi moi 2*'

(Kokko and Sjöholm 1997; Truong 1998; World Bank 1997b). The implication here is that at some point prior to the late 1990s there was a commitment on the part of Vietnam's leadership to a programme of change, a commitment which later waned.

But is this assumption of a slowed or stalled reform process correct? Answering this question is important not just as a matter of empirical fact, but because it goes to the heart of contemporary debates about how we understand Vietnam's political economy, including the relationship between 'ideas' and 'interests' in explaining change or the relative balance between 'policy' and 'informal activity'.[2] This chapter considers the relative importance of these concepts as a way of getting at the key issues in Vietnam's post-*doi moi* political economy. It does so by seeking to answer the following main questions:

- What is reform typically said to have consisted of, and how does this compare and contrast with reality?
- How do we explain the direction that change has in fact taken?
- Is there any evidence that at some point in the 1990s, a decision was made that reforms had gone too far and needed reining in? If we cannot identify such a decision or set of decisions, was this in fact what happened?
- How do we explain the rapid increase in private-sector activity since the end of the 1990s? That is, was it because of policy or in spite of it?

The chapter will conclude by asking how, given our findings, Vietnam's political economy might be expected to evolve in the future.

Reform in theory

According to most accounts, reform of centrally planned economies involves 'doing certain things'. First, reform is said to be outward or export-oriented. Second, the reform process is said to be pro-foreign investment. Both these policy approaches are seen to mark a shift from more autarkic, inward-looking policies associated with central planning in the era of the Cold War. Vietnam passed a Foreign Investment Law in December 1987, which in terms of its drafting was regarded as very liberal (Beresford 1997: 190). Select trading firms were said to be experimenting with trading on the international market from the 1980s (*Thanh Pho Ho Chi Minh Hai Muoi Nam* 1996). Moreover, despite a variety of ups and downs, the 1990s saw a dramatic increase in Vietnamese exports and inflows of foreign direct investment (Business Monitor International 1994, 1999). Third, reform is commonly associated with greater acceptance of the private sector. Gareth Porter notes a series of decrees issued in March 1988 which 'recognised the long-term importance of private industry, guaranteeing its existence as part of a "multi-component economy" and lifting all limitations on its hiring of labour' (Porter 1993: 149).

While *doi moi* (renovation) is usually viewed as dating from the Sixth Party Congress in December 1986, many accounts recognise that partial, reform-oriented changes occurred before this. These go back as early as the late 1970s when limited market incentives were introduced in both agriculture and industry (Beresford 1997: 187). Nevertheless, the planned economy remained very much in place (Fforde and de Vylder 1996: 13–15).

If partial reforms occurred before 1986, most accounts of reform give pride of place to changes introduced in 1989 against the backdrop of a seriously deteriorating fiscal situation. In separate accounts, Gareth Porter and Melanie Beresford write:

> At its Sixth Plenum in March 1989, the VCP leadership decided to end budget subsidies to state enterprises immediately … The dismantling of special privileges for state enterprises came as part of a broader package of liberalising reforms in 1989 … the VCP broke completely with orthodox Leninist economic policy on prices. It pledged that the state would, henceforth, use only economic levers, such as tax and fiscal policies, rather than administrative measures to influence prices … These measures were accompanied by two other economic stabilisation measures: a rise in interest rates and a currency devaluation … In just eighteen months, the SRV [Socialist Republic of Vietnam] regime had gone from cautiously edging towards economic liberalisation to carrying out a package of adjustment and stabilisation measures that even the bastion of conservative capitalist banking [the International Monetary Fund (IMF)] found exemplary.
>
> (Porter 1993: 150–1)

> During 1989 the government abolished official prices (except for a handful of government monopolies), floated the exchange rate and introduced positive real interest rates in the banking system … Direct subsidies from the state budget to SOEs [state-owned enterprises] were effectively ended. Positive real interest rates … were used to encourage savings, halt the 'dollarisation' of the economy, eliminate SOE subsidies via cheap credit provision, halt the growth of the budget deficit and bring inflation under control.
>
> (Beresford 1997: 191)

Thus, freeing up prices, devaluing the currency, raising interest rates and eliminating cheap credit to state enterprises either through the budget or the banking system are regarded as key reforms.

Reform is also associated with decentralisation and a smaller state.[3] The rationale here is that with the dismantling of the central plan and greater reliance on the market, there is a need to devolve decision-making to local authorities and enterprises, which are better placed to respond to market imperatives in their geographical locale or sector. Thus the late 1980s and 1990s saw state enterprises granted greater autonomy to manage their affairs. Provincial and city authorities were also given greater control over local expenditure, notably on infrastructure, and increased freedom to approve foreign investment projects (see Fforde and Seneque 1995; Porter 1995; *Vietnam Investment Review*, 20–26 March 2000). In terms of the size of the state, the rationale here is that as the state relinquishes its planning role and stops interfering in the market, it will also reduce in size.

The actual components of reform since the changes of 1989 are often less clearly spelt out. However, the mantra of the international financial institutions has been the need for further progress on key structural reforms. These are commonly said to include public administration reform, trade reform, state enterprise reform, and banking reform (IMF 1996; World Bank 1999b). In this sense, reform in the 1990s can be understood as involving a deepening or extension of previously introduced changes.

Reform in practice

In fact, there are many problems with the above characterisation of reform. Leaving aside the question of whether there was ever a reform 'blueprint', or the way in which the above account overly emphasises the role of policy as a component of change (which will be addressed later), this depiction of reform is also a rather poor record of what has actually happened. To illustrate why this is the case, we will now focus on four aspects of the above characterisation of reform. The claims are that reform:

- is export oriented
- emphasises the private sector
- implies that the state should shrink
- involves a tightening up of access to credit on the part of state enterprises.

The chapter will also examine a fifth aspect of the above characterisation, namely the association of reform with decentralisation. However, this will be dealt with later in the chapter, when the question of whether it is appropriate to talk in terms of reform slowing is addressed.

Export-oriented reform

The literature on East Asian development models distinguishes between an export-oriented economic strategy and one which relies on import substitution. Countries are usually seen to be pursuing one or other strategy, although as domestic industries strengthen they often switch from import substitution to export-led growth (Haggard 1990). Vietnam is commonly depicted as pursuing an export-oriented development strategy – a fact seemingly confirmed by the four-fold increase in exports between 1990 and 1996. However, this is not the whole story. The period since 1986 has also seen large amounts of import substitution. At the centre of this activity are state enterprises targeting the domestic market and shielded from international competition by high tariff barriers, quotas and import licenses. High levels of protection have the effect of creating a captive market for local producers. Moreover, while the international financial institutions are associated with calls for trade liberalisation, foreign investors have invested substantial amounts of capital in protected companies engaged in import substitution. This has usually been in the form of joint ventures with state enterprises, which was the dominant pattern for foreign investment in Vietnam in the 1990s.

Ari Kokko has suggested that a significant portion of Vietnam's imports, which increased six-fold during 1990–6, were destined for import-substituting firms, not export-oriented ones. He also notes the existence of an overvalued exchange rate as a telltale sign of an import-substitution trade regime (Kokko 1997: 14, 16). Key import-substitution sectors include steel, cement, coal, sugar, paper and fertilisers. Here, the government has typically been vulnerable to lobbying from interest groups within these industries pressing for a continuation of protection. It was against this backdrop that state enterprises continued to outstrip private enterprises in terms of industrial growth right up until the last year of the 1990s.

The role of the private sector

Reform is commonly associated with the growth of the private sector. However, aside from a rapid expansion of household enterprises, growth in the private corporate sector was a much more limited affair during the 1990s. Instead, at the forefront of moves to take advantage of business opportunities which emerged with reform were state business interests. This process comprises three principal strands: first, existing state enterprises diversifying into new sectors; second, the formation of large numbers of new state enterprises, especially at the city and district level; and third, the establishment of private companies with state share-holders, the latter often involving asset-stripping from the state sector. These companies have tended to operate in a clearly defined set of sectors, namely foreign and domestic trade, real estate and construction, hotel and tourism, and light manufacturing. The choice of sectors was no coincidence. These were areas which saw rapid growth in the 1990s. They also included areas, such as foreign trade, where entry was restricted at least until the end of the 1990s. State business interests were also well-placed to take advantage of preferential access to contracts, licenses, land and credit – areas where private firms generally did not do so well (Gainsborough 2003: 16–39).

Some of these companies that emerged in the 1990s have been so successful that they have begun to resemble diversified business conglomerates, with interests extending well beyond their core business. Apart from having subsidiary or associate companies active in a range of business sectors, a defining characteristic of these new conglomerates is that they have developed interests in banking. Even in Ho Chi Minh City, a city widely associated with the private sector, 64 per cent of domestic industrial output was derived from state companies in 2000. This is little different from the nationwide average, where the share is 65 per cent (*Nien Giam Thong Ke 2000* 2001).

The size of the state

With its emphasis on growth of the market and the dismantling of the mechanisms of central planning, reform is often associated with the retreat of the state. However, the picture in Vietnam is much more ambiguous. Looking at patterns in state sector employment as an indicator of the size of the state, the trend was for a consistent rise during the second half of the 1990s, after a fall in the first half. This pattern is also evident in data distinguishing between centrally and locally employed public sector workers (*Nien Giam Thong Ke 2000* 2001 and *Nien Giam Thong Ke 1995* 1996). In Ho Chi Minh City, widely associated with reform in the popular lexicon – and hence where one might expect a smaller state sector – the trend in state sector employment was upwards for most of the 1990s. Thus the numbers employed by the state sector in the city were larger at the end of the 1990s compared with the beginning. Some of the most significant increases were in the area of party and state management and construction (*Nien Giam Thong Ke Thanh Pho Ho Chi Minh 1997* 1998).

Access to credit

Reform is widely associated with a hardening of soft budget constraints for state enterprises, thereby ending the practice whereby firms obtained credit either directly from the budget or from state-owned commercial banks with little attention paid to performance. Porter talks in terms of the immediate ending of budget subsidies to state enterprises in 1989, while Beresford talks of the elimination of cheap credit provision for state enterprises following the raising of interest rates in the same year (Porter 1993: 150–1; Beresford 1997: 191). However, there is little evidence that these changes actually happened. In the absence of greater transparency in terms of public finances or patterns in bank lending, any assertion that there has been a hardening of soft budget and credit constraints has rather to be taken on trust. Moreover, what evidence is available suggests that even if direct subsidies from the state budget might have become less common in the 1990s, access to cheap bank credit for state enterprises remained widespread.

Underpinning a continuation of soft credit constraints during the 1990s was the continued influence of politicians and enterprises over banks. Thus, if politicians (in their capacity as heads of enterprise-controlling institutions) made representations to a bank instructing it to lend to one of their firms, the bank was usually powerless to resist. Banks were similarly weak when it came to trying to call in overdue loans, especially if an enterprise had exercised the right to borrow without putting down collateral – as was permitted in the second half of the 1990s. Furthermore, bank vulnerability to political pressures has not just been a problem affecting the state-owned commercial banks. The shareholding structure of the joint stock commercial banks is heavily dominated by state business interests, so that bankers are also vulnerable to political pressures (Gainsborough 2003: 32–7).

A good illustration of how the lending process actually worked came to light in proceedings associated with the trial of a Ho Chi Minh City-based party company, Tamexco, which was taken to court on alleged corruption charges in 1997. While this is just one example, a common refrain at the time was that many of the practices for which Tamexco was prosecuted were commonplace.[4] In the extract below, the Deputy General Director of the state-owned Bank for Foreign Trade (Vietcombank) is asked in court to explain why Vietcombank continued lending to Tamexco despite its debts:

COURT: By December 1992, Tamexco's total debt at Vietcombank was $15.6m, wasn't it?

MR LO: It was only $10m.

COURT: Why then did you continue to lend a further $3m?

MR LO: At this stage, we did not want to lend but because Tamexco was a fertiliser importer – importing fertiliser for the winter–spring harvest – this was a duty entrusted to us by the office of the government.

COURT: Why did they not entrust it to a firm which could do business profitably?

MR LO: The court ought to ask this question to the Ministries of Agriculture and Trade; why did they give [fertiliser import] quotas to Tamexco?

(*Tuoi Tre*, 28 January 1997)

When Lo was pressed further as to whether he was aware that lending to Tamexco, given the circumstances of its debts, contravened bank regulations (*sai so voi phap luat ngan hang*), he said that lending to the company was guided by Document 8 (*van ban 08*), issued on 8 April 1991. Document 8 apparently permitted certain bank clients to borrow beyond the normal ceiling set at 10 per cent of a bank's legal capital for a single client. According to Lo, it was the result of collaboration between different institutions in Ho Chi Minh City, including the local Party committee:

Document 8 was signed by [Deputy State Bank Governor] Chu Van Nguyen, and was the result of a collaboration between the State Bank and the Standing Committee of the Ho Chi Minh City party committee. It had the ability to overcome obstacles (*no co gia tri thao go*).

(*Tuoi Tre*, 28 January 1997)

Lo did not say who had signed for the Party, and to this day the question remains something of a mystery.[5] According to the prosecution, Document 8 had been superseded by new regulations issued 28 days later by the then State Bank Governor, Cao Sy Kiem. Called to give evidence, State Bank Governor Chu Van Nguyen said that Vietcombank Ho Chi Minh City must have known about this. Lo, however, said that Document 8 continued to apply in Ho Chi Minh City, even after the new regulations were issued. Despite repeated high-level assertions of a commitment to reforming the banking system from the 1990s onwards, the influence of politicians over banks remains widespread.

Explaining change

If this is the reality of reform – import substitution in the context of continued protectionism, a constrained private sector, an expanding state bureaucracy, and a tendency for the credit constraint to be soft – how do we explain the direction that change has taken? Why is the private sector not bigger? Why has there not been more export-oriented economic activity and why has the state not withdrawn more from the economy? It is here that a distinction between 'ideas' and 'interests' may be usefully employed.

Interests

The direction that reform has taken can to a large extent be explained with reference to interests which became established in the party-state under central planning. As the plan broke down or was dismantled, these interests – located in state enterprises and the bureaucracy – did not just roll over: rather, they sought to preserve what they had, whether it be control over material or financial resources, or the right to carry out certain regulatory functions. Where this was not possible, state institutions proved adept at re-inventing themselves. Thus, offices which had formerly been a cog in the wheel of the central plan took on new roles linked to the market economy. These included issuing licenses to foreign investors or private businesses, or regulating or overseeing activities linked to the emergence of the land market, or even the introduction of new taxes (Gainsborough 2003: 30–7, 60–6).

State enterprises which had performed a circumscribed role under central planning did not simply sit back as markets in the former Eastern bloc disappeared, or demands for their products dried up. Rather, they too sought to adapt to new opportunities which had emerged under reform. While this frequently involved embracing the market – including engaging in speculative activity often involving foreign exchange and land – state enterprises were also complicit in undermining its free play. If quick profits could be had by producing for the local market under heavy protective barriers or keeping out the competition, enterprises wasted no time in lobbying for such protection.

It is this metamorphosis from guardian of the plan to gate-keeping the market economy and exploiting new business opportunities which explains the increase in the size of the state. In all cases, the boundaries between public and private remained blurred, with politicians, bureaucrats and enterprise directors quick to reap the rewards of office.

Ideas

Ideas are also important in explaining the direction change has taken in Vietnam. While the government has signed up to structural adjustment programmes with the IMF – involving plans to tighten access to credit by state enterprises, and to lower tariff barriers – it is worth asking what Vietnam's politicians really believe in. After all, the philosophical tradition on which Vietnam draws regarding the role of the state in the economy is quite different from that of the West. In this respect, it has not gone unremarked that there may be a possible link between present-day hostility towards the private sector and the lowly status of commerce in the pre-colonial era (Fforde 1995: 5–6). Moreover, calls by the West for renewed liberalisation following the Asian financial crisis are not viewed in countries like Vietnam simply as the innocent application of the 'right policy', but rather as something much more political. Calls for the government to withdraw from the economy are often regarded suspiciously as possible attempts by the West to undermine state power. Liberalisation, meanwhile, is not seen simply as being 'good for growth' but rather being motivated by a desire to force open Asian markets, so that Western firms may benefit (Higgott 1999: 101–4). Given such perspectives, it is hardly surprising that import substitution has been so prominent, and that 15 or so years after the Sixth Party Congress state involvement in credit allocation remains the norm.

The role of policy

While writings by the international financial institutions and some academics often place heavy emphasis on policy, both in its description and explanation of the change, a growing body of literature on Vietnam downplays the importance of policy in explaining how reform emerged. Popularised terms such as 'fence-breaking' – or the idea that the market emerged out of the plan – encapsulate the view that the illegal involvement of state enterprises and bureaucratic institutions in markets during the era of planning laid the foundations for the market economy, ahead of any substantive moves towards reform by the state (Fforde and de Vylder 1996: 5–6). According to such accounts, policy-makers have played a much more passive role in determining the direction of change, often responding after the event.

If the above account offers a valid interpretation of the years immediately preceding *doi moi*, does it adequately describe the situation now given that the state has now formally adopted a policy of reform? To a large extent, the answer appears to be yes. State institutions and societal actors continue to operate in ways which are not formally sanctioned, but where the stipulations of policy-makers are widely flouted. The way in which the land market has emerged over the last decade – the land market heated up in Ho Chi Minh City in anticipation of changes expected with the 1993 Land Law which authorised the sale of land use rights – is a good example (Gainsborough 2003: 35–7).

Nevertheless, it would be wrong to suggest that policy has no relevance in explaining the direction of change. The state may be weak in a technical sense, insofar as it has difficulty getting different institutions to work towards a common goal, but it still exerts significant influence in setting – at the very least – the outer parameters within which informal activity happens. Thus, speculation in the land and foreign exchange markets only makes sense in the context of state restrictions on land prices and control over the exchange rate. Equally, illegal revenue collection by provincial or local authorities, or underdeclaring the total amount of revenue raised, only occurs in the context of a particular way of structuring intergovernmental fiscal relations, which is the result of policy.

In addition, the state still retains the ability to discipline those who step too far out of line. This was evident during the 1990s in the periodic clampdowns on speculative activity in the land and foreign exchange markets and in a number of court cases in which acts of alleged corruption were brought to book (Gainsborough 2003: 70–7, 78–97).

Did reform slow?

It was noted at the beginning of the chapter that a common explanation offered to explain widely diverging depictions of Vietnam either side of 1995 was not simply that perceptions had changed but rather that there had occurred a substantive change in Vietnam itself – hence the idea that reform had slowed. Given what has just be said about reform, namely that it frequently has a momentum of its own largely divorced from the action of policy-makers, it is worth asking whether it is meaningful to conceive of reform as something which can be turned on or off like a tap. Many commentators clearly believe so. Former Australian ambassador Boyd suggested as much when she spoke about the 'forces of control' receiving a renewed mandate in the run-up to the Eighth Party Congress in 1996. Carlyle Thayer talks of party conservatives seeking to reimpose control in 1989 in response to liberalisation moves introduced by the then Party General Secretary, Nguyen Van Linh (Thayer 1992: 117).

How precisely reform is said to have slowed is not always clear. Part of the problem is the contradictory nature of change in Vietnam both at a macro-level (for example, import substitution and export-oriented economic activity occurring alongside each other) and at a micro-level (for example, calls for banking sector reforms versus actual practice at the level of the firm). Consequently, it is hard to be sure whether a certain development represents an actual slowdown, or just a reaffirmation of an existing policy or approach.

There is, however, one development that may constitute a substantive change in direction, namely the trend towards re-centralisation mentioned earlier as being the fifth 'counter-intuitive' hallmark of Vietnam's reforms during the 1990s. This may well be what commentators are picking up on when they say that reform has slowed.

Reform is commonly understood in terms of decentralisation, and rightly so, for the reasons outlined earlier. The process of decentralisation also provides a good example of the limits of policy in determining the direction change has taken. While some moves towards decentralisation are formally granted by way of policy changes – the right to approve foreign investment, for example – many others are the result of unsanctioned behaviour. The rise of new state business interests at the lower levels of the party state, which has had far-reaching implications for the political balance of power between the centre and the lower levels, is a case in point. At best, this activity is very loosely overseen by the higher levels, and much of it is not overseen at all.

However, it appears that at some point in the early 1990s steps were taken to try and reassert central control, in the face of what were regarded as worrying levels of decentralisation which had occurred during the 1980s and especially after 1986. A reduction in provincial representation on the Party Central Committee at the Seventh Congress in 1991 has been cited as an illustration of a reversal of the decentralisation which occurred at the Sixth Congress.[6] Other examples include: an attempt by the Prime Minister's office to gain greater control over the appointment of provincial and city People's Committee chairmen (1992) (see Gainsborough 2003: 43–52); the reorganisation of state enterprises into *tap doan* and *tong cong ty* in an attempt to concentrate control over state resources (1994–5) (Jerneck 1997); and an increase in big corruption cases in the second half of the 1990s. The big corruption cases, which include Tamexco, Minh Phung-Epco and Tan Truong Sanh, are understood here less in terms of the state clamping down on corruption *per se*, and more about the centre disciplining the lower levels of the party-state in an attempt to counter decentralisation (Gainsborough 2003: 78–97).

Perhaps in view of its wealth, Ho Chi Minh City has been very much on the receiving end of moves towards re-centralisation. Since 1991 the Party Secretary in the city has always been a member of the Politburo – when previously he was not. This fits with the idea of re-centralisation, with the state seeking to lock the local Party Secretary into central decision-making processes. The formation of the Chief Architect's office in Ho Chi Minh City in 1993, with a strong central mandate to oversee activities in the city's land market, represents a further attempt by the centre to reassert its authority in the localities (Gainsborough 2003: 62–3). Whether such moves are conscious or instinctive, or represent a slowdown in reform, is a matter for debate. However, there is no denying they are having a significant impact on the nature of Vietnam's political economy.

The rise of the private sector

The characterisation of Vietnam's political economy offered here places heavy emphasis on the rise of new state business interests under reform, countering the usual tendency associating reform with the rise of the private sector. However, there is a sense in which this is changing. State business interests still predominate in Vietnam, but private firms are becoming more important. This became apparent in the aftermath of the Asian financial crisis. Since 1999, growth in the non-state sector has consistently outstripped that of the state sector, reversing a trend previously sustained since 1988 (*Nien Giam Thong Ke 1995* 1996 and *Nien Giam Thong Ke 2000* 2001). Understanding why this has happened is important in terms of our efforts to understand the key determinants of change in Vietnam's post-*doi moi* political economy. A search for an explanation also feeds into the debate about how much importance to attach to policy in explaining change.

Certainly, there is no shortage of policy measures relating to the private sector. In December 2001, the National Assembly voted in favour of a constitutional amendment stipulating that the private sector should be treated equally with the state sector. Much emphasis has also been placed on explaining the private sector take-off following the passage of the Enterprise Law, which came into effect in January 2000 (Business Monitor International 2002: 14–15). Certainly the law's implementation was followed by a surge in company start-ups, and private entrepreneurs confirm that setting up a company is easier than it used to be. Nevertheless, it would be unprecedented for a law in Vietnam to have such a ready effect, suggesting that other factors might be important.

In all likelihood it appears that a mixture of non-policy and policy measures are important. The Enterprise Law introduced in January 2000 was one of a number of measures introduced by the government following the Asian financial crisis, which together have led to enhanced confidence among private business-people. An important measure was the lifting of restrictions preventing private firms from exporting directly. However, a number of non-policy measures are also relevant, including the need for would-be entrepreneurs to accumulate practical experience in areas such as how to run a business, including mobilising capital through informal networks and learning how to negotiate tricky social relationships. This takes time. Thus it was not until the end of the 1990s that the effects of such processes started to become apparent. Also important in explaining private sector growth are various informal processes involving the migration of capital from the state sector, often known as asset-stripping (Fforde 2001c: 25–6). Thus, a convincing explanation for private sector growth includes a range of factors in which policy is one of a number of variables.

Conclusion

It has been argued that Vietnam's post-*doi moi* political economy can be aptly characterised with reference to five broad components: import substitution against a backdrop of continued heavy protection; the continued importance of state business interests, many of which have developed quite successfully since the late 1980s; an expanding state bureaucracy, moving from administering the plan to gate-keeping the market economy; a drive by the central state to re-centralise power; and the continuation of strong political involvement in credit allocation to state enterprises. Moreover, all this has occurred in an environment where the direction of change is determined by the interaction between informal, illicit activity and state policy, where the latter is often rather an insignificant factor.

A final question concerns whether what we have observed is simply a transitional stage on the road to a more reformed economy. In some respects, this is almost certainly the case. We have noted faster growth in the private sector since 1999. The government has also signed up to far-reaching liberalisation measures through agreements with the international financial institutions, the Association of Southeast Asian Nations and the United States. Vietnam's desire to join the World Trade Organisation promises further such changes. Nevertheless, based on what we have seen over the last 15 years or so, state power in Vietnam has proved adept at reinventing itself and finding cracks in the reformed system in order to steal a march on others. Thus it is likely that the impact of the anticipated liberalisation measures will turn out rather differently from how they were originally conceived. It may be that the drive towards re-centralisation which has occurred during the 1990s – while resisted in some quarters – could lead to the emergence of a stronger, even more technocratic, state. More than a decade after outsiders first started talking about the need for politicians to withdraw from credit allocation to state enterprises, this remains an area of unfinished business. This highlights the way in which aspects of Vietnam's political economy, which we have suggested draw on deep philosophical underpinnings regarding the relationship between state and market, are likely to prove rather resilient.

Notes

1 For more details, see Chapter 13 by Freeman and Nestor in this volume.
2 Emphasising the informal dimensions of change has been a major theme in the work of Adam Fforde. See Fforde and de Vylder 1996.

3 This is more talked about in the literature on China than on Vietnam; while the idea of reform leading to a smaller state derives from the writing of neo-classical economists. See Duckett 1998; Nevitt 1996.

4 This inevitably raises the question as to why Tamexco was taken to court. For a discussion of this issue, see Gainsborough 2001.

5 One source suggested almost as a passing comment that it was the then Party Secretary in Ho Chi Minh City, Vo Tran Chi. Interview 4 February 1998.

6 See Thayer (1997c). However, developments at the Ninth Party Congress in 2001, which saw a sharp increase in provincial representation on the Central Committee, make sustaining this kind of analysis difficult, unless of course there has been a marked shift away from re-centralisation, which seems unlikely. See Abuza 2002.

5 Politics in mountain communes

Exploring Vietnamese grassroots democracy

Claudia Zingerli

Vietnam has been undergoing tremendous economic and societal changes during the past two decades. The launch of comprehensive reform programmes (*doi moi*) has opened Vietnam towards the world market and to many other global influences. Vietnam's transition from a planned economy to a market economy under state management is characterised by a heady fusion of socialist and capitalist ideas, the combination of which have created enormous socio-economic forces in Vietnam.

Reforms of the Land Law (1993) and the Law on Enterprises (1999) provided the impulse for economic growth and diversification, based on the reassignment of responsibility for the means of production to organisations, households and individuals. Vietnamese citizens have developed a tremendous desire for entrepreneurial liberty and innovation. The depoliticised 'mass man' of totalitarian communism, characterised as unable to articulate his needs and powerless to express himself in a organised way (Ehrenberg 1999: 182), has evolved into a 'homo economicus' exposed to a wide range of different influences and pressures making him less susceptible to the appeals of radical and anti-democratic ideas (Gill 2000: 4). In this new socio-economic situation policies and programmes require adjustment.

Although the Vietnamese leaders initially intended to reform the economy without major changes in the political tradition, the launch of *doi moi* has contributed to fundamental transformations of both the economic and the political spheres (McCormick 1998: 129). Market reforms have given birth to a legalised private sector, while the resulting economic forces have led to the revitalisation of groups and organisational activity at the local level and the emergence of associations formed as a result of local initiative (Thayer 1995: 52; Gill 2000: 4). The increased diversity of the economy and the enhanced complexity of economic decision-making have forced the Vietnamese leadership to turn its attention towards the regions and localities where new economic roles are assumed. It has also put the issue of political participation back on the agenda, a recurrent theme throughout Vietnam's modern history.

However, the Seventh Party Congress of 1991 firmly rejected calls for any form of political pluralism and a loosening of the Party's monopoly role. Rather, the Congress agreed to endorse gradual and limited efforts at political reform

(Thayer 1995: 51). The government's political commitment to governance reform was acknowledged by adopting central principles, such as participation, transparency, accountability, effectiveness, efficiency and rule of law (United Nations Development Programme [UNDP] 2001: 7). These principles are regarded as guidelines in the process of strengthening socialist democracy in the economic transition period.

In 1998, the Vietnamese Communist Party (VCP) and the government issued Decree 29/1998/ND-CP on the exercise of democracy in the communes (Politburo of the Communist Party of Vietnam 1998; Government of the Socialist Republic of Vietnam 1998). The political leadership in Hanoi declared:

> Democracy is the nature of our regime and State. Our Party and the State always respect and bring into full play the people's mastery, creating an enormous strength and making a decisive contribution to the success of our revolution.
>
> (Government of the Socialist Republic of Vietnam 1998: 14)

In order to address such violations of the 'people's mastery' as increasing bureaucracy, democratic deficits, inequality and bribery, the VCP and government embarked on steps to (re)establish and strengthen democratic regimes in the localities. They based the principles of exercising democracy in the communes on the words of Ho Chi Minh: 'people know, people discuss, people execute and people supervise' (Government Committee for Organisation and Personnel 2000: 29). The four levels of participation specified in Decree No. 29 were information sharing, consultation, participation in decision-making, and monitoring and supervision.

Decree No. 29 came to be called the 'grassroots democracy decree' and received wide attention. It largely nurtured expectations for the pursuit of bigger political projects of decentralisation and democratisation, advocated more by liberal Party members, and frequently supported by international development agencies involved in institutional and administrative reform in Vietnam. However, the concept of democracy promoted in the grassroots democracy decree involves many paradoxes and dilemmas.

This study explores the meaning of democracy and grassroots democracy in the context of Vietnam and asks how it is implemented and what it changes in the localities. The concept of democracy advocated by the VCP is followed down to the local political contexts of mountain communes, and is discussed by taking account of views held by those on the ground.

Notions of democracy in Vietnam

During Vietnam's transition period, calls for political participation and democratisation by both party members and international donor agencies have become louder. These calls are largely based on the assumption that greater democracy would contribute positively towards economic development (Crawford 1995: vii).

However, notions of democracy differ greatly between countries and political regimes. Officially, Vietnam's understanding of democracy is rooted in Marxist–Leninist ideas and the theory of the 'dictatorship of the proletariat' (Ehrenberg 1992: 2). Vietnamese socialist democracy was established during the revolution in 1945.

In its official interpretation 'socialist democracy' is a term used for a certain version of democracy, which emphasises social justice and is considered to be superior to 'bourgeois democracy' (Wilczynski 1981: 535). In Vietnam, socialist democracy is defined as a regime where people are the owners (*lam chu*), and where every interest and power belongs to them (Government Committee for Organisation and Personnel 2000: 27). According to the theory of the 'dictatorship of the proletariat', the working class can use this power to oppose the dictatorship of the bourgeoisie and to suppress any attempts at counterrevolutions (Ehrenberg 1992: 2). The essential characteristic of Vietnamese socialist democracy, which largely distinguishes it from liberal democracies, is that the VCP plays the sole leading role. Polyarchic features and the multiparty system of Western democracies are not compatible with the Vietnamese idea of democracy. It follows the principle that 'Vietnam's Communist Party is the country's leader, Vietnam's government is the country's manager, and Vietnamese people are the country's owners' (Dau Hoan Do *et al.* 1999:12). The VCP asserts that the regime is democratic in nature because it represents the interest of the majority of the population: the peasants and the proletariat. However, only three per cent of the total population are Party members (Abuza 2001: 2).

The standard operating procedure of democracy in Vietnam is the concept of democratic centralism. Pluralist opinions and conflicting views should be freely expressed and widely discussed at all levels of the Party hierarchy. The Party should take these opinions into account when making a decision but once the decision has been made the policy must be unquestioningly accepted and carried out by all Party members. This concept theoretically permits dissent, but in reality it allows very little upward flow of views and opinions (Robertson 1993: 130). Democratic centralism is also defined by 'the part submitting to the whole, the minority yielding to the majority, lower ranks obeying upper ranks, and localities obeying the centre' (Marr 1994 in MacLean 2001: 16).

Despite many intra-party debates and changing economic realities, the monopoly of political power held by the VCP is untouched. The Vietnamese notion of democracy differs significantly, therefore, from understandings of liberal democracy which are based on political pluralism, competition and rule of law (Gutmann 1993: 413; Nuscheler 1995: 220). Also, the export of democracy through agendas such as 'good governance' advocated by international institutions like the World Bank and the International Monetary Fund (Laasko 1995: 217) has not yet encouraged polyarchic political features. Democracy in Vietnam has the character of a political project implemented in a top-down manner, rather than underpinned by an active civil society. Vietnamese socialist democracy involves the risk of the arbitrary use of power by political leaders. This makes many Western observers sceptical about the democratic substance of the whole political system; critics often point out Vietnam's totalitarian and authoritarian tendencies (see also Ehrenberg 1999; Gill 2000; Abuza 2001).

Grassroots democracy: a political project

Since the promulgation of Decree No. 29 on the exercise of democracy in the communes, direct democratic arrangements of the political structure at the local level have been promoted. All delegates are revocable, bound by the instructions of their constituency, and organised into a pyramid of directly elected committees (Held 2001: 199). Enhanced participation and more transparency of political and economic decision-making in issues concerning livelihood and well-being in the communes are central elements of the grassroots democracy decree. It redefines roles, responsibilities and obligations in everyday politics in the communes, and seeks to strengthen the direct democratic links between the public and the authorities (Government of the Socialist Republic of Vietnam 1998). Decree No. 29 indicates a trend toward more accountability and debate in political practice in Vietnam.

The government and the VCP have recognised that putting in place effective governance structures at the local level is essential for a well-functioning economy, and for spreading the benefits of growth widely among society. They have acknowledged the need for re-orienting the all-encompassing government of the planning era, towards a more enabling set of activities supporting and complementing individual involvement in economic decision-making at the grassroots level. Decree No. 29 represents a set of legal rules that encourages local authorities actively to apply democratic principles when exercising their daily work duties, and it provides grassroots people with legal rights to take part in village- and commune-level economic and political decisions.

However, democracy in the communes – so-called grassroots democracy – has the character of a political project that is likely to be abandoned when political, economic and social circumstances change. There is a constant struggle between the need for a strong central administration to enforce laws and impose order, and the need for constraints on state bodies' power to create space for individuals' rights at the grassroots level (Dau Hoan Do *et al.* 1999: 12). Held (2001: 199) points out that for democracy to flourish today it has to be reconceived as a double-sided phenomenon, concerned, on the one hand, with the reform of state power, and, on the other hand, with the restructuring of civil society. This entails recognising the indispensability of a process of 'double democratisation', the interdependent transformation of both state and civil society.

However, the political leadership's attitude in Vietnam is rather reluctant concerning the emergence of an active civil society and reactive in granting more political participation. Typically, the leadership looks at a small number of alternatives for dealing with a problem, and tends to choose options that differ only marginally from existing policy. Policy-making is serial, and new approaches to problems are continuously developed. As mistakes become apparent, policies are re-adjusted. The model suggests that major changes occur through a series of small steps, each of which does not fundamentally challenge the whole system (Sutton 1999: 10). The political leaders justify their approach by referring to the experiences of other socialist countries in Eastern Europe and the former Soviet Union. They are eager to prevent any political instability, and argue that the monopoly power of the VCP is the only way to prevent political and economic turmoil (Abuza 2001: 5). This strategy has encountered many criticisms from both VCP members and external observers, as it involves a voluntaristic component in the democratisation efforts.

Another characteristic of Vietnam's grassroots democracy is that its scope is conscientiously circumscribed by the central level of political decision-making. Grassroots democracy is an idea formulated by the Party, which has defined its political scope with reference to Marxist doctrine. In contrast to advocates of liberalism, who developed a theory of civil society because they sought to democratise the state, Marxists developed a theory of the state because they wanted to democratise civil society (Ehrenberg 1999:174). Grassroots democracy in Vietnam therefore does not result from an emerging civil society claiming basic democratic political rights, but has been implemented from the centre to the locality. This top-down character of Decree No. 29 places massive constraints on its implementation. Officials of government institutions and administrative bodies at the provincial, district and commune level are advised to adjust their daily work to the principles of grassroots democracy. Actual empowerment and sharing final decision-making depend tremendously on the authorities' capabilities, capacities and conviction. Many officials tend to see implementing 'democracy' as simply another administrative duty. They frequently argue that the people do not need to be informed about all matters (MacLean 2001:16). Such working attitudes hamper a continuous and rapid implementation process. Grassroots democracy tends to be perceived as a political experiment, which materialises only when the state and VCP provide budgets for training courses, workshops, and regular meetings for government officials. The role of local authorities is crucial to the implementation of the decree, since their attitudes concerning the expression of opposing views and the representation of the local people determines whether or not concerns raised at the grassroots level are transmitted to higher decision-making arenas.

Local autonomy and democratic components of the political system

Since the grassroots democracy decree, relations between local authorities and the central state have been put back into focus. Turley (1980: 185) reported that these links had been repeatedly strengthened during the Indochina Wars to enhance resistance and popular support of the VCP, but that their importance had diminished during peace time. Taylor (1993: 318) and Glassner (1993: 341) refer to the ambiguity of the local state. Different interests from those of the national dominant groups can control particular localities. Simultaneously, local groups can use the local state to promote their own policies, in opposition to those of the central state. Local–state relations are, therefore, typically loaded with tensions between the centre and the locality, mostly because of the unequal distribution of power between the two. Uneven development inevitably forces the central state to organise control of its territory through some local autonomy.

In Vietnam, the local state organises local agents in order to manage the country's territorial diversity. Historically, local authorities in Vietnam had a relatively large amount of discretion in applying central policies, whether in times of guerrilla warfare, or in the wake of economic renovation when many reforms originated from the political periphery (McLeod 1999: 360; Dang Phong and Beresford 1998: 18). The central state's constant wariness of opposing social initiatives on the political periphery gave, however, rise to thorough control mechanisms, such as the household registration system or the network of neighbourhood police stations that kept almost all citizens under close surveillance (McCormick 1998: 124). In recent times these mechanisms have lost much of their rigour, and individuals as well as organisations and associations can operate more freely than ever before (Gray 1999: 711).

The political system of the communes includes elements with direct democratic characteristics. The National Assembly and the People's Councils represent the people most directly. At the local level the People's Council raises local concerns in the commune meetings and feeds the contents of resolutions and government programme activities back to the villages. These regulations on the responsibilities and administrative duties of the communes, the smallest administrative unit closest to grassroots people, were set in place in the early 1980s (Council of Ministers 1981). Decree No. 29 was supposed to strengthen these existing democratic elements.

The direct and representative democratic elements have always been strongest in the communes (Turley 1980: 181). The interlinkage between the People's Council, village headmen and local people is supposed to facilitate direct democratic political participation (see Figure 5.1).

The diagram shows the political system with administrative bodies and mass organisations at the commune level. The arrows indicate the way the commune administration is established. The ellipse indicates the direct democratic realm between grassroots people, their direct representatives, and the commune administration.

In this realm of direct democratic exchange lies the potential for democratisation and decentralisation. However, the role of the People's Council and National Assembly remains rather formal and weak, although directly elected state organs have gained more real power and have been able to give more substance to their work since the launch of *doi moi* (Dang Phong and Beresford 1998: 91). Their direct link to the grassroots people makes the direct representatives who populate these organs, though only ideologically, the 'most powerful organ in the commune' (personal communication with People's Council chairmen, December 2000). However, their lack of budgetary power and independence from the party-state restricts their influence. The structure of direct democracy as vested in the People's Council and the National Assembly is a system of delegation which is, in principle, complemented by separate, but somewhat similar, systems at various levels of the VCP. Held (2001: 199) claims that in practice complementary systems have meant Party domination.

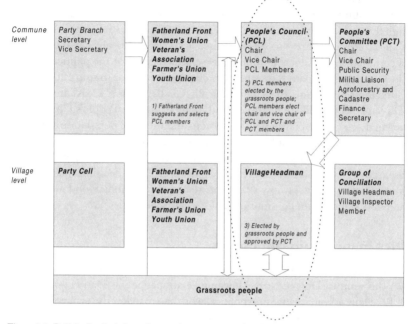

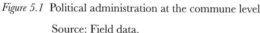

Figure 5.1 Political administration at the commune level

Source: Field data.

Ultimately, it is the VCP through its local cells, embodied in all local institutions, that remains the sole political power at all levels of state administration. The VCP retains a broad-based legitimacy, since it has placed its members in strategically influential positions. Strengthening these interactions would require other state bodies, such as the VCP, the Fatherland Front, and the People's Committee, to begin to share a considerable part of their influence and power.

Politics in Vietnam are, however, characterised by ambiguous policy guidelines and edicts which provide scope for a lot of interpretation at lower levels. It is this flexibility and relative pluralism in the system which allowed experimentation with modified economic concepts, and ultimately contributed to the abandonment of the planned economy at the beginning of the 1980s. Local modification and even rejection of centralist Party rule are common features of Vietnamese local politics. Dang Phong and Beresford (1998: 77) show that during the early stages of economic renovation, for example, policies were no longer planned according to any theory or resolution, but arose spontaneously from the day-to-day needs of the population. This 'foot-dragging' process reflected not only the economic crisis confronting the centrally planned economy, but also political tensions over the gap between the national interest as articulated by the top leadership, and local interests as articulated by lower-level officials (Dang Phong and Beresford 1998: 79). A certain degree of flexibility in local politics was therefore common, but did not reflect the existence of strong opposition against the regime.

In the villages, a level below the commune which is not recognised as an individual administrative unit, party directives and policies are disseminated through the members of the Fatherland Front and the village headmen. However, social and cultural life are also still organised according to local rules and customs and a certain degree of local autonomy are characteristics of the political system. An old Vietnamese maxim states that 'the emperor's rule has to stop at the village gate', and this still contains an element of truth (Chaliand 1969: 21; Kleinen 1999a: 11). Directly elected village headmen and members of the People's Councils act as intermediaries between the political system and the local population. They are responsible for explaining policies to the people so that they know what is going on, discussing policy details and plans for implementation, supervising the representatives' work, and actively participating in local decision-making. The following section discusses how grassroots democracy is understood and implemented in two mountain communes of northern Vietnam.

Politics in mountain communes

After an initial experimental phase with grassroots democracy in some communes all over the country, Decree No. 29 became a national policy (Dau Hoan Do *et al.* 1999: 12). Daily administrative and political work had to follow the principle 'people know, people discuss, people execute, and people supervise'. In the northern mountain district of Ba Be, in Bac Kan province, the grassroots democracy decree was introduced in the years 1999 and 2000. The communes' People's Councils and People's Committees of Dong Phuc and Nam Mau received training by the Government Committee of Organisation and Personnel, a government agency very close to the VCP. The training concerned the implementation of democracy in the communes. The training material outlines that government activities and policy purposes need to be made more transparent, and the responsiveness to local people's needs and socio-economic conditions requires to be enhanced (Government Committee for Organisation and Personnel 2000).

As understood by local cadres, democracy in the communes is closely linked with equitable socio-economic development, since more political transparency creates better conditions for rational decision-making and better allocation of productive resources. The chairman of a commune People's Committee said in an interview that

> the People's Committee has the power to manage the commune and to force people to follow the law. According to grassroots democracy, people must know about the decisions and resolutions. If some organs failed to let people know the socio-economic situation would not improve.

A VCP branch secretary argued that

> if grassroots democracy was implemented correctly then there is no opportunity to violate the interest of local people. [However,] once people

know and discuss they also have to carry out. If they fail to do so the authorities will treat them according to the law.

He continued by saying: 'Local people must know about policies and resolutions. Within a certain frame people are free. This is democracy.' This understanding of democracy is prevalent in the communes, and does not challenge the narrow notions of socialist democracy discussed earlier. Democracy is a bounded framework in which people are free to act and to raise their concerns. Their influence to change political and economic decision-making is, however, limited. The same VCP branch secretary summarised this very clearly: 'When local people want to respond to policies they can. Theoretically, people can influence higher level decision-making but in reality it never happens. Finally, people have to follow the Party's objectives.'

Politics in the communes strongly depends on the low-level cadres' understanding of socialist democracy and policies. Most of the local cadres are firmly rooted in commune life and village society, acting simultaneously as household heads and farmers, people's representatives and the long arm of the VCP and the government. They assume multiple responsibilities as social and political change takes place through their intermediary function, and according to locally interpreted VCP directions. Being so close to local people, low-level cadres are generally responsive and accountable to local people's needs and aspirations. A local leader said: 'There is a general solidarity between the villagers, being local leaders or ordinary people, because all of them face the same livelihood needs and difficulties.'

Despite the seeming mutual respect between local authorities and grassroots people and shared attempt to work on better socio-economic conditions, there is also criticism. Some villagers blame local officials for a lack of sensitivity to their needs and knowledge. They complain that officials use a language that is not comprehensible, although the leaders' responsibility is to help and to support the people. A Party member raises the concern that

> It is really difficult for the villagers to keep up with the local officials who have allowances, pensions and who are enjoying benefits from the government policies because they know better what is going on. They are also able to send their children to school.

Such officials are better able to invest in their future than ordinary villagers. The relationship between local officials and villagers is also still influenced by the experiences of the collective period. A village elder argued that local officials do not take care of the people, referring to former times when co-operative members were always hungry and the co-operative headmen effortlessly received better and more food from the co-operative stores. Incidents of abuses of power and information also occur, such as illicit land claims or partial behaviour in situations of conflict resolution. Such developments erode popular trust in local leaders.

Local cadres, on the other hand, report that they sometimes face difficulties in letting people participate and encouraging discussion according to the democracy decree directions. They say that due to the villagers' low level of political and abstract knowledge, they experienced difficulties in discussing concepts such as land use planning and forest zoning. Claims that villagers have insufficient levels of knowledge are often used as an excuse for not consulting grassroots people. Paternalism is widespread among government authorities. Dau Hoan Do *et al.* (1999: 9) go a step further by exploring the uneven relationship between farmers and local authorities, or lower ranks *vis-à-vis* upper ranks, in which the former are always subject to the unassailable superiority of the latter.

Despite occurrences of discontent, exchange between the villagers and the local officials take place on a regular basis in the two communes. Village meetings are held at least twice a month, while People's Council meetings are held every six months. The equitable development of the whole village and commune community is still the major goal of politics in mountain communes. This reveals the vitality of socialist ideology in both official and unofficial life. Dang Phong and Beresford (1998: 94) as well as Papin (2000: 12) point in the same direction, and emphasise that socialist ideology remains particularly strong in the remoter areas. Low-level cadres remain the stronghold of the VCP.

Policy implementation: adhering to grassroots democracy?

Local leaders, as the mediators between grassroots people and the commune and district departments, are responsible not only for information dissemination but also for policy implementation in ethnically and ecologically diverse environments such as in the northern mountain region of Vietnam. The better their knowledge and the better their information policy towards the village communities, the smoother and more successful the policy process. Their abilities to mediate between local complexities and central generalities are reflected in adapted forms of policies often referring to customary law and social practice, and therefore frequently differing from national policy guidelines (Sikor and Dao 2000: 33).

In Nam Mau and Dong Phuc communes, the responsiveness of local authorities to both local needs and governmental programmes finds its expression in diverse approaches to – and the varying pace of – policy implementation, as the following examples will show. In 1999, the Ministry of Agriculture and Rural Development (MARD) issued Circular No. 56/1999, which outlined the role and responsibilities of local communities for forest protection (Ministry of Agriculture and Rural Development 1999: 17; Nguyen Thuong Luu *et al.* 1995: 32). By referring to the grassroots democracy decree, MARD advised local authorities to work out village conventions for forest protection together with the local population. This turned out to be a difficult task. Local cadres in Dong Phuc commune say that 'It was not possible to let people discuss the land use planning scheme because of their low level of knowledge ... Some people do not understand the content of the discussion, and this is when policy implementation fails.' The policy outcome of forest land allocation and land use planning is so far very diverse. Some village communities accepted the formal institutional guidelines suggested by the government. Others resisted them, and regulated their access to and control of productive forest resources according to local customs and social habits. The local authorities did not insist on pushing through an environmental policy concept that was not yet accepted by all local residents. Their working attitude gave rise to a non-linear policy process that respects and reflects a relatively slow local learning process about policy change by both local people and low-level cadres. Diverse responses, whereby official policy guidelines are not taken up in village rules and commune resolutions, is a form of local autonomy characteristic to the rural communes. It faces problems, however, when policy frameworks are applied more rigidly by external actors.

This is the case in Nam Mau commune, which has been attracting growing national and international interest since Ba Be National Park was established in 1992. A unique mountain environment with great biodiversity potential encouraged national and international conservation and nature preservation efforts. Since 1999 the National Park management board, made up of two central-level government officials, has been assisted by a multilaterally-funded project for protected areas and resource conservation. The socio-political as well as the institutional situation for the local people living within the National Park boundaries has changed fundamentally. Policy instructions and environmental programmes of the MARD are pushed through in an increasingly strict manner, cutting down the livelihood opportunities of the local people, as well as their control over and access to natural resources which are essential for their well-being. Despite the policy guidelines of Decree No. 29 on consultation and participation of grassroots people in aspects concerning their daily lives, biodiversity conservation and natural resource management underlie the sole command of the National Park management board. Formally, some attempts had been made to consult people according to the grassroots democracy idea. The flow of information in externally organised village meetings concerning the elaboration of village conventions for the protection and development of forests was however highly biased. The MARD and Forest Protection Department representatives did not react to people's concerns and petitions regarding the imposed restrictions in natural resource use. They merely informed the villagers about their obligations, explaining the fines and sentences they would face when not behaving according to the regulations. Ready-prepared village conventions were distributed to bind the local residents to the guidelines for protection and development of the forest resources. One of the village headmen of Nam Mau commune reports that 'People feel forced and obliged to follow the National Park directions although they feel deprived of their rights. The payments for forest protection and patrolling are not adequate.' The commune authorities meanwhile try to keep the village communities co-operative. They say that, eventually, 'the villagers will benefit from the infrastructure the National Park provides'. However, they do not know what the National Park management board is about to decide because it seeks consultation and permission only at the provincial and central level.

The two examples of Dong Phuc and Nam Mau commune show that there are different modes of enabling participation of local residents in decision-making as stated in Decree No. 29. In Dong Phuc, local residents enjoy some form of self-determination and local autonomy in responding to policy changes concerning their livelihood systems. The local authorities are open to customary law and social habits that are valued for their community-stabilising factors. The second example of Nam Mau commune reveals a case where central rules pass over local concerns despite the grassroots democracy decree. Participation is formally enabled through discussion, but is generally ineffective. The paternalistic behaviour of the National Park management board and the representatives of government ministries assigns pre-defined roles to local people. This attitude does not enhance participation and representation of local public interests in a wider political arena.

Grassroots people's active participation in decision-making appears to be a function of the extent of central state interest in the locality. Where state interest is strong then the level of self-determination is small; if it is weak, then local politics is more deliberate and involves both official and customary rule. The grassroots democracy decree does not seem to enable consistent democratisation and decentralisation processes in the communes.

Conclusion: steps in a new revolutionary stage?

When the Vietnamese leadership issued the decree on the exercise of democracy at the commune level, it was responding to the socio-economic changes initiated by the economic renovation and to the requirements for establishing effective governance structures. The government speaks of a 'new revolutionary stage' that has been reached with the turn of the century (Government of the Socialist Republic of Vietnam 1998: 19). Another official document states that it is time to 'perfect' democracy (Government Committee for Organisation and Personnel 2000: 16). Decree No. 29 intends to strengthen the relationship between the public, the VCP and the government via political participation, and reflects attempts to enhance the VCP's legitimacy in the eyes of the public.

The concept of Vietnamese socialist democracy strongly implies the controlled implementation of democracy; it does not yet enable effective participation and discourse at lower levels of political and economic decision-making. Calls made by liberal VCP members for more freedom to express and to debate political and economic directions and policies are getting louder (Abuza 2001: 32). Criticisms concerning the slow change of working culture, and the unwillingness of some power-holders to retreat, touch on the self-image of the VCP and how it explains democracy. In the current understanding democracy is a political project to be implemented from above. It sets a frame within which freedom to express ideas and opinions is allowed. The VCP, however, strongly fights against opposition and social initiatives that might threaten its monopoly of power. Political participation symbolises one of the biggest challenges for the VCP today. In the transition period, the economy has become ever more complex and people are exposed to manifold influences with stronger international relations and conventions. The right to participation in economic and political decision-making may soon be claimed by more than just the three per cent of the population who are active VCP members.

The decree on the exercise of democracy in the communes was implemented in 1999 in the studied mountain communes. Local authorities reacted positively to the decree, and sought to amend their working practices according to grassroots democratic principles. However, the implementation of Decree No. 29 is diverse. In one commune local people enjoyed relative autonomy and their political participation had a direct influence on the policy context of the locality. Their neighbours, however, were struggling within a more tightly controlled institutional and political framework, which did not enhance consultation with the people. Their political participation in decision-making concerning their livelihoods and well-being was heavily circumscribed.

The implementation of Decree No. 29 is also much influenced by the communication flow between local authorities and grassroots people. The political attitude of the local authorities, influenced by historical events, prejudices and social behaviour, is decisive in the implementation process. The strengthened role of local authorities through the democracy decree has often led to arbitrary use of power and knowledge. Other studies on the implementation of grassroots democracy reveal that only a minority of people are well informed about policies and programmes, rights and obligations, and especially that ethnic minority groups of the northern mountain region have become politically marginalised (Dau Hoan Do *et al.* 1999: 21; Government-Donor-NGO Working Group 1999: 94). Such circumstances impinge on the processes of democratisation and decentralisation in the localities.

Democratisation and decentralisation efforts in Vietnam are moreover slowed down because they are not actively embraced by the public. Politics in Vietnam have never really been in people's hands. Local people in the studied mountain communities considered political issues too risky to become involved with. Brocheux (1994: 89) talks about the public's refusal to get engaged in political matters, whereas officials argue that local people lack sufficient knowledge, and that they are 'backward'. These views provide for many authorities' explanations for economic crisis and political lethargy in the peripheral areas of the country. There is some evidence that local people have begun to believe such explanations themselves (Jamieson *et al.* 1998: 28). The VCP's monopoly of power is therefore not much challenged by the citizenry on the political periphery.

Despite a lot of paradoxes and limitations, the decree on the exercise of democracy in the communes suggests a significant shift in guiding the authorities towards more consultation with the people, and encourages exchanges of views and information between citizens and political leaders. Although the steps in this 'new revolutionary stage' are still small, the grassroots democracy decree indicates a trend towards more discursive politics in Vietnam. Politics at the lower levels are supposed to become more responsive to local needs and people's aspirations. Given its claim to be the leading representative of the whole people, the VCP is now required firmly to face changing societal realities. In order to make the interaction between the public and the state work, however, it is high time for the VCP to shape a vision of an active Vietnamese citizenry that plays a strong role in the projects of democratisation and decentralisation.

Acknowledgements

This chapter draws on research facilitated by Helvetas Vietnam and financed by the Swiss Agency for Development and Co-operation. I am immensely grateful to the people in the Dong Phuc and Nam Mau communes, and to the local authorities who co-operated with my field research. Very special thanks go to my research assistant Tran Thu Huong. Catherine Locke, Cecilia Luttrell and Duncan McCargo provided valuable comments on previous versions of this chapter. Of course, I remain solely responsible for any errors of fact or interpretation.

Part II
Economy

Vietnam's economy

Currency:	Dong (VND)
Exchange rate:	US$1 = VND 16,183 (January 2004)
GDP:	$168.1 billion (PPP*, 2001 est.)
GDP growth rate:	4.7% p.a. (2001 est.)
GDP per capita:	$2,100 (PPP*, 2001 est.)
GDP composition by sector:	*Agriculture*: 25% *Industry*: 35% *Services*: 40% (2000 est.)
Inflation rate:	2.9% p.a. (2002)
Labour force:	38.2 million (1998 est.)
Labour force by occupation:	*Agriculture*: 67% *Industry and services*: 33% (1997 est.)
Unemployment rate:	6.4% (2000 est.)
Government budget in % of GDP:	*Revenue and grants:* 18.9% *Expenditures:* 25.4% (2001)
Population below poverty line:	37% (1998 est.)
Annual production of food staples:	34,254 thousands of tons, with 7.5% annual increase (1999)
Industries:	Food processing, garments, shoes, machine building, mining, cement, chemical fertiliser, glass, tyres, oil, coal, steel, paper
Industrial production growth rate:	10.4% p.a. (2001 est.)
Agricultural products:	Paddy rice, corn, potatoes, rubber, soybeans, coffee, tea, bananas, sugar, poultry, pigs, fish
Electricity production:	25.775 billion kWh (2000)
Electricity production by source:	*Fossil fuel:* 40.74% *Hydro:* 59.26% *Nuclear:* 0% (2000)
Electricity consumption:	23.97 billion kWh (2000)

Note * based on purchasing power parity (PPP).

Sources: CIA (2002) *The World Factbook 2002*, Washington, DC: CIA; ADB (2001) *Key Indicators 2001: Growth and Change in Asia and the Pacific*; VVG Economic Indicators, *August 2003*, available online at http://www.vvg-vietnam.com/economics_cvr. htm#Rates; IMF (2002) *Vietnam: Selected Issues and Statistical Appendix*, IMF Country Report No. 02/5.

6 Growth and reform since the Eighth Party Congress

Ari Kokko

At the time of the Eighth Party Congress of the VCP in 1996, Vietnam appeared set to join the ranks of 'Asian tiger' economies. The economic reform programme introduced after the Sixth Party Congress in 1986 had gradually decentralised decision-making and replaced central planning with markets and prices, with impressive results. In agriculture, chronic food deficits turned into large export surpluses. Industrial development accellerated when individual firms, mainly state-owned enterprises (SOEs), were allowed to determine their own prices and production. Foreign trade grew rapidly, albeit from a small base, and thousands of foreign investors were attracted to Vietnam, bringing with them more than US $2 billion per year by the mid-1990s. Altogether, the reforms translated into annual gross domestic product (GDP) growth rates exceeding 9 per cent in the mid-1990s, with corresponding improvements in living standards for large segments of the population.

However, the late 1990s were disappointing. The GDP growth rate fell gradually from its peak at 9.5 per cent in 1995 to below 5 per cent in 1999 (see Figure 6.1). Both import and export growth rates stagnated and the inflows of foreign direct investment (FDI) fell dramatically after 1997. The downturn was caused by a combination of domestic structural weaknesses and spillovers from the Asian crisis. The first signs of recovery did not appear until 2000, when stronger export demand boosted production. By 2001 and 2002, growth rates were firmly back in the region of 7 per cent.

The purpose of this chapter is to make a brief assessment of selected economic developments in Vietnam since the Eighth Party Congress in 1996. After a review of the development debate in the mid-1990s, the chapter focuses on some major challenges for economic policy-making, especially: trade policy, SOE reform, and the private sector. A key question is: Do recent improvements in economic performance mean that the structural problems plaguing the Vietnamese economy during the second half of the 1990s have now been remedied?

Vietnam in the mid-1990s: growth with structural imbalances

In the mid-1990s, Vietnam was considered one of the most promising markets and investment locations in Pacific Asia. The gradual shift from traditional central

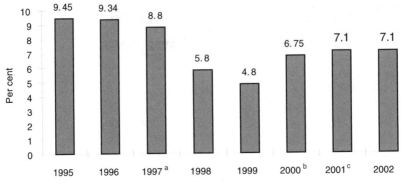

Notes

a ADB statistics: 8.2%

b World Bank statistics: 6.8%; IMF statistics: 5.5%

c World Bank statistics: 6.8%; IMF statistics: 4.75%; ADB statistics: 7%

Figure 6.1 Vietnam GDP growth (%), 1995–2002

Source: Vietnam Government Statistics Bureau.

planning to a market-oriented economy, which started officially in 1986, had led to dramatic improvements in economic performance. The GDP growth rate averaged almost 8 per cent per year during the period 1990–5, with over 9 per cent recorded in 1995 and 1996. Domestic savings and investment increased in absolute amounts as well as in shares of GDP. Exports grew from 25 per cent of GDP in 1990, to 33 per cent in 1995, with even faster growth for imports. Foreign direct investment emerged as an increasingly important source of capital and technology, with the inflow of FDI reaching US $2.3 billion (or 11 per cent of GDP) in 1995. In addition to high growth rates, the reform programme produced macroeconomic stabilisation. Most importantly, the rate of inflation was reduced from over 60 per cent in 1990 to less than 13 per cent in 1995, the current account of the government budget recorded a surplus by 1994, and the financing of the current account deficit in the country's balance of payments did not appear to be any major problem.

The reforms also contributed to Vietnam's integration into the world economy. Inflows of overseas development aid (ODA) increased significantly from the early 1990s, several bilateral trade agreements with foreign countries were established, the US embargo was lifted in early 1994, and Vietnam joined the Association of Southeast Asian Nations (ASEAN) in July 1995. Vietnam's relations with multilateral financial institutions such as the World Bank, the Asian Development Bank (ADB) and the International Monetary Fund (IMF) were normalised; by 1995, Vietnam held a Structural Adjustment Credit (SAC) from the World Bank and an Enhanced Structural Adjustment Facility (ESAF) from the IMF. These credits were important, not only because they provided financial resources, but also because they signalled that Vietnam's economic development was progressing satisfactorily. Both SAC and ESAF are normally granted on condition that the recipient country pursues 'appropriate' policies when it comes to structural reforms and fiscal and monetary management. One consequence of the perceived success of reforms during the early 1990s was that the Vietnamese authorities revised their economic targets for the period from 1991 to 2000. Instead of aiming for a doubling of the country's GDP over this period, as was originally intended before the Seventh Party Congress in 1991, the target was changed to a doubling of GDP per capita (Socialist Republic of Vietnam [SRV] 1994). Assessing the achievements of the reforms, many foreign observers concurred, concluding, for example, that 'Vietnam appears well-positioned to become a new East Asian "dragon"' (Irvin 1995: 725).

However, these impressive achievements could not completely hide some of the structural and systemic weaknesses of the economy. By 1996, donors and foreign observers had highlighted several problems related to the import-substituting trade regime and the role of the state, in particular the continuing reliance on SOEs as the main vehicle of development (Kokko and Zejan 1996; Ljunggren 1996; Mallon 1996; United Nations Development Programme [UNDP] 1996).

On trade policy, concerns focused on the distorted incentives provided by the complex, non-transparent and highly restrictive trade regime. The combination of tariffs, quotas, import licensing requirements, foreign exchange controls and various other trade barriers created strong incentives in favour of import substitution in consumer goods and selected heavy industries – and a bias against export-oriented production. One paradoxical result was a rapid increase in imports: import-substituting industry in Vietnam, as elsewhere, was heavily dependent upon imported machinery, raw materials and intermediates. Consequently, although exports grew rapidly, import growth was even faster, resulting in growing trade and current account deficits. By 1995, the current account deficit exceeded US $2.6 billion, or 13 per cent of GDP. Several problems were imminent. Would it be possible to finance large deficits without endangering future growth and macroeconomic stability? How would Vietnam's commitments to liberalise trade from around the year 2000 – mandated, for example, by Vietnam's membership of the ASEAN Free Trade Area (AFTA) and ambition to join the World Trade Organisation (WTO) – be realised? Would the promises to reduce tariffs be neutralised by the emergence of strong interest groups benefiting from, and therefore lobbying for, continued protectionism?

The last question was intimately related to concerns about the role of SOEs. These were the main beneficiaries of Vietnamese import substitution, in many cases in joint ventures with foreign investors. Although the foreign joint venture partners provided badly needed technology and skills, it was still clear that most SOEs operated with obsolete machinery and equipment, with perhaps one-third of the capital stock being completely useless (Le Dang Doanh 1996). The Central Institute for Economic Management (CIEM 1997) reported that most state enterprises were running at a loss and that only 300 enterprises accounted for 80 per cent of the SOE sector's contributions to the state budget. Many SOEs survived only thanks to loans from other state enterprises and preferential credits from state-owned banks, creating a significant debt burden (although the absence of transparent accounting practices still makes it impossible to quantify the total amount of SOE debt). It was not only uncertain whether high and sustainable economic growth could be achieved in a system almost entirely based on state-owned industry: the combination of import substitution and SOE dominance created additional problems. Protection from foreign competition was not expected to contribute to badly needed SOE reforms, including stricter performance requirements, harder budget constraints, and increased efficiency. On the contrary, it was feared that isolation from international markets would allow weak firms to survive without having to undertake necessary reforms.

The fact that the beneficiaries of protectionism were also the most powerful actors in the Vietnamese economy was another cause for concern. The SOEs (sometimes in joint ventures with foreign multinational corporations) were economically important, but also intimately connected with various levels of political decision-making, and in a position to use their political influence to oppose trade liberalisation or other reforms that might reduce their privileges. The lack of a detailed publicised time plan for promised, future tariff reductions increased the risk for this kind of backlash, since it implied that the scheme for trade reform was still open for negotiation.

Another area with severe problems was the banking sector, where lending to inefficient SOEs had created large stocks of problem credits. Official figures indicated that only 8 per cent of the loans in the banking sector were non-performing at the end of 1995, but the real problems were significantly larger than that. However, weak regulations and accounting practices, together with the repeated rollover of loans to SOEs (including the extension of new loans to service old debt), made it impossible to accurately quantify the problem (IMF 1999). Still, the pressure on the banks' balance sheets was beginning to affect their lending. Most private enterprises had to accept very strict collateral requirements, but were still largely unable to get any medium- or long-term credits. SOEs, on the other hand, were not bound by collateral requirements and other restrictions – after all, the state was not expected to default on its obligations.

The development of the private sector in general was disappointing. Private sector growth was stunted by the complex regulatory environment and the competition from SOEs benefiting from political contacts and privileged access to capital, land and other resources. The GDP share of the domestic private sector, excluding farmers and informal household enterprises, reached only about 7.5 per cent in 1995, while the 'modern' private sector, consisting of limited liability companies and shareholding companies, accounted for at most one per cent of GDP (Webster 1999; Kokko 2000). The lack of a dynamic private sector was worrying, particularly since it was becoming increasingly clear that the inefficient SOE sector would not be able to generate enough jobs for the rapidly growing labour force. In 1995, the SOEs employed only 1.8 million people out of a total labour force of nearly 35 million and over one million new entrants each year. In addition, it was clear that thorough public administration reform would be needed in order to manage reforms in other sectors. Some of the reasons for these reforms were of a structural nature. For instance, at least half of government revenues were generated through protectionism, in the form of direct taxes on trade or profit taxes from SOEs that were profitable mainly because they could set their own prices. Other reasons focused on the efficiency of public administration. The Vietnamese business environment not only suffered from excessive regulation and red tape: reports of outright corruption were widespread.

The reform agenda

These structural problems and contradictions in economic policy were by no means unknown to the Vietnamese authorities. On the contrary, the agenda for the dialogue between Vietnamese authorities and the multilateral and bilateral donors included all of the concerns discussed above, and several were also addressed in the government's reform plans in the mid-1990s. Some of these plans were summarised in a Policy Framework Paper (PFP 1996) prepared with the assistance of the World Bank and the IMF. This document laid out the country's general economic objectives for the medium term, including detailed reform commitments reflecting agreements with the World Bank and the IMF. Meeting these commitments was a condition for both the Bank's SAC and the Fund's ESAF. A look at these reform plans is helpful in describing Vietnamese expectations and reform priorities at that juncture.

PFP (1996) identified five main areas for reform for the late 1990s: trade and FDI policy, SOEs, the financial sector, the private sector, and public administration. In the area of international trade and investment, the primary aim was to simplify trade regulations. The stated ambition was to abolish import permits and import shipment licenses and to allow all enterprises to engage in international trade. Measures focusing on the foreign exchange market, especially the aim to eliminate all restrictions on current account transactions, were also notable. One reason for these quite radical liberalisation proposals was that the authorities did not anticipate problems in handling a continuing current account deficit: in fact, PFP (1996: 7) expected significant improvements in the current account, and noted that 'over the medium term, some appreciation cannot be ruled out as productivity improves'. This suggests that neither the Vietnamese government nor the multilaterals were, at the time, very concerned about the import-substituting character of the Vietnamese trade regime. As a result, the measures intended to reduce the level of protection were relatively weak. Although the document discussed the need to start preparing to meet AFTA tariff reduction commitments and future WTO accession, as well as the need to eliminate non-tariff barriers to trade, there were no concrete targets or time plans, except for a reduction of the maximum tariff from 100 per cent to 60 per cent. In the FDI area, reform proposals were also marginal, which is not surprising considering the large inflows of funds to Vietnam. For instance, in 1996, inward FDI commitments still amounted to more than US $8.6 billion (see Table 13.2, this volume).

The objectives for SOE reform were more far-reaching, mainly because both the World Bank and the IMF considered this a priority area (World Bank 1995). The State Enterprise Action Plan was expected to stipulate a clear timetable for the restructuring of the SOE sector, including the identification of strategic enterprises to be retained under government ownership and a programme for the divestiture of non-strategic SOEs. In particular, it was stated that the equitisation of SOEs would accelerate, although no numerical targets were given. In the equitisation process, SOEs are transformed into shareholding companies that are often partially privatised.

The main thrust of the measures intended to support private sector development was on legal reform. Comprehensive revisions of the Commercial Law, Company Law and Private Enterprise Law were announced, with special emphasis on a simplification of the regulatory framework for private enterprise. It was stated that 'licenses will be required only in cases where public safety or national security are involved. For all other businesses, a registration procedure will be introduced that does not require administrative approval' (PFP 1996: 8). In addition, the programme included plans to strengthen land use rights and to improve the transferability of non-agricultural land, in order to develop a market with a level playing field for individuals, private firms, and SOEs.

The reform plans for the financial sector covered two areas. First, the programme included several measures to strengthen the instruments for monetary policy. The primary objective was to start a gradual move away from direct controls (interest rate regulations and credit ceilings) to the use of indirect instruments, such as open market operations. Second, it was clear that the banking system needed to be reformed. In addition to revisions of banking laws and efforts to strengthen banking supervision, the four state-owned commercial banks were to undergo detailed audits, and the findings of these audits were to be used to formulate and adopt detailed reform programmes for each of the banks. The resulting reforms were expected to be quite radical; PFP stated that the programmes:

> will include provisions for increasing bank capital through issuance of shares, recapitalisation where necessary, and reform of operating procedures. These include holding bank management accountable for the commercial performance of the banks, giving the banks the autonomy to determine staffing and salary levels, and freeing them from specific lending directives.
>
> (PFP 1996: 9)

Considering the weaknesses of the banking system, with intimate connections to SOEs, large but undisclosed problem credits, and a lack of experience with market-based operations, it was obvious that the objectives for banking reform were also remarkably ambitious.

Public administration reform also covered two areas. On the one hand, there was an ambition to make the mobilisation of public revenue more efficient. In 1994, taxes on international trade accounted for one-third of total tax revenue, while taxes paid by SOEs comprised half of revenue (PFP 1996: 4). It was understood that the impending trade reforms would reduce these sources of income, and a broader tax base was therefore needed. On the other hand, reforms were needed on the expenditure side as well, increasingly to focus public investment on infrastructure and other projects complementary to private sector investment.

However, these reforms were not implemented as scheduled between 1996 and 1998. One reason was Vietnamese resistance against the ambitious SOE reform plans. It was clear that extensive privatisation and the SOE reforms contradicted the rhetoric of Vietnamese politics as well as the interests of the organisations controlling the SOEs. For instance, the Eighth Party Congress in early 1996 explicitly restated the objective that the state should hold a central position in the country's economic development, which many (though far from all) Vietnamese interpreted to mean that SOEs should dominate industry. Moreover, the reorganisation in 1994 and 1995 of some 2,000 SOEs into 18 General Corporations and over 70 Special Corporations – large conglomerates incorporating the SOEs operating in specific industries or specific geographical areas – essentially identified all large state enterprises as strategically important. Several observers therefore argued that more radical trade reforms should precede SOE reform, because protectionism made many SOEs look artificially attractive to the organisations 'owning' them. For instance, Kokko and Zejan (1996: 26) predicted that 'large-scale privatisation of SOEs will meet fierce opposition as long as the government, individual ministries, regional authorities, and other public entities draw a large share of their revenue from the SOEs they presently control'.

Consequently, in the 1996–7 SAC extension negotiations, the World Bank put additional stress on trade reform. A more open and outward-oriented trade regime would not only generate high growth rates by allowing the economy's comparative advantages to determine the allocation of investment resources, but also facilitate the necessary institutional reforms in the SOE sector. The main new requirement concerned the formulation and implementation of a clear time-bound action programme for trade reform, including schedules for the fulfillment of Vietnam's AFTA commitments regarding tariff reductions and phasing out of non-tariff barriers. In the SOE sector, numerical targets were introduced: at least 150 enterprises were to go through the equitisation process during the 1997–9 period. Strict requirements for the collection and analysis of key financial and performance indicators for the largest SOEs were also discussed.

It turned out to be impossible to reach an agreement. The Vietnamese authorities were unable to present any timetable for trade reform and a World Bank mission in early 1997 failed to get access to requested basic data on the financial status and performance of the SOE sector. The negotiations ended without results, and the structural adjustment credit was discontinued. With rapidly growing exports and around US $2 billion in FDI inflows in 1995 and 1996 (see Table 13.2, p. 186 this volume), Vietnam did not seem overly worried about losing the US $300 million SAC.

It is likely that the disagreements between the Bretton Woods institutions and the Vietnamese authorities would have been resolved during 1997 and 1998 if discussions had proceeded 'normally'. This was not to be the case. In July 1997, conditions changed sharply because of the outbreak of the Asian crisis. Vietnam was not directly hit by the financial turbulence, since the asset markets were weakly developed or controlled by the state. The exchange rate was strictly managed through trade restrictions and controls on the allocation of foreign exchange, there was no real estate market, nor was there any stock market. Instead, the crisis was felt through a reduction in the inflows of foreign capital. The crisis reduced export growth, because of tougher competition from countries with depreciating currencies and weaker purchasing power among Vietnam's regional trade partners. It also led to a dramatic fall in inward FDI, because the regional investors who had accounted for most of the FDI flows to Vietnam were concerned with their domestic financial problems. The reduced availability of foreign savings revealed the weaknesses in Vietnam's import-substituting development strategy and forced the authorities to introduce stricter controls in foreign trade and exchange markets – the opposite of what was called for in the structural adjustment programmes. In fact, most reform and liberalisation plans, including the formal structural adjustment programmes, were put aside while the causes and consequences of the regional crisis occupied the minds of Vietnamese decision makers.

Thanks to very cautious macroeconomic policies, Vietnam managed to avoid an acute crisis, but growth slowed significantly. Table 6.1 illustrates how developments in many areas stagnated between 1996 and 2000, in particular in comparison with the rapid progress that was recorded during the preceding five-year period. GDP growth fell from over 9 per cent in the mid-1990s to below 5 per cent in 1999. FDI inflows shrank by nearly 60 per cent, and the large net inflows of foreign capital recorded in the mid-1990s turned to outflows. Government revenue as share of GDP fell, and the share of public expenditures devoted to social services stopped growing. Trade was the one area where significant growth was recorded.

It was not until 2000 that clear signs of economic recovery were seen: according to official figures, GDP growth in 2000–1 averaged 6.7 per cent (CIEM 2002: 110). Economic reforms also reappeared on the policy agenda, and disagreements with the multilateral donor agencies have largely been ironed out. Vietnam is one of the pilot countries in the World Bank's current Comprehensive Development Framework

Table 6.1 Macroeconomic indicators, 1991–2000

	1991	1996	2000
GDP per capita (current US $)	228.0	337.0	390.0
GDP growth (per cent)	6.0	9.3	5.5
Inflation (CPI* increase, per cent)	67.0	5.7	1.7
Aggregate investment (per cent of GDP)	15.1	28.1	25.6
Domestic savings (per cent of GDP)	13.2	17.6	27.3
Foreign savings (net inflows of foreign capital, per cent of GDP)	1.9	10.5	−1.7
FDI inflows (US $ million)	220.0	1,800.0	800.0
Exports (US $ million)	2,042.0	7,330.0	14,449.0
Imports (US $ million)	2,105.0	10,480.0	14,071.0
Government budget revenue (per cent of GDP)	13.5	22.9	21.1
Government expenditure on social services (per cent of GDP)	4.4	7.5	7.5

Source: UNDP (1996); IMF (2002).

Note: * CPI = consumer price index.

programme. In this context, Vietnam has prepared a Comprehensive Poverty Reduction and Growth Strategy (CPRGS) in collaboration with the donor community (SRV 2002), and qualified for Poverty Reduction Support Credits from the World Bank. The CPRGS and the credit facilities linked to it in principle replace the Policy Framework Papers and Structural Adjustment Credits dating from the mid-1990s. But to what extent have the structural problems from the mid-1990s been resolved? The following sections look in some closer detail at what has happened since the mid-1990s in trade policy, SOE reform and the private sector.

International trade and trade policy

Although trade liberalisation was slow in the mid-1990s because of tough opposition from interest groups lobbying for continued protection, there was some cautious progress until the Asian crisis. For instance, most domestic firms were given export rights in January 1997, when import licensing requirements for a large number of consumer goods were eliminated. The Asian crisis put a halt to further reforms. In fact, many trade restrictions were tightened between 1997 and 1999, when authorities felt compelled to restrict imports of 'non-essential' goods in order to allocate the increasingly scarce foreign exchange to the import-dependent industrial sector.

However, concerns about the detrimental long-term effects of high trade barriers grew rapidly. There were also concerns about the need to meet the trade liberalisation targets set up by AFTA. During the first years of AFTA participation, Vietnam had been able to fulfill its formal annual tariff reduction commitments by listing product categories where it had comparative advantages or products that already met the 5 per cent maximum tariff requirement. It was clear that real tariff reductions would definitely be required from 2000, at the latest. Trade reform therefore reappeared on the policy agenda as soon as the acute worries about contagion from the Asian financial crisis dissipated. Trade has arguably been one of the areas with the fastest progress since then.

The most important result in terms of formal policy may be the agreement about a Bilateral Trade Agreement (BTA) between Vietnam and the US, which was signed in July 2000 and ratified in late 2001. The BTA is an important step towards Vietnamese membership in the WTO, and perhaps also a key step in Vietnam's continuing economic reforms. Unlike the AFTA agreement, which is based on consensus and does not prescribe severe sanctions against member countries that do not fulfill their commitments, both the BTA and eventual WTO membership are likely to come with stricter conditions, enforcement and sanctions. Moreover, the BTA allows Vietnam to reap some of the benefits (in terms of access to US markets) early on, while the perceived costs (resulting from opening the Vietnamese market to US firms) will come later. It is possible that these two features will strengthen the reform process: it will be difficult to default on reform promises once they have generated thousands of jobs that may be lost if promises are not fulfilled. The continuing increase in exports is another sign of progress in this area. In 1999 and 2000, exports grew at an annual rate of over 20 per cent, which was more than four times the rate of domestic demand growth. This shows that an increasing share of the Vietnamese economy is integrated with the international economy, and that there is probably a gradual shift in the balance of power from groups favouring inward-oriented policies to groups relying on contacts with the international economy. In fact, the current Ten-Year Socio-Economic Development Strategy sets up the goal that the export growth rate should be twice as high as the planned 7.5 per cent GDP growth rate during the period 2001–10: if the target is achieved, the ratio of exports to GDP will exceed 90 per cent by 2010.

Other important reforms have been made on the import side. Import tariffs have been reduced gradually, in line with Vietnam's AFTA commitments, and the road map for future tariff reductions under the agreement was published in early 2002. The tariff reduction scheme constitutes an important step to facilitate the long-term planning of Vietnamese producers: with a clear time-bound plan in place, there is less scope for interest groups to lobby for extended protection. Most quantitative restrictions have also been removed, and all domestic enterprises are now allowed to import any goods that are not subject to quotas. Yet some problems remain. The tariff structure remains complex. There is great dispersion of tariff rates in the range from zero to 100 per cent, with higher rates on import-substituting goods and lower ones on imported inputs. This provides high effective rates of protection for local market-oriented industry. Various administrative measures, such as temporary import bans, have also been used to restrict imports of consumer goods. Summarising a review on trade policy, CIEM (2002: 126) notes that this shows how 'many policy decisions tend to aim at "dealing with the problem on a case by case basis" rather than resolving it based on a consistent and overall approach'. Foreign trade transactions can also be controlled and restricted by the allocation of foreign exchange. The State Bank of Vietnam controls and approves remittances of foreign currency abroad, and State Bank authorisation is required to borrow foreign currency, to convert dong to dollars, and to open offshore escrow accounts. Exporters are obliged to surrender a large share (at present 40 per cent) of their foreign exchange earnings to the State Bank. For a long time, state enterprises and agencies had privileged access to foreign exchange (World Bank 1999b), and it is possible that these preferences still apply.

Table 6.2 summarises the Vietnamese balance of payments for the period 1995–2000, confirming the impressive trade growth. The table also provides a comparison between the actual outcome and the projections for 2000 made in PFP (1996). The first notable observation is that although the overall growth rate fell far below the projections from the mid-1990s, this was not due to weak performance in external trade. Both exports and imports in 2000 exceeded the projections from PFP (1996) by a wide margin. In fact, exports were a full 40 per cent higher than predicted only five years earlier. An important part of this export success was an increasing outward orientation among private firms and foreign multinational corporations, both in oil and non-oil sectors. This suggests that problems with lagging growth were mainly caused by weaknesses in other parts of the economy, that is, the more inward-oriented SOE sector.

Table 6.2 Balance of payments, 1995–2000 (US $ million)

	1995	1996	1997	1998	1999	2000	2000 proj.
Trade balance	-3,155	-3,143	-1,315	-981	1,080	378	-3,404
Exports f.o.b.*	5,198	7,337	9,145	9,365	11,540	14,449	10,552
Imports	-8,353	-10,480	-10,460	-10,346	-10,460	-14,071	-13,956
Factor services (net)	-279	-427	-611	-669	-412	-597	-1,344
Receipts	96	140	136	133	160	185	
Payments	375	567	747	802	572	782	
Non-factor services (net)	159	-61	-623	-539	-597	-615	636
Receipts	2,409	2,709	2,530	2,604	2,668	2,695	
Payments	2,250	2,770	3,153	3,143	3,265	3,310	
Transfers (net)	627	1,200	885	1,122	1,181	1,476	1,271
Private	474	1,050	710	950	1,050	1,340	1,080
Official	153	150	175	172	131	136	191
Current account	-2,648	-2,431	-1,664	-1,067	1,252	642	-2,396
Excl. official transfers	-2,801	-2,581	-1,839	-1,239	1,121	506	
FDI inflows (gross)	2,276	1,813	2,074	800	700	800	2,390
Equity	1,287	891	1,002	240	301	320	
Loan disbursements	989	921	1,072	560	399	480	
FDI loan repayments	8	55	174	372	603	601	
Medium and long-term loans (net)	-253	98	375	432	605	729	715
Disbursements	443	772	1,007	1,121	1,036	1,411	1,030
ODA loans	189	336	550	796	970	1,361	
Commercial loans	254	436	457	326	66	50	
Scheduled amortisation	-696	-674	-632	-690	-431	-682	-315
Short-term capital (net)	311	224	-612	-644	-1,036	-1,700	120
Capital account	2,326	2,079	1,662	216	-334	-772	3,225
Errors and omissions	299	71	-2	327	-150	247	

continued …

Table 6.2 continued

	1995	1996	1997	1998	1999	2000	2000 proj.
Overall balance (incl. official transfers)	−23	−281	−4	−524	768	116	*384*
Change in net foreign assets (increase −)	−405	−260	−319	−15	−1,316	−116	*−384*
Arrears and rescheduling	428	541	323	126	548	−9,691	
Debt relief	0	0	0	413	0	9,961	
Memorandum items:							
Current account balance in % of GDP	−13.5	−10.5	−6.9	−4.6	3.9	1.7	*−7.7*
Export growth, %	28.2	41.2	24.6	2.4	23.2	25.2	*15.5*
Import growth, %	41.1	25.5	−0,2	−1.1	1.1	34.5	*13.3*
GDP growth rate	9.5	9.3	8.2	3.5	4.2	5.5	*9.5*

Sources: IMF (2000) for 1995–9; IMF (2002) for 2000. Projections for 2000 are from PFP (1996).

Note: * f.o.b. = free on board

Second, it is clear that another major miscalculation in PFP (1996) concerned the scope to finance the persistent current account deficits that were established in the mid-1990s. It was expected that Vietnam would be able to finance an import-substituting development strategy by attracting external financing at a rate of 8–9 per cent of GDP for an extended period of time, mainly in the form of FDI inflows averaging more than US $2 billion per year. However, this forecast turned out to be severely wrong, partly because the Asian crisis made investment capital more scarce, and partly because inflows of FDI fell as a result of the weaker than expected performance of many foreign-invested enterprises in Vietnam. As a result, FDI inflows stayed below US $800 million in 1998–2000.[1]

Third, the contributions of Vietnam's donor community have met or even exceeded the expectations from PFP (1996), in spite of the temporary setbacks in the relations with multilateral donors when the structural adjustment programme was halted in 1997. ODA disbursements have grown rapidly since the relations with the World Bank and IMF improved in 1999, with annual inflows of grants and soft loans exceeding US $1 billion since that time. In addition, private transfers have increased significantly since 1999, although reliable data are hard to come by: the figures for private transfers are estimates, since only the part that is transferred via the official banking system is officially recorded.

How sustainable is Vietnam's export recovery? With preliminary data for 2001 in hand, there is reason for some caution. Export expansion has slowed down in tandem with the international business cycle – overall export growth was only 4 per cent in 2001 and exports fell significantly in early 2002 – and it is hard to extrapolate long-term trends from developments during the last three or four years. The main reason is that the international oil price has had a profound impact on Vietnam's exports and imports. The dramatic increase in international oil prices in 1999 translated into nearly 70 per cent increases in export earnings from oil during the following two years (so that oil now accounts for about a third of total exports). This means that nearly half of the total export growth during these two years was due to the increase in oil exports. Similarly, the slowdown in exports in 2001 and 2002 has to some degree been related to falling oil prices. Hence, it is difficult to forecast Vietnam's trade performance in the medium term, since the international oil price is a completely exogenous variable. At the same time, it is notable that the fluctuations in non-oil exports have been smaller, although there are distinct differences between industries. Some sectors, such as garments, footwear and seafood, have recorded reasonably healthy growth through 2001, while others, like electronics, rice and other agricultural products, have suffered from heavy price declines since 2001. Performance in these sectors is still to a great extent determined by the Vietnamese policy environment, and the policy reforms discussed above give cause for some optimism regarding the future. Although the continuing slump in Organisation for Economic Co-operation and Development demand and the tough competition from China are difficult challenges, trends in this area are positive.

State enterprise reform

The state sector continues to dominate the Vietnamese economy, in spite of the gradual shift towards a market economy through the reform period, and despite the emphasis on SOE reform and privatisation in the structural adjustment programmes formulated since the mid-1990s. One reason is that the official political doctrine is still communism, and public ownership of the means of production – at least in 'strategic' sectors – remains an important element of the ideology. Vietnam's SOEs have also proved to be more resourceful than has been the case in many other transition economies. The share of large, centrally controlled SOEs was small until the mid-1990s, and most enterprises in the state sector were instead controlled by provincial and municipal authorities. In most cases, it was even possible to identify the specific 'owner' of an SOE – a ministry, a local People's Committee, an army division, or some other part of the public sector or Party organisation. This decentralisation of decision-making, with considerable managerial autonomy in operations as well as financial matters (including the right to decide how a significant share of the profits were to be used) explains why many SOEs were able and willing to respond to post-*doi moi* opportunities (Mallon 1996). Hence, in many ways, Vietnamese SOEs have resembled Chinese township and village enterprises rather than Soviet-style state enterprises.

This notwithstanding, the SOE sector suffers from many problems that are more or less generic to state enterprises in developing countries. Soft budget constraints, restricted competition and the ability to influence the policy environment have resulted in severe debt problems and weak productivity growth. Some SOE dominance is at the expense of the private sector. Only very recently has the private sector been officially recognised as an important element of the economy; SOEs are still favoured by various rules and regulations, particularly related to land holding and financing.

The dominant position of the state is confirmed in official statistics on the Vietnamese economy. Table 6.3 shows that the aggregate GDP share of the state sector hovered around 40 per cent during the second half of the 1990s. This is only about 4 percentage points lower than the state share in 1986, although the country's GDP has more than doubled in real terms since that time (Mallon 1997). Most state sector activities are found in the relatively fast-growing parts of the Vietnamese economy, namely industry and services. Less than 250,000 of the 3.4 million state employees are in agriculture, while about 1.7 million are engaged in SOEs, most of them in manufacturing. The non-state sector, on the other hand, is overwhelmingly agricultural. Nearly 70 per cent of Vietnam's 33 million-strong non-state labour force is employed in agriculture, producing less than one-quarter of the country's total output.

The apparent state dominance is less overwhelming if we look separately at the industrial sector (Table 6.4). SOEs accounted for more than 50 per cent of industrial output in the mid-1990s, but their share had diminished to about 42 per cent by 2000.[2] The main reason was slower growth and productivity development in SOEs than in foreign-invested enterprises, which increased their output share from 25

Table 6.3 GDP by sector and ownership, 1995–2000 (per cent of GDP)

	1995	1996	1997	1998	1999	2000
GDP	**100.0**	**100.0**	**100.0**	**100.0**	**100.0**	**100.0**
State	40.2	39.9	40.5	40.0	38.7	39.0
Non-state	59.8	60.1	59.5	60.0	61.3	61.0
Agriculture	**27.2**	**27.8**	**25.8**	**25.8**	**25.4**	**22.9**
State	1.2	1.3	1.1	1.1	1.0	...
Non-state	26.0	26.5	24.6	24.7	24.4	...
Industry and construction	**28.8**	**29.7**	**32.1**	**32.5**	**34.5**	**36.6**
State	14.5	14.4	15.4	15.4	15.5	...
Non-state	14.3	15.3	16.7	17.1	19.0	...
Services	**44.1**	**42.5**	**42.2**	**41.7**	**40.1**	**39.1**
State	24.6	24.3	23.9	23.5	22.2	...
Non-state	19.5	18.3	18.2	18.2	17.9	...

Sources: IMF (2000); IMF (2002).

Table 6.4 Industrial production by ownership, 1995–2000 (per cent of industrial production)

	1995	1996	1997	1998	1999	2000
State sector	**50.3**	**49.3**	**48.0**	**45.9**	**43.4**	**42.0**
Non-state sector	**24.6**	**24.0**	**23.1**	**22.1**	**21.9**	**22.4**
Co-operative	0.6	0.6	0.6	0.6	0.6	...
Private	2.2	2.4	2.4	2.2	2.2	...
Household	17.6	16.1	14.7	13.8	13.0	...
Mixed	4.2	5.0	5.5	5.5	6.1	...
Foreign-invested sector	**25.1**	**26.7**	**28.9**	**32.0**	**34.7**	**35.5**

Sources: IMF (2000); IMF (2002).

per cent to 35 per cent between 1995 and 2000. The sluggish performance of the SOE sector is closely related to weaknesses in technical and management skills, as well as to the bottlenecks that emerged between 1997 and 1999 when the Asian crisis led to the tightening of import restrictions. However, as noted earlier, several problems were evident already before the Asian crisis hit the region. Most importantly, the state sector had not managed to create any significant increase in employment opportunities since economic reforms were launched in the mid-1980s. The inward-oriented trade regime encouraged investment in capital-intensive import-substituting industries where few jobs have been created. Pool (1999) reports that state enterprises accounted for over 85 per cent of the total registered capital of all new firms established between 1991 and 1997. Yet, employment in state enterprises decreased from 1.9 million to 1.8 million jobs during the same period, although the total labour force increased by about 6 million people. The average capital cost to create one new job in SOEs during this period was about US $7,500, whereas each new job in private small and medium-sized industrial enterprises cost US $1,000–2,000.

Another problem has been the accumulation of large debt, including non-performing debt, in the SOE sector. The IMF (1999) reported that at least two-thirds of the SOEs were classified as permanent or temporary loss-makers in 1997, and that the aggregate debt of the SOE sector exceeded its total assets by a wide margin. It was also estimated that the non-performing loans (NPLs) in state-owned commercial banks amounted to 30–5 per cent of their total lending already in 1997, before the Asian crisis, with a somewhat higher figure for joint-stock banks (IMF 1999: 29). If these estimates were correct, Vietnam's problems with bad credit were worse than those of Thailand and Malaysia before they were hit by severe financial crises in 1997. The situation has probably improved somewhat since that time, but information is scarce and official figures tend to underestimate the problem: still, official data reveal that some 10 per cent of outstanding bank loans were overdue in 2001 (IMF 2002: 75).

One explanation for the weak performance of the state sector is that Vietnam has no comparative advantages in many of the industries where import-substituting SOEs operate. An added problem in many of these sectors is that smuggling is highly profitable – the difference between domestic and international prices is large – which cuts into the profits of SOEs. Another problem is that many SOEs are also shielded from domestic competition – through various rules, regulations and administrative practices that discriminate against private firms – meaning that there is relatively little pressure on them to meet high performance standards. Furthermore, many Vietnamese SOEs do not appear to be subject to hard budget constraints. Loss-making SOEs have systematically been rescued through the write-off of non-performing loans and cash injections from state-owned banks, the National Investment Assistance Fund, Social Security Funds, and other sources. For instance, the IMF (1999) noted that several of the most severely indebted SOEs were able to increase their total outstanding debt by 50 per cent or more in 1997, mainly by recourse to the state banking system. The softness of budgetary constraints is particularly problematic because the incentives for SOE managers to maximise profit are weak (for a more detailed discussion, see Chapter 7 in this volume).

While equitisation will be helpful in severing the intimate connection between various levels of government and individual enterprises, it is uncertain how much it will contribute to the overall problems in the SOE sector. First, it is not likely that the equitisation and divestment targets will be met. There is still some resistance against equitisation, particularly from employees and managers who feel that jobs in the state sector are more secure. This type of resistance will remain as long as the actors in the market feel that there is no level playing field for all types of firms. Hence, the success of SOE reform is to a great extent dependent on the business environment for the private sector.

Second, although the equitisation programmes involve many enterprises, they are mainly small and medium-sized, and play a limited role for economic development in general. Together, the National Corporations and Special Corporations absorbed around 2,000 of the 6,300 SOEs that existed at the end of 1994. They account for an estimated 50 per cent of employment and some 80 per cent of the resources and production capacity in Vietnam's SOE sector. The motives for the establishment of these conglomerates were to secure the leading role of the public sector by establishing state control over a number of strategic industries, to achieve economies of scale in production and management, and to make it possible for Vietnamese SOEs to compete on a more equal basis with foreign multinational corporations (Mallon 1996). The problem is that it is not obvious how attempts to centralise management and reduce competition in important industries will lead to the necessary improvements in technical and financial performance. Not surprisingly, a review of the National Corporations conducted in early 1999 noted serious problems related to low productivity, high costs and the emergence of monopolies. However, the review did not conclude that restructuring would be needed. Instead, it was proposed that the National Corporations should be maintained and strengthened: in practice, this meant more bank credits and higher barriers to competition. It is estimated that the government provided about 2.2 per cent of GDP annually between 1997 and 1999 in supplementary capital, subsidies, tax exemptions, debt write-offs and preferential credits to the SOE sector (World Bank 2000a). Against this background, it is likely that SOE reform will remain a medium-term problem area.

Private sector development

In addition to the continuing dominance of the state sector, Table 6.4 also shows the small share of the private sector in industrial output. The aggregate share of private firms fell from nearly 25 per cent in 1995 to 22.4 per cent in 2000. This reflects the complicated business environment in Vietnam, where the domestic private sector has been struggling not only against a complex bureaucracy but also against SOEs with various privileges. Moreover, the bulk of the private sector is made up of household enterprises, which operate at a very small scale and with very simple technologies. The perhaps most remarkable characteristic of the private manufacturing sector is that only 466 private firms had managed to grow to a size exceeding 100 employees in 1998. Few of the largest firms sought their customers on the domestic Vietnamese market, presumably because they were unwilling or unable to challenge the SOEs active in these markets: instead, they were largely focused on food and beverages, garments, leather products, and wood products for exports (Webster and Taussig 1999).

The complex and thoroughly regulated business environment in Vietnam has made it difficult to identify the relative importance of various obstacles to enterprise development. Still, it is easy to recognise several problem areas that appear frequently in discussions about private sector development. A core issue concerns the legal framework for land use rights. According to Vietnamese law, all land belongs to the people and is administered by the state. Individuals and companies may have a legal right to use land, but never to own land. The right to use land is documented in special land use certificates, which define the accepted uses of the land for example, agriculture, industry or housing. These certificates can be traded with some restrictions, as well as inherited. They are also required if land is used as collateral. Without a certificate, firms – especially new firms – will find it very hard to secure loans from the banking system, and they will be restricted to operating on leased land, where the long-term user rights are uncertain.

Private enterprises have typically found it very hard to obtain the documents required for land use certificates, particularly in urban areas. There are many complaints about the lack of a unified public registration system for the transfer, lease and mortgage of land. The government approval process for each application for land use rights has been cumbersome, arbitrary and discriminated against private enterprises. The value of land use rights has been determined administratively by governmental officials, rather than by market forces, and land lease procedures have varied from place to place. In urban areas, long-term land use rights have mainly been allocated to SOEs. This has enabled them to obtain the bulk of the credits from the banking system, and also enhanced their ability to form joint ventures with foreign investors. In many cases, the only tangible contribution of the Vietnamese partner has been their land use rights, which have surprisingly often been valued at 30 per cent of the total project value. Private enterprises have not been attractive as joint venture partners because they have rarely had any land to offer – and, of course, because foreign investors have been well aware of the less-than-whole-hearted official support for private firms.

Another central problem area is taxation. Complaints about the complicated tax system, with differential sales tax rates for different sectors and much scope for discretion in assessing tax rates, were common before 1999. Some of these complaints have been abated by the introduction of value-added tax (VAT) at the beginning of 1999. However, complaints regarding profit taxes remain. Profit tax rates differ between business activities, but there are also differences between different types of enterprises in the same economic sector. For example, profit tax rates on domestic private enterprises are often twice as high as tax rates levied on foreign-invested projects and SOEs.

Other common complaints focus on the extensive licensing requirements in all areas of business. At the beginning of 2000, it was estimated that the Vietnamese authorities required some 400 various kinds of licenses from domestic companies, many of which – such as printing and photocopying licenses – applied to several areas of business. Although around 150 types of license were dropped from the books that year, the remaining 250 licenses constitute a significant administrative burden for most firms. They also introduce an element of uncertainty into business planning, because of the discretionary decision-making practices of Vietnamese authorities. Complaints about red tape and corruption are still common, as are complaints that the Vietnamese legal system has been assessed as one of the weakest in the region.

For domestic businesses, however, the greatest problem is access to investment finance. Analysing financing in a sample of 371 private enterprises, Ramamurthy (2001) noted that the great majority of enterprises relied on personal and family savings for investment and working capital. More than half of the surveyed enterprises relied solely on their own savings for the initial capital requirements. Only a few of the most successful enterprises were able to access credit from banks and other financial institutions; even in these cases, loans were small and of short maturity. Worker contributions, interest-free loans from friends and relatives, and loans from the informal sector were all much more important than the formal banking sector as sources of credit.

Most available formal credit resources have been directed to SOEs, many of whom have had problems servicing their debt. The resulting NPL problems have forced banks to restrict lending to all but their most strategically important customer: the state. Banking rules have directly discriminated against private enterprises, which need collateral to obtain loans – SOEs do not – and pay higher rates of interest than SOEs. Another reason is the low level of development in the private sector: the credit risks connected to loans to private small and medium-sized enterprises (SMEs) are high because of the unfavourable business environment. Investment capital remains a scarce resource in Vietnam because the banking system has not been very successful in absorbing domestic household savings. Pool (1999) reports that while domestic savings increased from 7.4 per cent of GDP to 16.5 per cent between 1990 and 1997, domestic banks only managed to attract one-fourth of these savings. The rest was reportedly kept in mattresses, invested in inventory and real estate, or channelled through the informal financial sector. Restricted access to credit has made private industry very self-sufficient – the average ratio of debt to assets among SMEs is around 25 per cent, compared with 60 per cent for SOEs – but it has also restricted its growth potential. Where the bulk of finance comes from retained earnings, only the most successful companies are able to expand and invest in reasonably modern technology.

While SOE reform has been erratic and sometimes disappointing, certain aspects of private sector reform have progressed surprisingly fast. A revision of the Law on Promotion of Domestic Investment in 1998, together with the implementation of the new Enterprise Law in 2000, have had a strong positive effect on the growth of formal private enterprise. The investment law provided new incentives for domestic investment, while the latter has contributed to a transformation of the business licensing system into a business registration system, with automatic approval of all applications that fulfill the requirements. Together with the elimination of nearly 150 business licenses that restricted entry in different sectors of industry, this has led to a very large increase in the registration of new private SMEs. Over half of the country's 70,000 SMEs have been registered since January 2000, with perhaps one-fifth of the new enterprises in manufacturing. It is likely that a large share of these new formal sector enterprises were former household enterprises, which means that the actual increase in private sector activity is smaller than the number of new SMEs indicates. Nevertheless, the growing propensity to register into the formal sector is encouraging. As long as household enterprises remained in the border area between the formal and informal sector, they were not able to qualify for external credit, sign long-term agreements with customers and suppliers, and employ additional workers in the formal labour market. The fact that a large number of household enterprises have decided to register as formal enterprises indicates that they expect a future business environment with significant earnings and growth potential. In addition, as noted by the World Bank (2002:16), the emerging private sector has outperformed the state sector in both employment creation and export growth in the last few years.

Another important development is the increase in donor support for capacity building in the private sector. Several donor-funded projects are now actively promoting the development of private SMEs and providing business development services to the Vietnamese private sector. In addition to several bilateral projects, major ventures have been established by the United Nations Industrial Development Organisation and the International Finance Corporation. The Vietnamese government itself has also set up several bodies to support and supervise development in the sector. One of the more notable bilateral initiatives has been taken by the Japanese, who are promoting private sector development through the Miyazawa plan. This plan was set up to support the post-crisis recovery of the Asian economies, and the US $400 million pledged to Vietnam are tied to a broad programme aiming to facilitate SME development.[3] The establishment of the Private Sector Forum, a non-governmental body bringing together domestic and foreign private investors, government, non-governmental organisations, and donors, is another initiative that has contributed to a more lively and open discussion on private sector development.

The cautious – and very slow – reforms in the financial sector are also potentially important for private enterprise. The most visible reform has been the introduction of a stock market in July 2000. Although it only lists some 20 companies at present, it provides an important signal regarding future reforms. In addition to an increase in the number of listed companies, it can be expected that an over the counter (OTC) market will be established in the future. The requirements for transparency and accounting practices on the regular stock market are considered too demanding by many firms, and an OTC market with somewhat less stringent rules would be a suitable first step for many firms. The number of company shares in circulation is also increasing rapidly with the progress of the equitisation programme, and there is presently no official market for these equities.

Banking reform has progressed relatively slowly, which is not surprising considering the likely extent of NPLs in the system, but the plans for future reform are ambitious and important. The banking reform plan includes measures to restructure joint-stock banks and to reduce their number from 52 in 2000 to about 25 in 2003. (Thirteen joint-stock banks had been closed or merged by mid-2002.) The plans also include restructuring of the four state-owned commercial banks, with focus on modern accounting practices, annual independent audits, increased managerial accountability, phasing out of non-commercial lending, loan-loss provisioning, recapitalisation, and other measures to implement commercial operating principles. Many of these measures were called for already in PFP (1996), and the fact that they are not addressed seriously until the present time testifies to the great difficulties involved. It is likely that measures on two fronts are needed to improve the private sector's access to capital. One essential reform requirement is to sever the connection between loss-making SOEs and the banking system, to avoid further weakening of the banks' balance sheets in the next few years, when the level of competition and losses in SOEs are likely to increase. In addition, it may be necessary to establish entirely new financial institutions focusing on the private sector. It is unlikely that the existing banks will manage their debt burden in time to provide the necessary support to the private sector during the coming five years (although the share of bank credit going to the SOE sector shows a clear downward trend).

There are several other areas where progress has also been relatively slow. Land regulations should be revised to make it easier for private firms to obtain land for their business needs, and to use land as collateral for bank loans. Tax regulations, particularly for profit taxes, should be simplified, and the tax treatment of private and public enterprises should be equalised. Vietnamese science and technology centres should be encouraged to establish networks with private business, to facilitate the diffusion of modern technologies. Yet the experiences of private sector reform from the last few years are positive, and it is likely that these challenges can be managed given the requisite political will.

Conclusion

This chapter has offered a brief assessment of selected economic developments in Vietnam since the Eighth Party Congress in 1996. The focus has been on some of the structural reform areas that were identified as development challenges in the mid-1990s by Vietnamese authorities and the donor community: trade policy and the roles of the state and the private sector.

The discussion has shown that there has been significant progress in two of these areas. Trade reform has been faster than expected in the mid-1990s, and trade performance has also been much better than predicted half a decade ago. Assuming that external developments are not too unstable, there is reason to expect further progress in this area. Negotiations for WTO membership have commenced, and the increasing export orientation of foreign investors and private entrepreneurs is likely to yield continued growth. Private sector development has also been surprisingly successful in recent years. The new Enterprise Law from May 1999 has contributed to tremendous growth in the formal private sector, and the continuing efforts to strengthen the business environment look promising. The role of the private sector has now also been recognised at the highest policy-making and symbolic levels: the constitution was amended in 2002 to give equal status to the private sector and the state sector (World Bank 2002: 22). The remaining challenges are mainly related to the financial sector, where debt problems and links between state-owned banks and SOEs are slowing down necessary reforms.

SOE reform has also been slower than prescribed in various plans and strategies. Despite some progress in the equitisation programme, there has been little progress in other areas. Moreover, only a relatively small share of state capital will be privatised: the sectors identified as strategically important (and therefore earmarked for SOEs) already account for some three-quarters of SOE capital. The reason for the limited progress is clearly resistance from interest groups that fear losing their privileges, either related to 'ownership' of state enterprises, or employment in state enterprises. Earlier SOE reforms have met more resistance than expected, and Vietnam lacks domestic interest groups that are able and willing to counterbalance the influence of SOE proponents. It is therefore possible that future strategies should focus on the development of the private sector while accepting more gradual reform of the SOE sector.

Although trade reform, SOE reform and private sector promotion are essential to achieve rapid and sustainable development in Vietnam, it should be noted that the discussion above only covers a small step on the road towards a more developed society. In the long run, reforms will also be needed in several other areas. The education system needs to adjust to the requirements of a more modern economy. For instance, vocational training programmes will be demanded as soon as the private sector moves into industrial production with higher skill requirements. The demand for business training already exceeds supply. Science and technology policies must be revised to provide the necessary inputs for a rapidly developing industrial sector. Reforms in the labour market will be needed to create stronger links between productivity and wages. Social sectors need to be strengthened, not only to protect redundant workers when SOEs are reformed but, even more importantly, to provide equal opportunities to all citizens in the areas of health care and education. Carefully designed support programmes are needed to reduce poverty among the most disadvantaged groups in Vietnamese society, in the urban informal sector as well as in rural areas far from the main metropolitan regions. These are all formidable challenges for the coming years.

Notes

1 The large sums recorded for debt rescheduling and arrears in 2000 are related to the renegotiation of rouble debts to the former USSR.
2 It is difficult to provide an accurate description of ownership structures in the manufacturing sector, since many FDI projects are set up as joint ventures with SOEs. For instance, Webster (1999) classified joint ventures into the state sector, which raised its shares of manufacturing GDP to well over 50 per cent. Moreover, several SOEs have started new companies that are often registered as private firms although they are financed with state capital.
3 It is likely that the 'carrot-and-stick' approach implicit in the Miyazawa plan facilitated several of the reforms set up in connection with the new Enterprise Law.

7 The social challenges of reform

Restructuring state-owned enterprises in Vietnam

Gerard Clarke

Seventy kilometres south of Hanoi lies Nam Dinh, Vietnam's 'textile town', a grim, sprawling industrial city with a population of 250,000 – home to the Nam Dinh Textile Company (Natexco), Vietnam's oldest, largest and proudest integrated garment and textiles company. Established in 1889, Natexco became one of Vietnam's industrial behemoths after the introduction of central planning in 1954; by 1988, 17,000 people were employed in its spinning, weaving, dying, sewing and other factories. As Nam Dinh's main employer, the company provided housing for a quarter of the town's population in its 4,000 apartments and maintained five crèches, three schools, a hospital and a holiday home by the coast for workers and their families. When market reforms were introduced in Vietnam in the late 1980s under the banner of *doi moi*, Natexco was poorly placed to cope. The company's mainly Chinese machinery was so antiquated – and production so inefficient – that Natexco sold the cotton yarn it spun to other state enterprises, substituting imported yarn for its own weaving workshops.

By 2000, Natexco's workforce had been cut to 7,000 and its housing, education and health care obligations transferred to other state agencies. A new spinning factory with Japanese machinery opened in 1993, and other plant and machinery was modernised with aid from the Dutch and Belgian governments. By 2000, the company was producing 10,000 tons of yarn per year and exporting garments to Japan, Europe, Russia and South Korea. The company remained loss-making, however, its products shunned by Vietnamese consumers in favour of the outputs of more efficient producers in the state and private sectors alike. Its buildings, some dating to the end of the nineteenth century, were dilapidated, its plant and machinery still inefficient and expensive to maintain and its factories still overstaffed. At a time of general economic hardship throughout Vietnam in the aftermath of the 1997 East Asian economic crisis, the company remained handicapped by its traditional responsibilities as the city's largest employer.[1]

State-owned enterprises (SOEs), as the example of Natexco illustrates, continue to represent a key component in Vietnam's ongoing reform process. Vietnam still has a small formal domestic private sector, accounting for less than 4 per cent of gross domestic product (GDP), 6 per cent of manufacturing output and 3 per cent of total employment (World Bank and ADB 2002: 32). By contrast, the country had approximately 5,500 SOEs in 2002, generating 38 per cent of GDP, consuming

40 per cent of total domestic credit and employing roughly 1.7m people (World Bank and ADB 2002: 21). Most of these SOEs are controlled by provincial or district governments, with the larger, more capital-intensive, firms controlled by central ministries in Hanoi or the Prime Minister's Office.[2] Economically and socially, the SOE sector is more important in Vietnam than in the developing world as a whole, where public enterprises typically account for less than 10 per cent of GDP (Galal *et al.* 1994: 576). SOEs, however, have been less important in Vietnam than in China or in the former Soviet bloc. Vietnam is less industrialised and more reliant on agriculture than its former communist peers. In addition, the virtually continuous state of war in which Vietnam found itself from 1954 to 1975 (and beyond in the case of intervention in Cambodia between 1978 and 1989) made it impossible to build up a broadly based industrial capacity (Harris and Lockwood 1997: 612). In 1986, for instance, SOEs accounted for 15 per cent of the total labour force, compared to more than 75 per cent in a number of former communist states in Eastern Europe (Probert and Young 1995). As a result, Vietnamese SOEs have traditionally been, and remain, relatively small, with typical capital of 5.7 billion Vietnam dong (US $370,000) and a typical workforce of 250 (World Bank and ADB 2002: 22).[3]

Given Vietnam's agricultural base, SOEs have traditionally been an important source of wage employment, not to mention an important power base for the Vietnamese Communist Party (VCP). SOEs constitute a significant impediment both to further reform and to long-term economic growth: 60 per cent of Vietnamese SOEs were classified as loss-making in 1997. By 1999, SOEs accounted for VND 126 trillion (US $9 billion) of bank debt, a significant proportion of which they are unable to service or repay (World Bank *et al.* 2000a: 32). In 1999, according to the World Bank, SOEs were responsible for 46 per cent of industrial output, yet they soaked up 60 to 70 per cent of banking system credit, crowding out other productive investment (World Bank 1999a: 61, 139).

SOE reform is widely seen as a central pillar in Vietnam's ongoing reform process, although the challenge of reform is mainly viewed (and contested) in the literature in political or economic terms. Gabriel Kolko, for instance, a staunch critic of Vietnam's *doi moi* era reforms, has criticised SOE reforms, including equitisation, for weakening the power of the state and for increasing corruption in the state sector. 'Essentially,' Kolko argues, 'the Politburo rented its SOEs to its managers, who stood to become rich from them if they made profits without subsidies' (Kolko 1997: 58). Porter (1993: 128), on the other hand, argues that SOE reform is an integral component in rolling back the official 'bureaucratic centralism and state subsidies system' (*co che tap quan lieu hanh chinh bao cap*), a process continually delayed and frustrated by 'the ability of the bureaucratic elite to fend off challenges to its interests'.[4] The economic significance of SOE reform is also disputed. Griffin (1998: 42, 44) argues that the Vietnamese government has successfully transformed the SOE sector into an engine of growth over the last decade, and that further reform should concentrate on the banking system rather than the privatisation of SOEs. Kokko and Sjöholm (2000: 258–9), however, claim that SOE reform remains vital in continued efforts to mobilise productive investment.

By contrast, this chapter focuses on the *social* challenges of SOE reform, a subject largely ignored in the literature,[5] linking SOE reform to other social challenges such as reforming Vietnam's elaborate social welfare system, easing tensions with ethnic minorities and reducing punitive taxes on farmers. Based on research carried out in April and May 2000 on behalf of the United Kingdom (UK) Department for International Development (DfID), it focuses on two sectors targeted for reform between 2000 and 2005: garment and textiles and coffee.[6]

The reform of state-owned enterprises (SOEs) in Vietnam

The reform of state-owned enterprises has been an integral component of *doi moi* since 1986, but its origins date back to the early 1980s. In January 1981, the Council of Ministers decided to give SOEs greater independence from the state with respect to production, trade and finance (Beresford 1988: 163).[7] The move quickly triggered demands for further reforms. 'Throughout the 1980s,' Porter (1993: 140) argues, 'debate continued within the VCP Political Bureau between those who believed that the state violated objective economic laws by maintaining tight controls over production and trade and those who were primarily concerned with the supremacy of the state sector in the economy'. In 1985, a resolution approved at the Eighth Plenum of the VCP Central Committee called for 'an end to managing the economy mainly with administrative orders and [a] switch to a period of correctly perceiving and applying the objective laws' (quoted in Porter 1993: 142). It was only after the Sixth Party Congress in December 1986 – and the appointment of Nguyen Van Linh as General Secretary – that the SOE reform process acquired real momentum.

Broadly speaking, the years from 1987 to 2003 can be divided into three phases of uneven progress. The first phase began with the Enterprise Reform Law of November 1987, which increased the autonomy granted to SOEs in 1981. In 1988–9, however, as economic aid from the Soviet Union was dramatically reduced, Vietnam was gripped by an economic crisis, including falling industrial output, severe food shortages and triple-digit inflation. In 1989 the government responded by launching a radical programme to reduce the number of loss-making SOEs, in order to contain Vietnam's ballooning budget deficit. Over the three years to mid-1992, the number of SOEs was reduced from 12,000 to roughly 6,000, through the closure and merger of the most inefficient and debt-ridden enterprises (Griffin 1998: 42; World Bank 1999b: 36). During this phase, roughly 800,000 workers in the SOE sector, or one-third of the SOE workforce, lost their jobs (World Bank 1999a: 43; Dollar 1999: 42). According to one estimate, 60 per cent of those who lost their jobs were women (Van Anh and Hung 1997: 106).

From mid-1992 onwards, a second phase began to take shape, one of cautious reform and consolidation. Over the five years to mid-1997, the number of SOEs was reduced by fewer than 500. During this phase, however, a number of significant new policies were put in place. In 1992, the government terminated the system of direct subsidies to SOEs, changing the incentive structure and forcing SOEs to compete more with private sector firms (Griffin 1998: 42). The same year, the government introduced measures to facilitate the 'equitisation' of SOEs: in other words, the conversion of enterprises into joint stock companies in which the state, employees and private investors alike could own and control share capital.[8] This allowed for a range of options including the privatisation of enterprises, where the government divested a majority of the shares, and more limited equitisations, where the state retained a substantial or majority stake. Despite the introduction of explicit provisions for *privatisation* in the 1992 decision, both party and government eschewed the concept, in favour of *equitisation*, a far less ideologically contentious concept. Reflecting this equivocation, the process proceeded slowly, due in significant part to opposition from managers and concerns about job security for workers. By the end of 1997, only 17 enterprises had been equitised (World Bank 1999b: 36). In 1994, the government created a new tier of General Corporations and Special Corporations, grouped around basic economic sectors, and transferred to them SOEs previously administered directly by central or local government (World Bank 1999b: 37).[9] General Corporations created included Vinatex, Seaprodex and Vinacafé, covering the garment and textiles, marine products and coffee industries respectively. Despite the slow pace of reform, however, these measures succeeded in improving efficiency and competitiveness.

The third phase, from 1997 to the present, is characterised by further policy reform but with a renewed commitment to substantially reducing the number of SOEs. This phase was also characterised, however, by significant ideological tension within the party and government, opposition from SOE managers and resultant slippage in the attainment of targets, in the lead up to and beyond the Ninth Party Congress of April 2001. The phase effectively began with the opening of the tenth parliamentary assembly in 1997, when Prime Minister Phan Van Khai called for an acceleration of the SOE reform process. In response, a number of new measures were introduced in 1998 and 1999. In 1998, the government simplified the equitisation process[10] and established the National Enterprise Restructuring Committee (NERC) to guide it, under the authority of the Deputy Prime Minister.[11] As a result, the equitisation process speeded up and by November 1999, an additional 224 companies had been successfully equitised, another 210 were in the process of equitisation and a further 434 enterprises had registered for equitisation with the NERC (World Bank 1999b: 37).[12] Most of these involved relatively small enterprises, however, with only a few involving enterprises with capital of over US $1m. Equally, the reform process in this phase, as in the previous one, involved very few liquidations due in large part to anxiety about the consequences of significant job losses (World Bank *et al.* 2000a: 33).[13] By the end of 1999, NERC had prepared ambitious plans, with the support of donors, to reduce the number of SOEs from an estimated 5,800 to 3,000 by 2005 and to reduce the number of workers in the SOE sector from 1.7m to 1.2m.[14] NERC identified garments and textiles, marine products and coffee as the priorities for reform in an equitisation pilot project,[15] sectors with significant potential for export and employment growth and for inward foreign investment and know-how. Aid donors such as the World Bank and DfID promised funding and technical assistance to support the process, but progress in 2000 was slow amid political inertia prior to the Ninth Party Congress.

That Congress, held on 19–22 April 2001, approved a ten-year socio-economic development strategy (2001–10) committing Vietnam to becoming a 'socialist-oriented market economy', in which 'the state economic sector [plays] the leading role' (Government of Vietnam 2001). The strategy also commits the party and government to a five-year programme of SOE reform, including a programme of equitisation. Despite these decisions, however, the Congress failed to agree on the overall direction of economic policy (Cohen 2001c). According to the 10-year strategy paper (Government of Vietnam 2001), for instance, 'A number of viewpoints, such as those related to ownership and economic sectors, the role of the state and market, the building of an independent and autonomous economy, international economic integration, etc. have not been clarified', indicating some of the issues dividing senior VCP cadres at the Congress.

Despite the ideological tension surrounding SOE reform at the Congress, the reform agenda was apparently quickening in pace. NERC, a relatively weak and under-resourced institution during its four years of existence, was abolished in the lead up to the Congress and replaced by the new interministerial National Steering Committee for Enterprise Reform and Development (NSCERD), chaired by the Deputy Prime Minister, Nguyen Tan Dung. Supporting the main elements of the NERC reform agenda, NSCERD proposed limiting the role of SOEs to a number of key sectors of the economy,[16] and a significant increase in the capital resources of SOEs.[17] It also proposed a new corporate model in which General Corporations acted as holding companies with subsidiaries which were entirely state-owned or in which share capital and profits were shared with other investors.[18] Speaking at the Third Plenum of the Ninth Party Congress in Hanoi in August 2001, Party Secretary General Nong Duc Manh described SOE reform as a 'vital and urgent issue' and called for renewed efforts to reorganise SOEs and improve their operational efficiency.[19]

In the months following the Congress, a raft of new legislation was approved to provide added impetus to the SOE reform drive.[20] Nevertheless, the tensions that materialised at the Ninth Party Congress continued to affect policy-making and the issue of SOE reform dominated the Third Plenum in August 2001. The Plenum approved a detailed Action Plan to accelerate the equitisation process,[21] but behind the scenes, debate in party circles remained intense, while SOE managers remained hesitant, delaying implementation.[22] Through the remainder of 2001 and into 2002, the pace of SOE reform slowed dramatically. A target of 400 enterprise transformations in the first year of the Action Plan was achieved, largely through the restructuring of enterprises managed by provincial authorities, but new SOEs were also created during the same period (World Bank and ADB 2002: 22). By the end of 2002, the five-year (2000–5) SOE reform programme was substantially behind schedule, despite progress in other areas of macroeconomic reform, including banking and trade reform (World Bank 2001a: 41). As the World Bank argued at the end of 1992, 'At present, the [SOE] reform mechanisms in place amount to an option, rather than a mandate', due to deep-seated fears of the consequences of job losses and the difficulty of clearing enterprise debts (World Bank and ADB 2002: 20). In addition to the ideological debate in party circles surrounding the role of the state sector in Vietnam's ongoing programme of economic reform, the SOE reform process has been hampered by the absence of a strong decision-making centre in the midst of a complex institutional milieu. As the World Bank notes, for instance,

> Not only are four ministries and agencies involved – Ministry of Finance, Ministry of Planning and Investment, Ministry of Labor, Invalids and Social Affairs, and the Office of Government – but actions in respect of specific SOEs like equitisation, liquidation, sale and restructuring can only be taken by owners such as provincial people's committees, line ministries and General Corporations. They in turn have to persuade enterprise managers to take action.
>
> (World Bank and ADB 2002: 42)

In addition, however, SOE reform has been delayed by debate about the social challenges of the reform process and about the institutional responses to these challenges.

The social challenges of reform

The plans of the NERC, and its successor, the NSCERD, have given rise to significant ideological tension on political, economic and social grounds. Social issues are a central source of tension in intra-party and intra-government debate and partly explain the cautious programme of reform for 2000–5. The government had not only to manage the process of retrenching 500,000 workers, or roughly 100,000 per year, from the SOE sector, but also had to provide social security entitlements for retrenched workers – an area of dispute between the government and foreign donors.

Employment is a sensitive issue for a number of reasons. Sustaining wage employment has traditionally been one of the most important objectives of Vietnamese SOEs. Roughly 800,000 SOE workers lost their jobs between 1989 and 1992 amid very difficult economic circumstances. Little appetite exists for further job losses on this scale. Furthermore, the Ministry of Labour, Invalids and Social Affairs (MoLISA) estimates that up to 30 per cent of the 800,000 workers retrenched between 1989 and 1992 are still living in 'difficult circumstances', and that many workers retrenched between 2000 and 2005 will be similarly unable to find new work.[23] MoLISA concerns are well-founded. An estimated 50 per cent of the Vietnamese population is under the age of 25. With the population growing at 1.65 per cent per annum, the economy needs to grow by 7 per cent per annum to absorb new entrants into the labour force, excluding those retrenched from the SOE sector. To prevent unemployment rising, the economy needs to create 1.2m new jobs each year. Yet the economic growth needed to create jobs has fallen from the high levels preceding the East Asian Crisis. Vietnam achieved average GDP growth rates of 8.4 per cent a year between 1992 and 1998, and urban unemployment fell as result from 7.7 per cent in 1992 to 5.4 per cent in 1998 (World Bank 1999a: 44, 50). The high economic growth of the 1993–8 period, however, translated into barely 1.6m new wage jobs over the five years (World Bank 1999a: 47), fewer than the number of people entering the labour force *each year*. By 1999, however, economic growth (GDP) had fallen to 4 per cent while urban unemployment had increased to 7.4 per cent (World Bank 1999b: i; World Bank 1999a: 50), transforming employment markets and increasing the sensitivity associated with retrenching SOE workers. GDP growth rose to nearly 6 per cent in 2000 and is expected to increase to 6.5 per cent for 2001 and 6 per cent for 2002 (World Bank *et al.* 2000a: 15–16; World Bank and ADB 2002 : 7), encouraging signs of recovery – but lower growth than 1992–8.

Anticipated growth over the five years 2000–5 will not be sufficient to absorb new labour market entrants nor those retrenched from the SOE sector. This increases the salience of the social security system and of proposed social security reforms. At present the social architecture for SOE reform rests on the Labour Code of 1994 and the Social Insurance Regulations of 1995.[24] Harris and Lockwood (1997: 623) claim that SOE employment in Vietnam confers few welfare benefits in comparison to Russia or China – yet the 1994 Code and the 1995 Regulations provide for retirement and redundancy entitlements which are generous by Western standards. In practice, SOEs also 'top up' redundancy packages, typically with an extra half month's pay per year of employment and a full or partial salary for the first three to six months following redundancy.[25]

In return for these entitlements, employees pay 5 per cent of their salary, and the employer 15 per cent.[26] Workers in turn are only entitled to benefits if they and their employer have paid amounts due to central government. Many loss-making SOEs, however, have accrued significant social security debts: many workers retrenched between 1989 and 1992 waited for considerable periods to receive compensation or pension entitlements.[27] Today, numerous small loss-making SOEs cannot be wound up, nor their workers laid off, until outstanding debts to the government are cleared. Staff of one Seaprodex member enterprise scheduled for closure, for instance, were assembling motorbikes in May 2000 in an attempt to clear the company's social security debts.

Existing welfare provisions reward civil servants and SOE employees – a constituency which has long provided loyal support to the VCP – rather than making equitable provision for the poor. In Vietnam, the social welfare system is dominated by social insurance payments to public and ex-public employees, in the form of pensions, redundancy packages and benefits for ill-health. Payments from the social insurance fund account for 82 per cent of the total value of social safety nets. Yet the wealthiest 40 per cent of the Vietnamese population, predominantly those with wage employment, command over 72 per cent of this social insurance provision, while the poorest 20 per cent command a mere 3.2 per cent. Only 1.1 per cent of social welfare expenditure is devoted to targeted anti-poverty programmes (World Bank 1999a: 124–5).

In mid-2000, however, MoLISA was considering the adoption of a revised Labour Code and further changes to the 1995 Social Insurance Regulations to provide even more generous entitlements to state employees.[28] Some MoLISA officials, for instance, believed that NERC's proposals to retrench 500,000 workers between 2000 and 2005 were unrealistic without further incentives to encourage workers to accept voluntary redundancy or early retirement. Yet any such measures would undermine the government's broader anti-poverty measures by consolidating the relatively blunt and poorly targeted social safety nets that currently marginalise the poorest.

In response to concerns within MoLISA and elsewhere in the government and party machinery, Prime Minister Phan Van Khai launched an Enterprise Restructuring Fund (ERF) in 1999 to cushion the effects of jobs losses.[29] Detailed implementation procedures were confirmed in Decree 41 of April 2002, including the establishment of a subsidiary Fund for Redundant Workers (FRW).[30] From August 2002, international donors began to contribute to the FRW and the estimated US $500m cost of redundancy pay, wage arrears and retraining for workers who lose their jobs in equitised corporations.[31] Donors are funding this element of the ERF to make it more attractive for SOE managers and workers alike to support equitisation. The government also hoped the ERF would help to clear the social security debts of newly-equitised SOEs, but aid donors have expressed reluctance to support this. A far greater problem is that the ERF does not provide additional compensation for workers who accept voluntary redundancy in enterprises that are not equitised because of their severe debts or labour over-capacity, or those not closed on the grounds of insolvency: in other words, the larger, more inefficient enterprises in greatest need of restructuring. This makes it more difficult for such corporations to secure agreement for redundancy programmes and hence to restructure their activities.

The social roles of SOEs

In Vietnam, SOEs were never burdened with social roles and obligations to the same extent as in China; and many such roles were curtailed during the radical reforms of the 1989–92 period. Yet today, SOEs are still legally obliged to pursue a mix of commercial and social objectives, many of which place onerous obligations on individual companies. According to the 1995 law on state enterprises, for instance, 'State enterprises … carr[y] out business … aimed at achieving the socio-economic objectives assigned by the state'. Another decree notes a number of these objectives, including 'the performance of obligations towards the locality', 'program[s] of action in support of the locality' and 'charity and humanitarian' functions.[32] Some decisions taken after the Ninth Party Congress in 2001 aim to protect these social roles.[33]

Legislation also provides a variety of party and mass organisations with influence over the affairs of state enterprises, including enterprise trade unions affiliated to the Vietnam General Confederation of Labour and the Ho Chi Minh Youth Communist League, ensuring that these social roles are fulfilled.[34] Article 4 of Decree 07/1999 seeks the 'enhance[ment] of Party organisations' leadership in State enterprises'. Generally, commercial objectives such as efficiency and competitiveness have recently gained priority, although more slowly than in China. The rationalisation of SOEs since 1988 has involved more emphasis on market-based relationships and a retreat from social service provision. In most cases, workers have lost their entitlements to enterprise-provided housing, education, health and childcare and in many cases have been compensated with an increase in wages to bring their conditions of employment closer in line with those in the private sector. Nevertheless, there have been no significant job losses in the SOE sector since the establishment of the General Corporations, which continue to have important social functions. Government strategy of retaining roughly 50 per cent of existing SOEs in the state sector beyond 2005 entails a commitment to defending this mix of commercial, social and political objectives for the foreseeable future. This has significant ramifications for the social dimensions of *doi moi*: the social roles of SOEs therefore represent another ideological battleground within the party and government for the foreseeable future.

Equitisation and employee participation

The party and government alike are keen to enable managers and workers to acquire substantial stakes in their companies as a result of equitisation, so enabling the state to maintain influence over equitised companies and diluting the stake of private, especially foreign, investors. To this effect, legislation provides generous incentives for workers to buy shares,[35] while 'poor' employees receive extra incentives.[36] 'Poor' workers are defined as those on less than one-third of average earnings:[37] in 1998, the average salary was 900,000 VND per month (US $60). Equitising enterprises can distribute surpluses from bonus or welfare funds to employees to enable them to buy shares.[38] Vietnam therefore risks repeating the débâcle in Russia where managers and workers acquired a majority of shares in state companies equitised in the early 1990s. Managers preparing their enterprises for sale undervalued their assets; under inflationary conditions, the state effectively transferred vast sums to privileged insiders (Harris and Lockwood 1997: 614).

Workers have the right to reassign or bequeath the right to their shares,[39] yet there is no established mechanism for dealing in the shares of equitised corporations.[40] At present, such corporations must update their list of shareholders annually. This allows for changes in share ownership between the compilation of lists. A 'grey' market in the shares of equitised corporations allows managers and others with capital to acquire workers' shares by a variety of means. Managers in equitised companies can persuade friends and relations to buy shares, enabling them to retain control and to protect their positions. The anti-corruption law stipulates that current directors and their families cannot buy more than 0.6 per cent of the shares of equitised companies. At present, however, the government is considering measures to allow managers to buy a greater number of shares and to control a greater percentage of the equity of equitised corporations. The enforcement of existing measures for share ownership by managers and workers is also weak, as are measures to ensure that workers who hold shares are given an equitable say in the running of their enterprises. Equally, SOE employees in general have very little understanding of 'shares' and by 2000 labour unions had not yet begun to explain the concept or implications of shareholding ahead of equitisation.[41]

Sectoral challenges

The social challenges or tensions of the SOE reform process noted above are all cross-sectoral, affecting SOEs as a whole. The two cases of the garment and textiles industry and the coffee industry also illustrate significant sectoral tensions, demonstrating the connections between SOE reform and other social challenges of the reform process, including improving the situation of women and ethnic minorities and reducing punitive taxes on farmers.

Vinatex and the garments and textiles industry

Vietnam has become a major player in the global garment and textile industry, now ranking with China and Indonesia among Asia's largest exporters. Along with cheap labour and reliable supplies of water and energy, the expansion of the private sector has been central to the growth of the Vietnamese industry, stimulated in large part by foreign investment. Nike, the American sportswear manufacturer, for instance, now employs 46,000 workers in six factories in Vietnam, all foreign-owned (Larmer 2001). Despite the growth of the private sector, however, the state remains a central player. Vinatex, the Vietnam National Textile and Garment Corporation, had 61 enterprises in early 1999, employing roughly 90,000 people or 12 per cent of the labour force in the garments and textiles industry.[42] In 1999, five enterprises were equitised and nine were scheduled for equitisation in 2000. By 2005, Vinatex should be reduced to 15 enterprises that are wholly state-owned.[43]

Vinatex factories are generally integrated garments and textiles production facilities, employing a predominantly (65–80 per cent) female labour force. Many have cut their workforces over the last 10 years, often dramatically, but excess labour remains a significant problem. Vinatex officials estimate labour overcapacity in member enterprises at 25–30 per cent. Many of its enterprises are loss-making. In the case of weaker, debt-ridden enterprises, Vinatex helps companies to restructure by funding compensation packages for workers who accept voluntary redundancy, using profits from its own activities and membership fees from member enterprises.[44]

Vinatex companies are often key local employers in the suburbs of Hanoi and Ho Chi Minh City or in key provincial towns. Many employ over 2,500 people directly, while other jobs are supported in downstream activities. Employment opportunities in the garments and textiles industry have traditionally benefited families with longstanding connections to particular companies or local party structures. Since companies often employ three or four members from the same household, such families are badly hit by the loss of multiple incomes when jobs are retrenched. In making workers redundant, however, Vinatex members try to ensure that at least one member per household retains a job. Many Vinatex members also continue to operate facilities such as schools and hospitals;

transferring these responsibilities to local government departments that are already overburdened and underresourced is a considerable challenge.

A more important social problem, however, is the disproportionate impact of labour restructuring on female employees. Women have been disproportionately affected by economic restructuring since *doi moi* began in 1986–7. In the 1960s and early 1970s, female participation in the wage labour force increased dramatically as men were inducted into military service.[45] From the late 1970s, female participation began to taper off as men were demobilised and returned to wage employment; but the rate of decline increased significantly from the late 1980s, as women were laid off in disproportionate numbers during the restructuring period of 1989–92 (Van Anh and Hung 1997: 104). For women who remain in SOE employment or for women who enter the SOE labour force for the first time, employment conditions have changed significantly.

Restructuring of the SOE sector since the late 1980s has led to the widespread use of fixed-term contracts, overwhelmingly for women, in contrast to men who are employed disproportionately on permanent contracts.[46] Women have to retire at 55 under the 1995 Social Insurance Regulations, and interviews with female workers in four factories suggest that the contracts of those as young as 40 are being terminated on health grounds (for example, poor eyesight or deteriorating manual dexterity), leading to considerable financial hardship. In addition, women can be laid off on a compulsory basis at the end of their contracts; they are ineligible for redundancy pay, regardless of the number of years of employment. It is thus easier to shed the jobs of female workers, even where labour overcapacity is concentrated in activities dominated by male employment (for example, machine tool manufacture and repair). Trade unions in Vietnam have expressed little interest in this issue and women's organisations are still virtually nonexistent, so the problem – a common one in developing countries with significant garment and textiles industries – is largely hidden in Vietnam.

Vinacafé and the coffee industry

The coffee industry, on the other hand, illustrates a very different set of social challenges. Vietnam has become one of the world's largest producers of coffee; production has increased dramatically over the last decade, stimulated in large part by rising prices on international markets. By 2001, Vietnam had 500,000 hectares of land planted to coffee (a 60 per cent increase on 1996) and the Vietnamese coffee industry accounted for 12.3 per cent of global production.[47] The private sector and independent coffee growers account for the bulk of production, but the state sector is a significant actor in the industry. The Vietnam National Coffee Corporation (Vinacafé) oversees state-run coffee farms in Vietnam and has 70 companies with a presence in 14 provinces. It controls 72,000 hectares of land devoted to coffee production, with other land holdings devoted to sugar cane and cashew nuts.[48] The bulk of its landholdings, however, are concentrated in the ethnically sensitive Central or Tay Nguyen Highlands, making its activities both politically and socially significant.

Vinacafé and its member companies employ 30,000 people, mostly farmers who grow coffee on plots of roughly a hectare provided by these companies. Most of these employees have additional land on which they grow coffee or other crops. In many cases, the farmers are members of ethnic minorities who were allocated individual parcels of land after their collective land rights were abrogated. Others are migrants from the Red River delta and other parts of Vietnam who received free parcels of land as compensation for their resettlement. Farmers produce a quota for the enterprise through which they are employed and sell surplus production to the company at free market rates or to other purchasers. Production quotas typically range from 0.8 to 1.7 tonnes per hectare,[49] but in many cases have proved onerous and pushed farmers into debt, especially following the global coffee price collapse of 1999–2000. Vietnam is unusual among developing countries in providing social security entitlements such as pension rights to farmers through wage employment on state-owned farms. Under the quota system, farmers pay in kind to secure social security and other entitlements that have monetary values. In some respects, the quota system protects farmers from price fluctuations; farmers receive fixed entitlements when they meet their quotas, regardless of the prevailing free market price. The effective rates at which these quotas are converted into monetary equivalents, however, represent a relatively penal form of taxation of farmers, including poor farmers,[50] and mean that farmers effectively pay more for the same social security entitlements as urban workers. The practice of valuing production at market rates also allows Vinacafé enterprises to transfer some of the risk arising from fluctuating coffee prices on international markets to farmers, including the poor.[51]

Vinacafé and its member enterprises maintain important social roles. It works primarily in remote and mountainous areas where low population densities give rise to weak government services and Vinacafé plays an important role in providing basic infrastructure such as roads, bridges and schools.[52] The Central Highlands as a whole remain desperately poor, with 52 per cent of households living below the poverty line in 1998 (World Bank 1999a: 16); food insecurity is a significant problem, due in part to the emphasis on cash, rather than subsistence, crop production. Nationally, coffee production has expanded significantly in recent years, from 186,000 hectares in 1995 to 362,000 hectares in 1998, to 500,000 by 2001. This growth reflects an increase in land area rather than in yields, which have fallen slightly in the same period. The Central Highlands accounts for the bulk of this expansion in the land area devoted to coffee production, although the non-state sector, as noted above, has been largely responsible.

The liberalisation of land tenure laws and the boom in coffee prices and production have stimulated the process of social differentiation in the Central Highlands. Many coffee farmers or traders have become prosperous and have expanded their landholdings and trading activities. Provincial capitals in the Central Highlands such as Buon Ma Thuot have a general air of prosperity. Most farmers, however, have struggled with the technical demands of coffee production (which are greater than for rice) and small landholdings, continuing to live in poverty.

Others are growing coffee in unsuitable climatic conditions. Employees of state-owned coffee farms count among these winners and losers alike.

The growth of coffee production, however, has also intensified resentment on the part of ethnic minorities. Minorities in the Central Highlands have opposed the VCP in the past and the government controls them more closely than minorities in the North. The Central Highlands' agricultural potential led to sponsored resettlement schemes from the late 1970s till the mid-1990s, which promoted the inward migration of Kinh (ethnic Vietnamese) people from the Red River delta and other overpopulated areas. This achieved the double objective of improving the livelihoods of poor Kinh and of hastening the absorption of ethnic minorities into mainstream Kinh society. The promotion of sedentary agriculture, notably coffee production, has been and remains a key feature of this strategy. This has led to considerable resentment on the part of minorities. Between 2 and 6 February 2001, for instance, roughly 5,000 Ede, Giarai and others demonstrated on the streets of Buon Ma Thuot and Pleiku (the provincial capitals of Dak Lak and Gia Lai), protesting against the influx of Kinh migrants and the encroachment of their land rights and culture. Troops and riot police used water cannon to disperse the demonstrators, and the crisis provoked a special meeting of the Politburo in Hanoi on 10 February (Cohen 2001a).

The collapse of global coffee prices compounded the social sensitivity of coffee sector reform, stemming from the ethnic diversity of the country's main coffee producing regions. Restructuring the state coffee sector is largely designed to enhance international competitiveness, but the reform process will have significant social consequences. In August 2001 the government, through the Vietnam Coffee and Cocoa Association (VCCA), announced plans to end coffee production on large areas of land and to reduce Vietnam's share of global production to 9 per cent.[53] Unlike urban-based industries such as garments and textiles where social safety nets, especially the proposed ERF, will cushion the effects on workers, no special measures have been announced to date to help farmers cope with the transition. Many farmers who grow coffee under harsh climatic and other conditions will benefit in the medium to long term from switching to other food or cash crops, but will lose out in the short term while they invest in nurturing alternatives. Ethnic minority groups will feature significantly among those affected, potentially heightening the political unrest seen in the Central Highlands in February 2001.

Conclusion

The reform of SOEs represented one of the most contentious issues before the Ninth Party Congress of April 2001. According to one journalist: 'the big decision' facing the Congress 'is what to do about state-sector reform' (Cohen 2001b). 'The party's elite,' Cohen writes, 'will meet in Hanoi facing their biggest and pressing dilemma—how to implement significant economic reforms while preventing those reforms from threatening the party's lock on power' (Cohen 2001b). Ultimately, the decisions reached at the Congress were equivocal, reflecting the cautious approach to reform that has characterised the whole *doi moi* era, but also reflecting significant ideological tension surrounding its future. In 'Strategy for Socio-Economic Development 2001–2010' – a key document approved by the Congress – party and government committed Vietnam to developing a 'socialist-oriented market economy' in which 'the state sector [plays] the leading role' (Government of Vietnam 2001: 6–7). The party, however, also supported government plans to reduce the number of SOEs to 3,000 and to reduce employment in the sector to roughly 1.2m by 2005. Nevertheless, the SOE reform process remains the subject of significant debate in party and government circles; it remains by no means certain that current targets for SOE reform will be achieved.

The ideological tension promoted by the SOE reform process derives from a variety of political, economic and social factors, many of them tightly intertwined. This chapter has examined the social challenges or dilemmas of SOE reform and sought to link them to other social dilemmas of the continuing reform process. The main social dilemma of SOE reform concerns the loss of jobs. Sustaining wage employment has traditionally been one of the most important tasks of Vietnamese SOEs; SOE reform was put on hold from 1992 to 1997, largely because of the fear of job losses. The SOE reform process as currently conceived, however, will lead to the loss of up to 500,000 jobs over the five years to 2005. In 1998, the state sector accounted for over 24 per cent of industrial employment (World Bank 1999a: 61): reducing employment in SOEs by one-third threatens significant social dislocation, especially since economic growth rates have yet to return to 1992–8 levels.

Many people laid off by SOEs will be unable to find new employment and will instead rely on Vietnam's social security system, a system which has traditionally protected state sector employees very well. To address this situation, the government introduced, in Decree 41 of April 2002, a generous compensation package for workers who accept redundancy from SOEs which are closed or equitised. Since 2000, MoLISA has explored the option of further expanding welfare entitlements for state employees, but this goal – along with the package contained within Decree 41 – conflicts with other aspects of the social security and poverty reduction agenda in Vietnam. There is an urgent need to broaden the coverage of social safety nets beyond the special interests traditionally supported by the VCP, and to improve their targeting and focus. Reforming this social security system represents another important social challenge over the coming years.

Between 2000 and 2005, the NSCERD, the successor to the NERC, will focus on restructuring the garments and textiles, coffee and marine products industries and developing mechanisms for further reform before and beyond 2005.[54] Reform in each sector, this chapter argues, gives rise to distinct social challenges, especially in the case of garments and textiles and the coffee industry. Restructuring of the garments and textiles industry, for instance, has significant implications for textile towns such as Nam Dinh. They have to cope, not only with job losses with the potential to cripple local economies, but also with the transfer of social services from SOEs to the local departments of line ministries. Reform also has implications for the predominantly female workforce. Female workers in the garment and textiles industry are predominantly employed on fixed-term contracts and do not enjoy the social security entitlements of permanent employees. As a result they suffer significant gender discrimination and stand to lose significantly from the SOE reform process.

Restructuring the state coffee industry has particular implications for sensitivities in the Central Highlands, and for ethnic minority and Kinh farmers alike. The successful promotion of cash crops, such as coffee, has been critical to the government strategy of forcing ethnic minorities to engage in fixed cultivation and live in fixed settlements, as well as helping poor migrants from the Red River delta and other parts of the country. The Strategy for Socio-Economic Development 2001–10 commits party and government to the further promotion of coffee and other industrial crops in the Central Highlands (Government of Vietnam 2001), yet the collapse in international coffee prices in 1999–2000 has prompted plans to cut coffee production, which will have significant effects on farmers. Coffee industry restructuring will also have implications for farmers who pay punitive taxes, but who nevertheless stand to lose social security entitlements when state coffee farms are equitised. The February 2001 riots in the Central Highlands illustrated and accentuated these sensitivities.

Vietnam has an enviable record for converting low levels of per capita GNP into high levels of human development,[55] and economic growth in the 1990s did little to exacerbate Vietnam's low level of income inequality.[56] Nevertheless, further economic reform, including the reform of SOEs, will weaken state control of the economy and associated social processes. SOEs, including their personnel and assets, have long represented an important power base for the VCP. Both the slow pace of SOE reform between 1992 and 1998 and the cautious programme of reform for 2000–5 are explained in large part by the fear of the consequences. Once lost, state control will be near-impossible to restore. Hence the social dilemmas of SOE reform represent a hydra-headed snake, a process with multifaceted components, all of which threaten the interests of party and government alike.

Given the absence of opposition political parties and autonomous trade unions or interest groups, the social and other tensions of SOE reform will be resolved within government and party organs with minimal influence conceded to mass organisations. Foreign aid donors, however, represent one of the few sources of external influence on the policy-making process; the *Vietnam Development Report 2001*, prepared jointly by the World Bank, Asian Development Bank and the United Nations Development Programme, represents an extended commentary on, and attempt to influence, the Strategy for Socio-Economic Development 2001–10 (cf. World Bank *et al.* 2000a, 2000b and 2000c). That influence is considerable. In the case of SOE reform, for instance, multilateral and bilateral donors were funding 19 different programmes concerned with SOE reform in 2001, costing US $36m (World Bank 2001b: 31–2). Yet donors also face many of the same social dilemmas in supporting the SOE reform process. In meeting the estimated $500m cost of the FRW, for instance, donors will ease a significant source of social tension by funding redundancy packages for SOE workers who lose their jobs when their firms are equitised or wound up. But in doing so, donors will be strengthening a social security system that benefits the relatively well off, the reform of which they have continually sought. Even in the case of their limited interventions, the social challenges of SOE reform presents donors with difficult dilemmas. Party, government and donors alike face an uncertain future, one which they can barely hope to control.

Acknowledgements

The research was undertaken as an input to the design of a programme of support to the National Enterprise Restructuring Committee (NERC) in implementing its SOE reform strategy 2000–5, to be funded by the UK Department for International Development (DfID) and the World Bank. The programme design work was led by the international management consultancy firm KPMG, and I am grateful to my KPMG colleagues during the research, Razab Chowdhury and Mark Bennett, for their help and advice. I am also grateful to Peter Balacs and Lindy Cameron of DfID for permission to draw on material from the research for this chapter. Neither DfID nor KPMG bear any responsibility for errors of interpretation or fact in this chapter. I am also grateful to Daniel Musson of the World Bank office in Hanoi and Jane Rintoul of DfID Hanoi for further help and advice.

Notes

1 The preceding paragraphs are based on interviews with Natexco workers and managers, 25 April 2000, and on the company's marketing brochure.
2 In 1989, locally-run enterprises outnumbered those run by central ministries by six to one (Probert and Young 1995: 501).
3 Of 2,268 SOEs surveyed by the General Statistical Office in 1992, 88 per cent employed fewer than 500 workers while only 22 employed more than 3,000 (Probert and Young 1995: 501).
4 See Painter (2003) for a discussion of the politics of SOE restructuring in Vietnam that is similarly sympathetic to the case for reform.
5 Kolko (1997: 61) alludes very briefly to the 'high social costs' of the SOE reform process, the World Bank (1999b: 41; 2000: 35) makes proposals for social safety nets for retrenched SOE workers, and Van Anh and Hung (1997: 104–6) discuss the impact of SOE reform on women, but otherwise the literature is bare.
6 The chapter draws on interviews with officials of the former National Enterprise Restructuring Committee, the Ministry of Labour, Invalids and Social Affairs (MoLISA) and of the two General Corporations that oversee two key sectors: Vinatex and Vinacafé. It also draws on interviews with managers, union officials and groups of workers in 11 SOEs allied to three General Corporations. Research also conducted on the marine product sector is not discussed in detail in this chapter, for reasons of space.
7 These measures were implemented in Decree No. 25-CP of 1988, which established the system known as 'three plans' (Probert and Young 1995: 507).
8 Decision of the Prime Minister No. 22-CT, dated 8 June 1992. This followed the launch of an SOE equitisation pilot project in 1990 (Decision No. 143-HDBT, dated 10 May 1990) (World Bank 1999b: 36).

9 Decisions 90 and 91 of the Prime Minister, dated 7 March 1994. Corporations created under Decision 90 required capital of at least VND 500 billion (except for special cases which required VND 100 billion) and are governed by line ministries or People's Committees (city or provincial). Decision 91 corporations are bigger, with capital of at least VND 1,000 billion, have responsibility for more strategic industries in which the state is involved, and are administered by the Prime Minister's Office.

10 Decree No. 44/1998/ND-CP, 'On the Transformation of State-Owned Enterprises into Joint Stock Enterprises'. Other policy commitments included Directive No. 20/1998/CT-TTg, which prescribed a method for equistising SOEs, and Decree No. 103/1999/ND-CP, which amplified on the framework for equitisation.

11 Decision of the Prime Minister No. 111-1998-QD-TTg, dated 29 June 1998.

12 The 224 successful transactions included 146 privatisations (that is, more than 65 per cent of the share capital was divested by the state), 37 equitisations (that is, 51–65 per cent of share capital was sold off) and 41 minority sales (that is, less than 51 per cent of the capital divested by the state) (World Bank 1999b: 37).

13 In addition, the World Bank notes 'the legal framework and procedures for liquidation remain cumbersome, making it difficult to enforce creditor rights and for the authorities to declare bankruptcies (World Bank *et al.* 2000a: 33).

14 Interviews with NERC officials.

15 This was in addition to a pilot programme to divest and equitise SOEs in Haiphong under the authority of the Haiphong People's Committee, which was underway by 2000, and a programme of SOE reform in Ho Chi Minh City still awaiting approval in late 2000. See World Bank *et al.* (2000b: 40) for details of these and other SOE reform projects supported by multilateral and bilateral donors. Most of the other projects are studies or capacity-building initiatives.

16 Oil and gas, electricity generation, metallurgy, mechanical engineering, cement, telecommunications, aviation, maritime transport, railways, chemicals, food, insurance and banking (Government of Vietnam 2001).

17 From an estimated VND 80,000 billion (US $5.7 billion) at present to VND 170,000 billion (US $12.1 billion) in five years' time.

18 *Vietnam News*, 13 August 2001.

19 *Vietnam News*, 14 August 2001.

20 Including Decree 64/2002/ND-CP (19 June) dealing with the transformation of SOEs into joint stock companies (replacing Decree 44/1998) and Decree 69/2002/ND-CP (12 July), which requires SOEs to settle their outstanding debts.

21 Set out in Decision of the Prime Minister No. 183/QD-TTg, dated 20 November 2001.

22 According to Painter (2003), the NSCERD itself contributed to the delays. '[I]n a highly complex and conflict-ridden field of policy', he writes, 'the [NSCERD] is generally viewed as a force for prevarication as much as an engine of reform' (Painter 2003: 38).

23 Interviews with MoLISA officials, April 2000.

24 Decree No. 12-CP, dated 26 January 1995.

25 Interviews with the Personnel Directors of General Corporations and Enterprises.

26 Some provisions have been superseded by subsequent decrees, notably Decree 93/1998/ND-CP, dated 12 November, covering social security regulations, and Decree 44/1998/ND-CP and its replacement, Decree 64/2002/ND-CP, covering the conversion of SOEs into joint stock enterprises.

27 Interviews with employees in SOEs, April–May 2000.

28 Interviews with MoLISA officials and with donor representatives.

29 Decision of the Prime Minister 177/1999/QD-TTg. ERF is an abbreviated version of the full title, the SOE Equitisation and Restructuring Support Fund.

30 Decree 41/2002/ND-CP, dated 11 April, Art. 3 Sec, 3b. The full title of the Fund for Redundant Workers is the 'Fund for Redundant Workers caused by SOE Restructuring'.

31   According to the World Bank (2000: 38), international donors are willing to meet the full $500m cost of reducing the SOE labour force.

32   Decree No. 07/1999/ND-CP, dated 13 February (on the exercise of democracy in state enterprises), Article 8, Section 7.

33   Decision 58/2002/QD-TTG dated 26 April, for instance, identifies a number of strategic areas or sectors where SOEs will remain state-dominated, including those concerned with the enhancement of living conditions in rural mountainous and remote areas.

34   For instance, Article 5 of the 1995 Law on State Enterprises.

35   All shares in equitised companies have a nominal value of VND 100,000: employees may buy up to 10 shares for every year of employment in the enterprise at a discount of 30 per cent. Decree No. 64/2002/ND-CP, Article 27, Section 1. A similar provision was made in Decree No. 44/1998/ND-CP, Article 14, Section 1.

36   Decree 64/2002, Article 27, Section 2.

37   Circular No. 03/1999/TT-LDTBXH.

38   Decree 64/2002/ND-CP, Article 14.

39   Decree 44/1998, Article 1, Section 1, Decree 64/2002 Article 27 Section 1, however, states that preferred stocks (that is, stocks acquired by employees at a discount) cannot be transferred within the first three years of purchase.

40   A stock exchange was opened in Ho Chi Minh City in 2000, but trading was limited to the shares in fewer than 10 equitised companies.

41   Interviews with SOE union officials and workers, April–May 2000.

42   Vinatex documents.

43   Interviews with Vinatex officials and Vinatex documents.

44   For workers who take voluntary redundancy, Vinatex in 2000 paid one month's salary for every year worked, plus 500,000 VND.

45   In 1960, women accounted for 15 per cent of employees in the state sector but by 1975 the figure had increased to 42 per cent (Van Anh and Hung 1997: 103).

46   Interviews with the Personnel Directors of General Corporations and of member SOEs, April–May 2000.

47   *Vietnam News*, 14 August 2001.

48   Vinacafé documents.

49   Based on interviews with managers, farmers and employees in three coffee companies as well as interviews with Vinacafé officials in Dak Lak, May 2000.

50   In the case of one site visited, for instance, Ea Tul district in Dak Lak, a hectare of land planted with mature coffee trees sells for VND 120–30m (US $8,000–8,600). Farmers with land belonging to the Ea Tul Coffee Company pay a production quota of 1.7 tonnes per hectare (worth roughly 34m VND [US $2,260] before the 1999–2000 global price collapse, 17m VND [US $1,130] after). In return they receive a salary of 400,000 VND (US $27) per month (4.8m VND or US $320 per annum) along with standard social security entitlements (mainly the right to a pension). Nevertheless, the effective rate of taxation, relative to both the value of the land and the entitlements received, is punitive.

51   For instance, if farmers fail to meet a production quota in a particular year, they become indebted to the company. The debts are marked up at prevailing market rates and carried over to the following year when the farmer must produce coffee of the same value at that year's prices.

52   Interviews with Vinacafé officials in Hanoi and Dak Lak, April and May 2000.

53   *Vietnam News*, 14 August 2001. The article mentioned VCCA plans to cut coffee production on 420,000 to 462,000 hectares of land, although the total land area devoted to coffee production in Vietnam is roughly 500,000 hectares.

54   This is in addition to separate SOE reform programmes in Hai Phong and Ho Chi Minh City under the administration of the respective People's Committees.

55 Vietnam's human development index (HDI) of 0.671 in 2000 placed it 108 out of 174 countries (UNDP 2000), considerably higher than its position in tables based on per capita gross national or domestic product.
56 Vietnam's Gini Co-efficient increased modestly between 1993 and 1998, from 0.33 to 0.35 (World Bank 1999a: ix).

8 Vietnam's rural transformation

Information, knowledge and diversification

Tran Thi Thu Trang

Since the mid-1980s, Vietnam has undergone a structural reform process based on *doi moi* (renovation) policies, transforming a socialist and rather egalitarian system into a more liberal market economy. One issue to which the Vietnamese government has paid particular attention is rural development, notably by promoting diversification of the agricultural sector. The government considers diversification as the principal means of promoting production growth, and even as a panacea for rural poverty. However, while public policy measures have certainly accelerated the diversification process, not all peasants have been able to diversify successfully.

This chapter analyses the processes by which some households have taken advantage of new opportunities, while others are lagging behind. It discusses decision-making by peasants based on their access to information and knowledge, means of communication and capacity to translate these resources into economic benefits. The chapter finds that while production assets were collectivised during the co-operative period and then distributed rather equally in the early 1980s, peasant groups have differentiated access to information and knowledge. This then has significant implications on their economic diversification strategies under various political and economic contexts.

The analysis is based on findings from field research conducted between March and December 2001 in a village[1] of Hoa Binh province. The fieldwork included extensive interviews with 25 households, about one-fourth of all families in the village. The selection of these households was done randomly across five income groups.[2] The research also includes interviews with district, commune and village authorities, as well as key informants. The chapter first discusses the co-operative period and the origin and nature of *doi moi*. It then briefly presents the settings and the specific aspects of collectivisation in the studied village, before proceeding to analyse the diversification process centred on sugar cane, which characterised the early transitional period. The chapter then examines the current context of market fluctuations, and the problems of diversification towards longan and lychee production, that result from a lack of access to relevant information. Finally, the conclusion underlines the various implications that information and knowledge have on peasant diversification strategies in given political and economic contexts.

Agricultural transformation: the co-operative period

Rural development in northern Vietnam has undergone dramatic changes since the 1954 land reforms. This was an important political move aimed at radically transforming the socio-economic structure of the Vietnamese countryside. Under the slogan of 'land to the tillers', the government confiscated land from landlords and rich peasants and redistributed it to the smallholders and landless workers. Through the mechanism of land reform, the government sought to reward poor rural people for their support for the armed struggle against the French, reinforce class alliances and gain legitimacy. Land reform also entailed a firm commitment from the government to implement socialism by dismantling exploitative class structures, and siding with poor peasants and workers (Bhaduri 1982: 34; Kleinen 1999b: 95–6).

However, peasant households were allowed to manage their agricultural production for only a few years. At the end of the 1950s, the government started collectivising land and other productive resources to establish co-operatives. Collectivisation was supposed to be a response to the concentration of land ownership that re-emerged soon after land reform (Bhaduri 1982: 34). It also aimed to expand the scale of production, since small landholding was seen as an obstacle to the application of new technologies, so limiting production. The collectivisation of the means of production and formation of co-operatives in rural Vietnam at that time therefore had both political and technical implications (Bhaduri 1982: 35–8). During the early stage of collectivisation and in the context of limited resources for agricultural mechanisation, co-operatives considered investment in irrigation infrastructures to be most appropriate for increasing land productivity. 'Irrigated area under annual crops made up 63.7 per cent of the cultivated land in 1960 against 53 per cent in 1957 and 42 per cent in 1955' (Bhaduri 1982: 42).

Peasants were grouped into production brigades and performed different agricultural tasks. They received points for each working day (known as workday contracts, or *khoan cong*); after the harvest, these points were converted into paddy. The amount of paddy per point varied according to the production output that each co-operative could obtain each season, minus taxes, inputs and services. Co-operative members then received their shares based on the total points that they accumulated throughout the season (Kerkvliet 1993: 5–6; Ngo Vinh Long 1993: 166). The improvement in water management as well as early peasant enthusiasm towards the new regime indeed contributed to increased grain production. During the first five years of the co-operative period, the productivity of land and workers almost doubled. 'Availability of rice in the North reached fifteen kilograms per person per month, the highest level in thirty years' (Ngo Vinh Long 1993: 166).

In the mid-1960s, the American War expanded both in scope and intensity. The northern Vietnamese government felt the need to consolidate co-operatives into high-level institutions that allowed large-scale specialised production and use of modern technologies. In addition, this model was seen 'as an essential means for mobilizing personnel, food, and other resources for the country's war against the United States and the Republic of Vietnam' (Kerkvliet 1993: 5). As a result, small co-operatives comprising single villages of a dozen families were grouped to form larger co-operatives, that could often include an entire commune of several hundred households. Given their larger size, co-operatives could then encompass several special brigades each focussing, for instance, on specific tasks such as irrigation, crop protection or seed preparation. The new co-operatives also had normal brigades performing basic production tasks such as planting, weeding, harvesting and other routine responsibilities (Ngo Vinh Long 1993: 167; Kerkvliet 1993: 5; Kleinen 1999b: 110). However, soon after the war, this model showed severe problems, reflected in a steady decline in agricultural outputs. 'For the entire northern half of the country per capita availability of paddy rice decreased precipitously in the late 1970s: 15.4, 12.0, 11.6, 11.9, and 10.4 kilograms a month in 1976, 1977, 1978, 1979, and 1980 respectively' (Ngo Vinh Long 1993: 173; see also Kerkvliet 1993: 7).

The co-operative system had become plagued with a number of problems. It had eliminated the traditional peasant economy by transforming peasants into rural labourers, with little control over the production process. In addition, it undermined social networks such as kinship, which were crucial in traditional agricultural work, by grouping peasants into different production brigades regardless of their family affiliations. This often degenerated into intra-brigade tension. Most importantly, the co-operative system could not apply an appropriate point system for different qualities, quantities and types of work, leading to production disincentive and negligence towards collective assets (Kerkvliet 1993: 7–10; Ngo Vinh Long 1993: 172).

The context of *doi moi*: implications for agricultural production

The above problems generated strong opposition and resistance from peasants. Many devoted considerable efforts to privately allocated household plots, which represented only five per cent of the total agricultural land, but from which peasants were allowed to keep all their outputs. While a significant proportion of co-operative lands were left fallow, private plots were used intensively, and provided productivity twice as high as that from collective land. Resistance was also found in various forms of foot-dragging and tricks to avoid tedious tasks and accumulate points more quickly (Kerkvliet 1993: 11).

Facing peasant resistance, 'co-operative leaders had to modify what central directives stipulated in order to meet some of villagers' needs and demands. Compromises were made especially at the brigade and sub-brigade level, where cadres had to interact daily with peasants' (Kerkvliet 1993: 17; see also Turley 1993a: 7). One of such types of arrangements was *khoan chui*, in which co-operatives unofficially contracted households for several economic activities that were in principle to be done collectively. Households had to return a fixed amount of output to the co-operatives but were allowed to keep all the remainder for their own use. This arrangement was beneficial to both parties, as it allowed co-operatives fulfilling production quota determined by higher authorities, while freeing them from management tasks. On the other hand, households could benefit from better earnings due to their higher productivity (Kerkvliet 1993: 13). *Khoan chui* was quite extensive in many localities, sowing the seeds for changes in agricultural policies in the 1980s.

The Sixth Plenum of the Central Committee in September 1979 recognised the importance of households' participation in the production process, and the need for material incentives for them to increase outputs. In January 1981 the Central Committee issued Decree 100/CT/TW, allowing co-operatives to assign paddy fields and unused land to individual households through production contracts (*khoan san pham*).[3] According to those contracts, co-operative brigades performed special tasks such as ploughing, water control, fertiliser and insecticide spraying. Contractors were responsible for basic production tasks such as transplanting and harvesting. Peasant households were allowed to keep their outputs beyond payment to the co-operatives of amounts contractually fixed, but were also held liable to pay in full when production was lower than the required repayment (Ngo Vinh Long 1993: 175; Kleinen 1999b: 138). However, administration and co-ordination problems persisted: peasant households were still dependent on co-operatives for part of their production tasks and the purchase of agricultural inputs. Moreover, land was not allocated for a long period, creating an unstable investment environment for peasants (Kerkvliet 1993: 19–20; Dao The Tuan 1995: 139; Jamal and Jansen 1998). After a peak in 1981–2, both cultivation areas and productivity of food crops decreased steadily (Fforde and de Vylder 1996: 180–1).

Although Decree 100 did not efficiently address problems in the agricultural sector, and merely legalised practices that were already common in many areas, it marked a significant step by the Party and government towards the 1986 economic reforms. This led some researchers to assert that reform policies were actually reactive rather than proactive, and changes in agricultural organisation, for instance, reflected the government's weakness in dealing with internal political threats from peasants (Fforde and de Vylder 1996: 1–5).

While the reform policies were clearly a response to crisis and to peasant resistance, this does not necessarily indicate the weakness of the Vietnamese state. In fact, the government might have been inefficient in formulating an adequate development strategy, but certainly had the ideological, political and repressive means of controlling opposition if and when needed. This ability was demonstrated by the elimination of the landlord class during the implementation of land reform, and the subsequent introduction and upholding of the co-operative system. The reluctance of the state to impose strict controls on production over peasant households during the co-operative period may therefore have resulted not so much from its weakness but mostly from a close relationship between the state and the peasantry. The revolutionary state came to power with much support from peasants, and continued needing that support to mobilise human and material resources necessary to fight the American War. On the other hand, the government also enjoyed legitimacy among a large sector of the peasantry thanks to the redistributive land reform.

Moreover, the government and peasantry can hardly be described in sharp opposition to one another. Without debating here the nature or scope of democratic representation in Vietnam, it can at least be argued that the politically empowered section of the peasant class has participated effectively in national governance, albeit not always for the benefit of the whole community. The government has not been a remote and abstract force, but materialised through cadres at the local level, themselves peasants affected by and influencing central policies. This explains how policy-making has often responded to specific local conditions in an interactive process, and not only in reaction to resistance or loss of legitimacy.

Launched at the Sixth National Congress in December 1986, *doi moi* marked the transition of Vietnam from a socialist and rather egalitarian system into a more liberal market economy, emphasising market demands as signals and incentives for economic production and allocation of resources, in which 'private entrepreneurship is encouraged and private ownership of means of production is accepted' (Ministry of Forestry 1991: 2). For agriculture, *doi moi* introduced various institutional changes regarding the ownership and management of resources. It stressed the important role of non-state sectors in economic development, sectors that had been neglected during the collectivisation period (Turley 1993a: 1–2; Kerkvliet 1993: 20; McNicoll and Durst 1995: 107). In 1988, the government implemented Resolution 10, which introduced household contracts (*khoan ho*, also called *khoan gon* or *khoan 10*), allowing co-operatives to distribute land to households, while retaining the right to adjust landholdings according to demographic changes. Agricultural land and other means of production were distributed equally to all peasants, based on the number of household members, with some variations in implementation between localities. Households were free to decide on the organisation and marketing of their agricultural production, while co-operatives simply played a supporting role and collected taxes (Kleinen 1999b: 110). This contract system marked the completion of decollectivisation in rural Vietnam, and resulted in a remarkable growth of production. Vietnam moved from 'importing about half a million tons of food annually in 1986–8, [to becoming] the third-largest exporter of rice by 1989' (Dodsworth *et al.* 1996: 4), and more recently the second-largest exporter (Glewwe *et al.* 2000: 1).

A Land Law was adopted in 1993, which could be interpreted simply as the continuation of Decree 100 and Resolution 10. Yet the new law qualitatively marked an important shift towards a reformed property rights system. Although all land remained under state ownership, households and individuals were henceforth allowed to exchange, transfer, lease, inherit and mortgage their land use rights (National Assembly 1993). The new Land Law facilitates a new land market and could have reduced the equal distribution of land that was until then the basis for political and economic structures in rural areas. However, a decade after the adoption of the new law, landholding in the northern part of Vietnam remained rather equal for a number of reasons, including limited alternatives in the non-agricultural sector, and the fact that current landholdings were barely larger than subsistence requirements. In this context, as we will see in the following sections, access to relevant information and knowledge through privileged networks of peers and resources has become a key factor in the success or failure of diversification in rural Vietnam. The relevance of such information has also varied over time as a result of changes in political and economic conditions.

The setting of the case study village

The studied village is classified as mountainous, but is in fact located in a relatively flat area. The village covers a total of 263 hectares of which paddy fields represent 10 per cent, other agricultural land accounts for 2 per cent, forest land 58 per cent, and garden land (including houses) 24 per cent. The rest of the area comprises roads, rivers and rocky mountains. The relative paucity of rice fields reflects the fact that most of the land is unsuitable for paddy, which has a significant impact on the nature of activities undertaken by peasants, and on their diversification strategies. Rice is indeed not the main source of income for villagers, while the most profitable activities take place in gardens and on other kinds of land.

The village is located one kilometre from road 12A that links it with other districts of Hoa Binh and the province of Ninh Binh. It is close to important political, administrative and economic centres, which facilitates transport, communication and trading. The village is divided into two hamlets, numbered 1 and 2, each with its own administrative officers. The village has a total of 105 households, mostly of Muong ethnicity, with the exception of one family of Chinese origin and three mixed couples comprising Muong and Kinh spouses.[4] Unlike other ethnic groups, the Muong are culturally and geographically similar to the Kinh, and probably share the same historical roots (Tran Tu 1996; Bui Tuyet Mai 1999). In 1961, due to a government policy of immigration and resettlement of the Kinh in mountainous areas, the commune established a new village of immigrants from Ha Nam Ninh province, and two villages of returnees from Thailand, within a total of 10 villages. Although this has not resulted in cultural integration, the presence of Kinh households has facilitated the development of commercial activities, since those families have been much more involved in trading activities than the Muong.

Village agriculture during the co-operative period

During the co-operative period, household economic activities were discouraged to the extent that a family could not be counted as a unit of production. The co-operative prohibited households from cultivating staple food crops in garden land, for fear peasants would concentrate their resources and labour on private instead of collective plots. In addition, peasant families had to pay duties to the government by selling a predetermined number of pigs and chickens each year at fixed prices, generally below market rates. Peasants could also raise their own buffaloes, but had to pay the co-operative for their grass.

Lack of incentives and other shortcomings of the co-operative system led to production deficits; peasants therefore had to search for alternatives to meet their food requirements and generate additional income. By the late 1970s, the two most important alternatives were rice cultivation in squatted forest land, and diversification of non-staple food crops in garden land. Such initiatives were tolerated by local authorities, at a time when the principle of co-operatives was coming under criticism.

Early diversification: the emergence and cultivation of sugar cane

Decree 100 of 1981 distributed agricultural land to individual households and allowed the latter more freedom in the organisation of production. It also recognised the importance of the family as a production unit. At that time, rice production had long been intensively supported by the government. Yet rice crops generated little return on investment from the standpoint of this new household economy. This was compounded by the impossibility of extensive cultivation due to the limited amount of suitable paddy land, roughly 10 per cent of the total area. In this context, rice was a food security crop for most households in the village, with just enough production for their own needs. It was however rarely a commodity, except for very poor or very rich households. Poor households often traded rice in case of contingency, while the rich speculated on seasonal price differentials. Thus, despite the predominance of rice in the rural economy, it could not generate significant income and resolve the scarcity of cash, already common in the village during the co-operative period.

Yet liquidity had long been needed to address contingencies, and became increasingly sought since the early 1980s due to the progressive integration of the village into the commodity economy. This was further accentuated in the early 1990s with the government enforcement of cash tax collection. Although in principle the tax was adjusted according to the price of paddy every season, the actual amount collected was often higher than the market paddy price. Moreover, the Muong used to live in wooden pillar houses built with logs gathered from communal forest land. Since the 1970s however, forest trees had become scarce and the commune exerted strict controls over the exploitation of that resource. These regulations meant that building houses henceforth required cash for the purchase of wood, cement, bricks or other materials.

With such a change in material needs, generating cash income became critical. Peasants also recognised that diversification would make them less dependent on a single source of income, and more resilient to contingencies. For most households in the village, however, diversifying towards non-farm economic activities that allow high profits was not feasible for lack of investment capital and skills. In turn, non-farm economic activities with low returns and of a temporary, precarious and exhausting nature (such as the quarrying of stone for construction) were undertaken, but only by poor households and as a survival strategy. Almost all village households therefore chose to concentrate their resources and labour in diversified agricultural production for which they could more easily secure inputs and acquire knowledge and skills.

In fact, the development of the village economy was associated with the introduction of violet sugar cane back in the early 1970s. Compared to other crops, including rice, violet sugar cane has the advantage of providing higher rates of return on investment and having little price elasticity, therefore maintaining its market value despite increasing production. For most village households, sugar cane has been the single most important source of cash, eventually accounting for 50 to 70 per cent of their total income, especially in the 1980s and early 1990s. When interviewed, villagers explained that all brick houses, motorbikes, televisions and other consumer goods were purchased from sugar cane profits. With the exception of the Chinese family, who produced agricultural tools, all households in the village continue growing sugar cane on a regular basis.

However, the research finds that the different times at which households started producing sugar cane and the scale of their production are the key factors in securing high levels of profit. Sugar cane was first introduced in the village in 1972, and planted on garden land. Households could not grow this crop elsewhere as the only other suitable area (*dat bai* or flat land) was under co-operative control. The *dat bai* used to be a housing area until 1972. Village houses were then moved to hillsides well away from the 12A road, to recover the space for rice growing and to escape the intensive American bombing of the road. The co-operative used tractors to level the land and make it suitable for rice. However, it was found that the water supply was insufficient for rice cultivation, and the land was planted with other cereals under co-operative control.

In 1990, the co-operative decided to rent that land to any households interested in growing sugar cane for a period of five years. At that time, sugar cane had been cultivated on garden land for more than a decade, and its economic benefits had become obvious to all. However, peasants' response to this opportunity varied between households, and between the two hamlets of the village. In Hamlet 1, only six households rented all the available land. In Hamlet 2, while all households rented equal shares of best quality land, only nine invested in less fertile but more extensive plots which were open to renting on demand.[5]

At that time, the investment for sugar cane in *dat bai* turned out to be very small, at approximately 15 per cent of the return. This was much lower than that in garden land since the *dat bai* soil was very productive, and for the first three years, households could use the same stems and needed no fertilisers to reach high yields. Households that secured larger areas of *dat bai* in addition to their garden land made significant profits, and are now all among the first two richest groups of the village. Other households expressed deep regrets at not perceiving and seizing the opportunity at the outset, and therefore having to wait five years for the next renting cycle before being able to use the *dat bai*. However, as everyone wanted to rent *dat bai* plots for the second cycle, the share available for each household was reduced significantly, from approximately 2,000 m^2 in 1990 to 600 m^2 in 1995. Thus, in the case of sugar cane diversification, early adoption was the key to securing high profitability, facilitated by the combined circumstances of low investment costs, and the relatively large amount of land available to individual households.

Information and sugar cane diversification

The research found that most households that rented extensive land in either hamlet were familiar with sugar cane, having previously grown it in their gardens in the 1970s and 1980s. Such households often had a member, usually a man, who had worked outside the village, or had joined the army during wars against the Americans, Chinese or Khmer Rouge. Soldiers who fought during these wars had travelled extensively, and were taught to remain autonomous from vulnerable military supplies. They were expected to grow their own food, raise animals and identify edible wild plants. While remaining mobile, solders needed also to integrate into local communities in order to receive material support and protection. Having served as a soldier therefore implied greater exposure to knowledge and experience of different agricultural production techniques and practices from various localities. Even a decade after the wars, Vietnam still 'had one of the largest armies in Asia, with an active force strength estimated at 1.26 million (… which) developed substantial production installations of its own, and grew a significant proportion of its own food' (Fforde and de Vylder 1996: 83).

Upon their return, these veterans and migrant workers significantly influenced the household decision-making process. They were often the first to introduce agricultural techniques new to the village, were more willing to experiment, and went as far as challenging traditional cultural rules and dominant discourses. For instance, the current chief of the commune, one of the richest men in the village, was the first to adopt Kinh pig-raising techniques in the early 1970s, which he learned while working in a state forest farm. These involved cloistering the animals into stables, as opposed to letting them stroll the gardens, allowing lower caloric losses and making them grow much quicker. Being exposed to other cultures also led him to abandon the traditional Muong wooden house, requiring regular maintenance, in favour of a brick structure. His initiatives, although meeting initial opposition both from his family and from the wider community, were quickly followed by others, mostly veterans and migrant workers themselves.

In addition, veterans often maintain informal ties with peers beyond district and even provincial boundaries, allowing frequent travelling and horizontal information flows. They also have an extended network institutionally supported by the state through the Association of Veterans. The association often organises meetings and training sessions on new agricultural techniques for members at different locations. The village chapter of the association receives monthly newsletters that provide information on the national political and economic situation, as well as on science and agricultural techniques. The association is also the most active organisation in the village with its own budget and credit programme. It also benefits from communal and district support for several economic activities. In fact, it was a veteran who had first introduced sugar cane in the village in 1972 after travelling to neighbouring Lac Son district. He planted the stems in his garden and subsequently sold new stems to other households in the village and elsewhere. Since sugar cane was not a traditional crop in the village, veterans benefited from their network to acquire information on cultivation techniques and marketing potential. In 1990, this enabled them quickly to seize the opportunity of investing in extensive sugar cane growing as soon as it was made possible.

The example above shows that with respect to diversification towards sugar cane, access to land in the context of an egalitarian society as well as investment capital were not the primary factors determining household production strategies. By contrast, information concerning relevant agricultural techniques and market opportunities was crucial to enable diversification. Yet the information needed to make the production of sugar cane profitable was relatively simple and remained valid over time, in both technical and marketing terms. The network of veterans was therefore sufficient to effectively facilitate formal or casual circulation of such information among members.

The shift to longan and lychee trees

As discussed above, the *dat bai* had been distributed equally to all households after 1995, making the share of each family much smaller. Households that first rented extensive sugar cane land in 1990 expressed their disappointment regarding the 1995 reallocation, which resulted in a significant loss of income. For several of those households, smaller lots were simply not worth the investment, and some neighbours negotiated to pool plots together and work them in turns. Furthermore, latecomers found their small areas less attractive: the land had become less productive after five years of intensive sugar cane growing, and the investment necessary to grow sugar cane had increased significantly since 1995. Households had to buy new stems every year and use much more fertiliser. Inputs now represented approximately 30 per cent of the returns, twice as much as a decade before. Despite a stable market, sugar cane had therefore become decreasingly profitable. Since the crop used to be the most important source of cash income, the loss in profit and opportunity threatened the overall household economic situation and compelled peasants to seek alternatives.

Since the mid-1990s, several families in the village have experimented with the large-scale planting of perennial trees such as longan and lychee, which offered higher profits than sugar cane according to the cost–benefit calculations at that time. With a plot of about 3,000 m^2 of garden land, for instance, a family growing sugar cane could make an annual net profit of approximately three million dong. Mature longan and lychee trees could generate as much as 30 per cent more profit, with capital investment necessary only in the first year, and little input or labour needed thereafter.

However, despite the economic potential of these crops, not all households could afford forgoing the income of sugar cane for a period of at least three years before the new trees could start bearing fruit. Since the villagers' cash incomes were already differentiated as a result of sugar cane diversification, only five well-off households have been able to substitute all sugar cane in their garden and undertake large-scale production of fruit trees.

Moreover, and most importantly, the heads of three of those five households are local cadres, although cadres represent less than 10 per cent of all village households. Holding official positions provides them better access to public media and political networks, thus granting privileged information on new crops and related government incentives. For instance, commune cadres often receive books on technical issues or advice from district extension services during official meetings. The commune also subscribes to newspapers, only circulated among the cadres. In addition, officials also have easier access to television sets, as a result of a post-1995 government programme aiming to facilitate information broadcasting to remote communities. Until the time of writing, the commune had received 12 colour televisions: one was kept at the office of the Peoples' Committee, while the rest were appropriated by cadres for private use. This privileged access to information had actually permitted the cadres, back in the mid-1990s, to learn about the government's intention to increase the area of fruit tree plantations by up to one million hectares over the period of 2000–10 (Philippe Cao Van *et al.* 1997: 120). The five households that decided to plant fruit trees on a large scale eventually benefited from related government incentives. In 1999, they each received 40 plants of young Huong Chi longan and a quantity of fertiliser as an incentive to diversification.

Besides these five initiators, other households had insufficient information to make a decision on large-scale plantations of longan and lychee trees in the mid-1990s. Most peasants did not have access to newspapers, due to relatively expensive subscription fees on the one hand, and to the fact that copies sent to the commune did not circulate beyond officials on the other (see also Bui Dinh Khoi 2000: 20). Radio does not seem to have become a significant source of agricultural information for reasons that still need to be clarified. Television has therefore become the main medium, yet 38 per cent of village households still did not have access to television at the time of fieldwork in 2001. This lack of access to public media prevented villagers obtaining up-to-date information on government policies and programmes, and long-term prospective analysis. Lack of information generated uncertainty about longan and lychee diversification, and encouraged households to inter-crop trees with sugar cane instead of devoting all their resources to the new crops.

This unequal access to information also influenced the selection of cultivation techniques. Households that were involved in large-scale fruit production bought young layered trees from recognised nurseries. The layering technique transfers all genetic characteristics of the parent tree to the plantlets, thus preserving the same quality over several generations. This also allows trees to bear fruit as soon as three years after planting – one-third of the time needed for seeded trees. On the other hand, those households that inter-cropped fruit trees with sugar cane tended to use seeds, or purchase cheap plantlets from uncertified itinerant merchants. Trees that grow from seeds often deteriorate quickly due to cross-fertilisation with crops of poor quality and take longer to bear fruit. Moreover, lack of information and knowledge about cultivation techniques made these households vulnerable to cheating by unscrupulous traders. As a result, their trees often developed poorly, forcing many of them to destroy part or all of the crops and to recover the space for sugar cane. Several households have had to abandon cultivation only two or three years after planting, without even waiting for the trees to bear fruit.

Thus, technical information was crucial to the successful undertaking of longan and lychee production, as shown by the five households that planted such trees on a large scale and which were more successful than others in obtaining a better quality and quantity of fruits, and significant profits for several years. Yet technical information alone was to prove insufficient to guarantee profitability. Successful growers have also encountered difficulties with the marketing of fruits. Villagers often commercialised longan and lychee for the purpose of both fresh and dry consumption. In 1996–7, the market for dry longan was very profitable due to substantial exports by informal merchants to China. In addition, in the same year Vietnam achieved its first significant export of fresh lychees to the French market (Tran Le 2000). This led to high demand and prices which benefited longan and lychee producers.

However, the trade with France ended only after a year of exports; while that with China was significantly reduced, as a result of mediocre quality, failure to meet hygiene requirements, and cheating on the part of informal Vietnamese merchants on the Chinese border. The Chinese market required frequent changes in quality and appearance of dry longan. Due to inadequate channels, such information could not reach Vietnamese producers in time, rendering them uncompetitive in relation to Thai farmers (Thanh Vu 2000). The combined increased production, inelasticity of demand, lack of knowledge and information on international trade, and limited know-how in post-harvesting technologies, led to a low level of exports and depression of prices (Food and Agriculture Organisation 2001). Between 1996 and 2001, the price of dry longan in Vietnam dropped by more than 80 per cent, severely affecting producers of fresh fruit. In the case of lychees, the price also went down despite a bad harvest nationwide in 2001. In the village, the volume of lychees harvested in 2001 amounted to less than 10 per cent of that harvested in 1996. Yet the commodity still sold for less than 60 per cent of its 1996 value. As a result, the five large-scale producing households of the studied village experienced severe marketing difficulties, and one of them destroyed all of its hundred longan and lychee trees and reverted to growing sugar cane. The other four households have so far decided to continue with the crop for one or two years, having learned from their political network that the district plans to build a longan and lychee processing factory in the foreseeable future.

Conclusion

This chapter has shown how information has crucially shaped the development of different agricultural diversification strategies in a Vietnamese village since the early 1970s. However, the impact of information has varied depending on the context. Successful long-term diversification into violet sugar cane, like the failure of longan and lychee after only a few years of cultivation, mostly resulted from the interaction between local information and knowledge networks, and the political and economic context at the national level.

Before the 1954 democratic reforms, the Muong village studied here functioned as a rather independent territory with its own governance and social rules. This system was referred to as *Nha Lang* (Lang family) with a clear division between a ruling family (*Lang Kun*), several administrators (*Au*), and ordinary peasants (*Mol*). This structure was rigidly maintained for generations, receiving little influence from the outside world. Agricultural techniques and practices as well as other social aspects also had little interference from other societies. In the early 1960s, the village was incorporated into the process of collectivisation and creation of production co-operatives. This brought the village closer to other communities, especially to the Kinh majority. The same period saw many villagers mobilised for the American War, fighting in the then southern Republic of Vietnam.

The eventual introduction of violet sugar cane resulted precisely from that opening process of the village, and the acquisition of knowledge and experience by veterans and migrant workers. With very limited access to formal education or media, villagers relied totally on their informal network for information and knowledge. It was the travelling of drafted soldiers and, later, the network of veterans that permitted exposure to and knowledge of sugar cane cultivation. Veterans gradually developed and expanded the crop over a 30-year period, testing cultivation techniques, learning about market conditions and consolidating their trading channels. As sugar cane is consumed domestically and has been in constant demand since the 1970s, its price has remained largely stable and unaffected by changes in international markets. During the transitional period from an egalitarian society to a market economy, opportunities and production assets were rather equally accessible to all. As a result, having privileged access to information and knowledge on agricultural techniques became crucial in influencing the time and scale for the taking of opportunities. This, in turn, was the key to ensuring the success of diversification towards sugar cane.

By contrast, longan and lychee remained in production for no more than five years, despite enormous efforts by the government. These crops were introduced in the village and elsewhere during the mid-1990s, when Vietnam started its integration into regional and global economies. While longan has a limited market, lychee is a crop with fierce competitors in the region and worldwide. Vietnam does not enjoy much comparative advantage in these crops in relation to Thailand, for instance; while exporters still lack experience in international trade and fail to meet strict criteria of hygiene, appearance and standardisation. Most importantly, policy-makers often have little capacity and resources for adequate market analysis and planning, which has led to numerous inaccurate estimates of market trends.

The most important failure of the new agricultural regime has been the incapacity of existing information systems to empower peasants with the necessary means of decision-making. It is true that since 1990, rural infrastructures, telecommunications and media services have greatly improved. Within a decade, two-thirds of the village has gained access to television, and the rest to radio. The government also established a cultural and information centre at the communal post office, which provides telephone and postal services, and especially free access to books and newspapers dealing with topics such as agricultural techniques and rural marketing. Yet these initiatives have largely failed to provide the information most needed by peasants. Television broadcasting is programmed and addressed either at national or provincial audiences, and content is often of little relevance to the specific problems of villagers. Furthermore, local television programming is poorly designed, and broadcasters lack the skills and financial resources to identify and answer peasant needs. On the other hand, the occasional television programmes relevant to economic activities of the village often get little attention, since entertainment shows are preferred by children and young people, at the expense of technical broadcasts. Books and newspapers are in turn not very helpful in providing information and knowledge because of their high costs, inappropriate language, and inadequate selection and content (Bui Dinh Khoi 2000: 20). Finally, the few existing extension services and their publications are largely discredited and of little interest to peasants, even if provided at no cost. These professionals are seen as having little field exposure and remaining unable to provide useful advice. As a result, these media and formal information channels remain underused or used for other purposes than for acquiring agricultural knowledge.

In this context, peasants prefer to rely on their own informal networks for knowledge transfer, even at greater cost and effort to themselves. Yet this organic information system has been hard-pressed to adapt to the stringent requirements of agricultural market globalisation. Diversification towards fruit trees has been a top-down process, with little technical and marketing support, offering no chance for peasants to experiment with the new crops and learn about their market requirements. They have become more dependent on production and trading decisions made by government officials and industrialists, who in turn have proven ineffective at market analysis and advice, let alone policy-driven oversight and leadership.

Moreover, this research has found that most Muong families have no extensive network of kinship or peers beyond their own and neighbouring villages on which to rely for information on new technical and marketing issues.[6] Instead, for example, they often seek practical information on matters such as fertilisers from merchants themselves, apparently failing to recognise their vested interest in maximising sales. Peasant households also typically expect that the information they need will be forthcoming from various local authorities. This is a legacy of the co-operative period, when knowledge and decision-making about production was centralised. On many occasions, local cadres stated that their guidance was essential for peasants to avoid problems, since peasants were perceived as lacking independent thinking. This was used to justify the cadres' privileged and gatekeeper position with respect to information within their jurisdiction, but did little to improve peasants' access to information.

When dealing with new global commodities, the current knowledge system of peasants has therefore proven inefficient in addressing production requirements and market fluctuations, largely beyond the reach of this system. Mere access to technical information, or being first to innovate in the growing of a new crop, was no longer sufficient to guarantee the success of diversification. The nature of information required had shifted towards more complex market prospective analyses, which allowed for planning and adjustment in the production and marketing of perennial crops. In this context, the rational reaction of peasants over the last couple of years has therefore been to retreat onto better-known terrain, reverting to crops they already understand and which present fewer risks, such as the violet sugar cane, for which their existing information system is appropriate.

The above suggests that if the Vietnamese agricultural sector is to integrate into global markets, on its own terms and for the benefit of its producers, a complete rethinking of the new information and knowledge systems required for this process is urgently needed. This will necessarily involve an understanding of the existing knowledge systems of farmers, and their integration with new national and global-level systems in a way that enables farmers to broaden their choices and ability to control the decision-making process of their economic activities.

Notes

1 The name of the village is withheld in order to protect the anonymity and privacy of respondents.

2 During a focus group discussion, about 10 peasants classified themselves and the rest of the villagers into five income groups ranging from number one, the richest, to number five, the poorest. There are 19 agricultural households and one non-farm family (an ethnic Chinese household that manufactures tools) in group number 1; 25 in group number 2; 30 in group 3; 12 in group 4; and 19 in group 5; representing 18 per cent, 24 per cent, 29 per cent, 11 per cent, and 18 per cent respectively. The wealth of a household is estimated from several criteria, defined by the focus group itself. These criteria include the diversity of household income sources, the quality and time of construction of their house, their access to consumer goods such as televisions and motorbikes, and the dynamism of household members in relation to economic opportunities. This classification is not only accurate with respect to the actual income of households but also suggests their future economic potential.

  The income of the richest group ranges from 10 to 20 million dong a year (roughly US $670–1,330, at 15,000 dong per dollar) while the poorest group earns from 1–3 million dong only. This difference is very significant considering the rural Vietnamese context.

3 Also called Decree 100 (*khoan 100*).

4 The Kinh form the largest Vietnamese ethnic group and are mostly lowland-based.

5 This is explained by the fact that most villagers of Hamlet 1 were reluctant to rent plots in the *dat bai* for fear of not being able to protect their crops, their settlement being at a distance. Instead of dividing approximately two hectares among more than 30 households, the land was leased out to six families. In Hamlet 2 however, peasants lived closer to the land and did not see crop protection as a major deterrent. Furthermore, they had been involved in sugar cane cultivation earlier than in Hamlet 1, as they were closer to the road and therefore more accessible to sugar cane wholesale buyers.

6 Due to space constraints, this aspect is discussed in 'Inheritance and marriage in social differentiation of a Muong ethnic community of Vietnam', paper presented at ICAS3, Singapore, September 2003.

Part III
Society

Key social facts about Vietnam

Population:	81,098,416 (July 2002 est.)
Population growth rate:	1.43% (2002 est.)
Urban–rural ratio:	*Urban:* 20.8% *Rural:* 79.2% (1995)
Age structure:	*0–14 years:* 31.6% *15–64 years:* 62.9% *65 years and over:* 5.5% (2002 est.)
Religion:	Buddhist, Hoa Hao, Cao Dai, Christian (predominantly Roman Catholic, some Protestant), indigenous beliefs, Muslim
Ethnic groups:	Vietnamese 85–90%, Chinese 3%, Hmong, Thai, Khmer, Cham, mountain groups
Language:	Vietnamese (official), English (increasingly favoured as a second language), some French, Chinese, and Khmer; mountain area languages (Mon-Khmer and Malayo-Polynesian)
Life expectancy at birth:	*Total population:* 69.86 years *Female:* 72.5 years (2002 est.) *Male:* 67.4 years
Infant mortality rate:	29.34 deaths/1,000 live births (2002 est.)
Literacy (those aged 15 and over who can read and write):	*Total population:* 93.7% *Male:* 96.5% *Female:* 91.2% (1995 est.)

Sources: CIA (2002) *The World Factbook 2002*, Washington, DC: CIA; *Atlapedia Countries*, Latimer Clarke Corporation, available online at http://www.atlapedia.com/online/countries/vietnam.htm; CNN *Vietnam at a Glance* available online at http://www.cnn.com/interactive/specials/0004/vietnam.polimap.

9 Rethinking Vietnam's mass education and health systems[1]

Jonathan London

Since its origins, the Vietnamese Communist Party (VCP) has professed a commitment to providing fair access to education and health services. The VCP has maintained this position even during periods of war and extreme poverty. Since the late 1980s, Vietnam has experienced unprecedented economic growth. Mainstream accounts of Vietnam's development have focused on the undeniable benefits of economic growth, such as improved living standards. However, Vietnam's market transition and its associated reinsertion into the regional and world economies entailed fundamental changes in the developmental and distributive roles of Vietnam's state, from the national level down to the grassroots. An appreciation of these changes, their political and economic antecedents, and their lingering institutionalised effects is essential for understanding the conduct and outcomes of education and health policy in contemporary Vietnam.

This chapter examines changes in the conduct and outcomes of mass education and health policy in post-colonial Vietnam. It explains how quasi-universalist education and health policies developed under the Democratic Republic of Vietnam (DRV) during the 1950s, gradually degenerated during the 1970s and 1980s, and were ultimately replaced by policies that shifted an increasing share of the costs of education and health from the state onto households. It shows that, since the 1950s, the VCP has indeed presided over gradual improvement in overall access to mass education and health services, but that the implementation and outcomes of education and health policies have frequently diverged from and even contradicted the announced goals and policies of both the VCP and the state. It also shows that Vietnamese today have unprecedented access to mass education and health services, but that the delivery of these services is increasingly subject to market principles and market institutions, which creates education and health outcomes increasingly at odds with the rhetoric of Vietnam's avowedly socialist state.

The chapter has two main sections. The first section briefly examines the conduct and outcomes of mass education and health policies between the 1950s and late 1980s, a period defined by national partition and anti-colonial and civil war as well as the development and breakdown of state socialist economic institutions. For reasons of space, the first section's limited aim is to underscore the distinctive principles and institutions governing access to education and health services under VCP rule during this extended period, accepting that such a brief sketch will inevitably simplify. The second section focuses on changes in the conduct and outcomes of mass education and health policy in Vietnam since 1989 when Vietnam's state abandoned core economic institutions of state socialism.

Mass education and health and the development and breakdown of state socialism

Between the early 1950s and the 1980s, patterns of mass education and health provision in Vietnam were powerfully influenced by the VCP's efforts to impose a soviet-inspired brand of state socialism, first in the north of the country – under the DRV – and on a national basis after 1975. A distinctive feature of mass education and health provision during this period lay in the universalist principles underlying the state's formal education and health policies, which promised all citizens fair access to education and health services as rights of citizenship. Between the 1950s and late 1960s the VCP's mass education and health initiatives did indeed dramatically improve overall access to education and health services in a society which, under prior Vietnamese and French administration, had denied broad access. At the same time, the state socialist system in which mass education and health policies were embedded also promoted a highly stratified society; the country's education and health institutions privileged state-affiliated and urban population segments over politically and economically marginal ones, and tended to reinforce this stratification outcome. Thus, mass education and health provision under the state socialist regime, while arguably revolutionary, was not strictly egalitarian. In assessing education and health outcomes during this period one observes four distinguishable phases: rapid expansion from the early 1950s through the mid-1960s, wartime resilience between 1965 and 1975, southward expansion after the war – when the VCP sought to extend state socialist institutions nationwide – and the 1980s, when the economic institutions of state socialism collapsed over the course of a decade.

Mass education and health provision in the DRV

The DRV's first education policies sought to increase literacy and to extend general education by building upon pre-existing village schools and the quite small number of independent and former colonial schools in the cities. By 1957, the number of primary students in the DRV alone was three times that counted in the entire country in 1939. In 1939 only 2 per cent of primary school students advanced to higher levels, whereas by 1957 this figure had risen to 13 per cent (Pham 1999). During the 1950s, Vietnam's health system also underwent a period of rapid expansion. The DRV's first health policies were designed to improve public health through health education and improved sanitation, achieve a network of preventive health services through the establishment of health centres in the communes, and to expand access to hospital care where possible through the development of hospitals at the national, province and district levels. State-led public health campaigns focused on eradicating communicable diseases through vaccinations and hygienic and sanitary measures. Correspondingly, the state's mass health campaigns emphasised behavioural changes among the general population, such as the adoption of simple technologies (such as latrines) for improved sanitation (Ladinsky and Levine 1985).

Arguably, the most important new health policy development at this time was the advent of the commune health centres (CHCs) which were to be responsible for a number of important public health functions, including: the local implementation of national health campaigns and programmes (such as vaccinations against cholera, smallpox, typhoid, tuberculosis, plague, diphtheria and polio); undertaking local measures to lower the incidence of trachoma and malaria; improving public sanitation; administering health education; and providing maternal and child health care.[2] Between 1957 and 1965, the number of CHCs in northern Vietnam rose from just 300 to 5,463,[3] while by the mid-1960s, all lowland villages and 80 per cent of upland villages had a CHC,[4] an expansion that helps to explain dramatic improvements in Vietnam's health status during that period (Merli and London 2002). Between 1965 and 1975, northern Vietnam saw increased (gross) enrollments and increased staffing at all levels of standard education. Between 1965 and 1971, the number of hospitals in northern Vietnam increased from 252 to 431, while the number of medical personnel swelled from 9,568 to 25,488, thanks in large part to the war effort (General Statistics Office [GSO] 1978).

The postwar years represented a third phase of development for the education and health systems under the state socialist regime. The newly constituted government of the Socialist Republic of Vietnam pronounced its commitments to education and health with revolutionary zeal. Postwar increases in quantitative measures of education and health development buttressed state ideological claims that the state was acting in the interests of 'the people': between 1975 and 1980, gross enrollments in primary, lower secondary and upper secondary education increased by 19, 25, and 28 per cent respectively; for the same period, the total number of health facilities (hospitals, outpatient clinics, sanatoriums and CHCs) increased by 28 per cent; and the number of hospital beds increased by 40 per cent (General Statistics Office [GSO] 2002).

An examination of Vietnam's education and health systems under the state socialist regime yields three principal insights. First, alongside its imposition of state socialist economic institutions, Vietnam's state undertook ambitious expansions of its education and health systems and, in the context of poverty and societal unrest, managed to improve the accessibility of education and health services to historically unprecedented levels. Second, these achievements notwithstanding, education and health services were provided at an extremely basic level. In practice, they promoted inequalities of access to education and health services, by reserving the best education and health services for state employees and other political constituencies and urban populations. Finally, and ominously (in the face of poor economic performance), mass education and health provision depended on economic resources generated through the state socialist economy; when these sources of state finance were compromised, so too was the quality of education and health services.

As late as 1979, VCP leaders reaffirmed their commitment eventually to provide universal and free access to basic education and health services as rights of citizenship. However, over the course of the 1980s, Vietnam's mass education and health systems gradually degenerated, as did the state socialist economy on which their financial viability depended. Politically, Vietnam faced exclusion and isolation under a Sino-US embargo. In the economic sphere, Vietnam underwent a transition from state socialism to a market economy, culminating in a fiscal crisis of the state. Appreciating the political and economic antecedents of this crisis is crucial for understanding developments in the country's mass education and health systems both during the 1980s and after. The sources of economic weakness – poor incentives, production bottlenecks, poor integration and a resistant grassroots populace – promoted economic disorder and forms of decentralisation that undermined the political powers of the central state. By 1986, at its Sixth Party Congress, the VCP formally announced its intent to pursue a new policy line of market-oriented reforms, known as *doi moi*, or renewal.

However, it would be misleading to view the demise of Vietnamese state socialism as a top-down government programme announced in 1986. Rather, the economic reforms that the VCP initiated during the 1980s were more frequently in response to – rather than anticipation of – developments at the grassroots. Ultimately, the disintegration of the planned economy weakened the powers of the central state *vis-à-vis* the localities and compromised the national state's fiscal integrity, setting in motion a prolonged fiscal crisis that ultimately led to the total abandonment of core state socialist institutions.

Continual declines in the quality of education and health services and the introduction of fees in 1989 depressed overall utilisation of education and health services. In the education system, the crisis was manifested in dropping enrollments: between 1989 and 1991, enrollment in lower and upper secondary education in Vietnam declined sharply – by over 40 per cent in many places – and would not recover to 1985 levels until the mid-1990s. While by the end of the decade Vietnam had registered a net increase only in its gross enrollment figures, it saw larger gains in the number of school-aged children during the same period. The collapse of the agricultural collectives during the 1980s created special difficulties for the CHCs. In 1980, the central budget assumed 42.6 per cent of the operating costs of CHCs; in 1985 this figure had dipped to 12.8 per cent (Ministry of Health [MoH] 1991). CHCs had become increasingly dependent on local finance precisely as the state's local capabilities began to collapse. While the declining quality of health services in the 1980s (owing chiefly to chronic funding shortages) had already produced declines in inpatient visits, it was 1989 and 1990 that saw the sharpest declines in the rate of outpatient consultations.[5] By the end of the 1980s, Vietnam's mass education and health systems were indeed in a period of crisis, precisely as the economy began to show signs of life.

Developments since 1989

Since the late 1980s, Vietnam has had one of the fastest growing economies in the world. However, the transition from state socialism to a market economy entailed basic changes in the developmental and distributive role of the state, and in the principles and institutions governing the provision of mass education and health services. Economic growth enabled expansions in both state revenues and household earnings, allowing unprecedented increases in total investments in education and health. Politically, the VCP survived the fiscal crisis of the late 1980s and effectively navigated Vietnam's reinsertion into world political and economic institutions. By the end of the 1980s, Vietnam's mass education and health systems combined large state subsidies – which allowed unprecedented access to primary and lower secondary education as well as preventive health services – with a host of 'socialisation' policies that both defrayed the state's education and health costs and impeded the access of relatively poor population segments to higher-level education and health services, such as preschool and upper-secondary education and hospital care.

Politics and markets, continuity and change

Vietnam's transition from state socialism to a market economy strengthened the political and financial powers of its Communist Party. At the same time, the transition required the party to reconstitute the economic and social relations binding state and society. The VCP achieved this outcome through a new developmental model that combined market-based accumulation strategies with authoritarian social regulation. Geopolitical developments in the region after 1989 saw the end of the Cold War for Vietnam. By the time the US lifted its economic embargo of Vietnam in 1994, Vietnam had already begun to attract sizeable foreign direct investment (FDI) from such regional economic powers as Taiwan, Singapore and Japan. By the time the US normalised relations in 1997, Vietnam had already joined the Association of Southeast Asian Nations (ASEAN). Domestically, the economic growth that Vietnam experienced during the 1990s aided the VCP and its state apparatus in political as well as economic terms. Arguably, it was revenues from oil and trade during the early 1990s that rescued the VCP from its fiscal crisis and sustained its continued monopoly on state power. With its abandonment of state socialist institutions, the state devoted its political energies to managing and regulating society in a way compatible with the state's own market-based accumulation strategies.

Mass education and health meet the market: the emergence of a hybrid regime

The distinguishing feature of mass education and health during the market period was the state's withdrawal from its historic commitment to the principles of universalism in its education and health policies, symbolised by the modification of the

1980 constitution in 1989, and the adoption of a new constitution in 1992 in which guarantees for access to education and health were conspicuous by their absence. The mass education and health systems that Vietnam developed during the 1990s combined state subsidies with market principles – given the advent of principles and institutions that have effectively shifted an increasing share of the cost of mass education and health services from the state onto consumers. On the one hand, Vietnam's state now provides a floor of basic education and health services, principally by providing free access to primary education and preventive health services, and by providing varying degrees of subsidies to secondary education and curative health services. On the other hand, accessing education and health services beyond the basic level increasingly depends on individual households earnings, a development clearly at odds with decades of VCP rhetoric. By the end of the 1990s, Vietnamese had unprecedented access to primary and lower secondary education and preventive health services. Yet Vietnamese consumers' 'out-of-pocket' expenditures accounted for perhaps 70 per cent of total (both state and private) mass education expenditure and nearly 80 per cent of total health expenditures.[6] The overall thrust of state policy toward mass education and health under the market regime has been to shift an increasing share of the costs of education and health from the state onto consumers. The VCP and state labelled these cost-shifting policies 'socialisation' (*xa hoi hoa*). 'Socialisation' here carries a meaning precisely opposite to the term's conventional North American and European meaning – that is, 'socialisation' in Vietnam refers to the shifting of costs from the state onto society.

At its core, 'socialisation' entailed three important policy changes. First, in the early 1990s, the state began to permit 'semi-public' and 'non-state' (that is, private) provision of some education and health services. Second, within both the education and health systems, the state undertook various measures to initiate and expand formal 'cost recovery' schemes, most importantly through the imposition of various fees, but also through state control over markets for basic education and health inputs, such as for textbooks and pharmaceuticals. Finally, within the education and health systems, the state undertook various cost-reducing measures, such as expanding class sizes and cutting numbers of medical staff.

Permitting 'non-state' provision

In the early 1990s, Vietnam's state introduced a number of policies that would permit private provisioning of education and health services. One of the earliest measures to allow for 'people founded' schools (that is, private provision of education services) came at the pre-primary level in 1990, when the Ministry of Education and Training's (MOET's) decision 124 sought to 'guide, manage and encourage the foundation of self-sustaining preschools' – a move initiated to address the collapse of agricultural collectives' capacities to finance preschool education (MOET 2000: 5). Resolution 90 of 1993 subsequently introduced a full set of rules permitting the foundation of 'non-state' school forms, including 'semi-public' (*ban cong*) schools, 'semi-public' *classes* within public schools, and 'people-sponsored' (*dan lap*) schools.

'Semi-public' schools and classes were partially subsidised through the state budgets, but students had to pay three to four times more than 'public students'. The 'semi-public' status was for students who performed below a certain level on lower and upper secondary school entrance exams and who had the capacity to pay the more costly tuition rate. 'People-sponsored' schools are, by contrast, financially autonomous from the state education budget, but are subject to state curriculum requirements. They are typically more expensive and exist only in cities. Both 'semi-public' and 'people-sponsored' forms were permitted at all levels of education except the primary level. In 1998, the latest year for which data were available, some 62 per cent of nursery school attendees and 50 per cent of kindergarten pupils were enrolled in 'people-sponsored' schools, whereas the figure was 0 per cent for primary education and just 5 per cent for lower-secondary education.[7]

The state permitted and promoted private provision of health services earlier and more comprehensively than in education. Furthermore, private provision of health services was formally institutionalised *within* the state health system and thus affected the character of health provision more profoundly than in education. Finally, the expanded accessibility of foreign pharmaceutical drugs occurred largely on a user-pays basis. Understanding the respective significance of fees, private health practice, private provision of health services *within* public institutions and patterns of pharmaceuticals drugs use helps to clarify the means by which the state shifted the burdens of health provision onto consumers. The most important impact of the state's sanctioning of private provision occurred within public health facilities themselves, where state doctors took on higher fee-paying private patients 'after hours'.

Cost recovery

Expanding 'cost recovery' through the imposition of fees and other charges took on increasing importance in both the education and health systems. In education, formal tuition fees became the principal mechanism for cost recovery. When they were first introduced in 1989, school fees applied to the fourth and fifth grades of primary school and to all secondary students grades. By 1993, school fees were no longer charged for primary school attendance, but were increased for lower and upper secondary school students.[8] For the remainder of the 1990s, the state increased fees continuously, while varying fees by region and between urban and rural areas. That said, in both urban and rural communities, the costs of attending school increased with each grade. In addition to tuition, local (both district and commune) authorities also collected annual construction 'contributions', compulsory payments earmarked for school upkeep and renovation. Survey data on household education expenditure reveal that, by 1996–7, school fees accounted for 46.1 per cent and 61.7 per cent of yearly education expenditures per lower and upper secondary student respectively (General Statistics Office 1999). Other education expenditures include those for books, transport and after-school 'extra-study'. Health service fees were also imposed from 1989. In addition to introducing fees for hospital care, the state marketised the distribution of drugs, previously available free. Since the early 1990s, both the availability of and dependence on (self-prescribed) drugs has increased significantly. Not surprisingly, the richest quintile's expenditure on drugs exceeded that of the poorest by three times (General Statistics Office 1994). For public health officials, the most disturbing aspect of increasing drugs use in Vietnam include easy self-prescription, widespread over-prescription and conflicting prescriptions.[9] Additionally, state production and sale of drugs has grown extremely rapidly and has become an important source of revenues in the health system.[10]

Outcomes of mass education and health provision in contemporary Vietnam

Outcomes of mass education and health under the market regime may be charac-terised in terms of both objective improvement and persistent, and sometimes intensifying, inequalities, often due to the unintended effects of state policies. The rapid economic growth that Vietnam experienced during the 1990s enabled increased overall investments in education and health, which improved the overall accessibility of education and health services and produced tangible gains in many important indicators of education and health, such as increased school enrollments, decreased incidence of infectious diseases, and improved nutritional status. Yet, while economic growth brought significant and broad-based improvements in Vietnam's education and health status, these improvements have been highly uneven, both spatially and between different economic strata of the population. Moreover, Vietnam's particular path of extrication from state socialism and the haphazard nature of state education and health policies during the early 1990s encouraged the development of vast informal education and health economies outside, within, and on the borders of state education and health institutions. Finally, nationally administered means-tested programmes, aimed at addressing mounting education and health inequalities, appeared to be legitimacy-seeking in their motivation yet meagre in terms of the resources involved and their effects.

The benefits of economic growth

The economic growth generated by market transition expanded investments in mass education and health by the Vietnamese state, households and foreign donors. From the early 1990s onwards, Vietnam's annual state investments in education and health increased at a faster rate than GDP growth. By the end of the 1990s, practically every one of Vietnam's 10,000 communes possessed a primary school and a commune health centre. The distributional effects of increased government expenditure on education and health clearly warrant consideration, yet it is worth noting the clear improvements Vietnam has experienced in the overall accessibility of basic education and health services.[11]

The increased average household earnings that Vietnam experienced during the 1990s were reflected in expenditure data on education and health: although between 1993 and 1998 this expenditure grew by a cumulative 44.6 per cent, household expenditures on primary, lower secondary and upper secondary education increased by 70, 65, and 70 per cent respectively.[12] Interestingly, average household expenditure on health decreased between 1993 and 1998, which the World Bank explains as an effect of declining drugs prices (World Bank 2001c). More recently, however, drug prices in Vietnam have soared, ironically due to the unintended consequences of state efforts to better regulate pharmaceuticals.[13] Still, increased consumption and household earnings appear to have had indirect health benefits. Nutrition indicators provide an example: in 1985, an estimated 60 per cent of Vietnamese children under the age of five suffered from stunting; as late as 1993, 56 per cent of children 12 and under were stunted; by 1998, stunting for the 12-and-under group had fallen to 42 per cent.[14]

Foreign aid represented an important source of increased education and health expenditure. Briefly, Japan, the Asian Development Bank, the World Bank, UN agencies, and the European Union were the most important contributors. The UN estimates that between 1993 and 1999, Vietnam's education and health sectors each received about US $500 million in overseas development aid. Between 1991 and 1998, foreign donors disbursed a total of US $442 million in the health sectors, while committing an estimated US $668 million (World Bank 2001c).

Improvements in Vietnam's education and health statuses

During the 1990s, Vietnam's populace witnessed significant improvements in its education and health status. In particular, the 1990s saw increased overall access to education and health services and significant gains in many important education and health indicators. Enrollment figures are a useful measure of a country's educational status in that they provide an indication of the size and proportion of the population accessing education and prove useful for tracking year-on-year change in the performance of a given country's education system. Data on enrollment gains in 1990s Vietnam are striking: between 1993 and 1998, net primary school enrollments in Vietnam increased from 78 to 93 per cent (General Statistics Office 1994, 1999), and by 1998 roughly 66 per cent of primary-school-aged children were actually completing their primary-level education (UN and Ministry of Labour, War Invalids and Social Affairs 1999). Gains in lower and upper secondary education appeared equally dramatic: between 1990 and 1998, gross lower secondary enrollment nearly doubled from 2.7 to 5 million, while net enrollment rates for lower secondary education increased to 61.7 per cent, and upper secondary enrollment rose to 28.6 per cent, surpassing previous record levels (General Statistics Office 1999). During this period, lower secondary school enrollment rates for girls and boys reached 61 per cent and 62 per cent respectively.

Quantitative data indicate important improvements in Vietnam's health status. During the 1990s, communicable diseases declined as a proportion of mortality. Incidence of malaria, for example, dropped from 16 cases per 1,000 persons in 1991 to just 6 in 1998. Progress in extending preventive health services to formerly underserved areas boosted the scale and effectiveness of the government's (donor-supported) inoculation programmes.[15] In international comparisons, Vietnam performs well for its low incidence of infant mortality,[16] low birth rate (2.67), and declines in mortality due to communicable diseases, which fell from 50–6 per cent to 22 per cent in 1997 (World Bank 2001c: 10).

Persistent and intensifying inequalities

However significant, achievements in Vietnam's education and health systems during the 1990s have been qualified by persistent and sometimes increasing social inequalities within the education and health systems. These differences were observed in the accessibility and quality of education and health services.[17] Social inequalities in Vietnam's education and health systems reflected widening social inequalities in Vietnam. In education, the 1990s saw a strong relationship between households' expenditure and households' ability to access higher-level education services. Importantly, all regions and all socio-economic strata experienced gains in their educational enrollment. Yet, beyond the lower secondary level, the gap between rich and poor regions' and rich and poor households' access to education widened. Between 1993 and 1998, the gap in enrollment figures between the richest and poorest quintiles of the population fell for the 6-to-10 and 11-to-14 age groups, but rose for the 15-to-17 group. In 1998, the wealthiest 15- to 17-year-olds were more than 12 times more likely to be enrolled, up from 11.5 per cent in 1993. In that same year, 18- to 23-year-old students from the wealthiest quintile were some 61 times more likely to be enrolled in school than those from the poorest quintile. These figures reflected a widening gap between Vietnam's richest regions – the Southeast (including Ho Chi Minh City) and Red River Delta (including Hanoi and Hai Phong), and five other geographical regions.

Similar dimensions of inequality could be observed in the health sector. The data indicate, for example, a strong relationship between households' incomes and their ability to access higher-level health services, virtually all of which takes place in hospitals. Throughout the 1990s, the top expenditure quintiles were significantly more likely to seek treatment at public hospitals, even as the overall decline in hospital use between 1993 and 1998 suggests either declining demand for inpatient services or declining provision of outpatient services by state-run hospitals (World Bank 2001c: 36–49). It is also illuminating to examine health contacts according to the economic composition of all users of particular types of health providers. Poorer segments of Vietnam's tend to rely on CHCs, whereas the wealthier population segments tend toward heavier use of hospitals. This reflects major rural–urban differences in the distribution of medical facilities. Using data from the Vietnam Living Standards Surveys, scholars calculate that urban and town-based households were almost twice as likely to visit a hospital as their rural counterparts (Vo Than Son *et al.* 2001: 176).

Informal economies: the unintended effects of policy change

Vietnam's particular path of extrication from state socialism and the state's subsequent efforts to reform the education and health systems produced important unintended effects. Among the most significant of these are the vast informal economies that operate outside, within and on the borders of nominally public education and health institutions. Slow increases in education and health workers' wages, combined with rapid economic growth, occasioned the development of informal economies within the education and health systems built upon unregulated, and often under-the-table, payments to public education and health personnel. The preferred medium of exchange became an envelope, or *phong bi*, filled with bills bearing the likeness of Ho Chi Minh. These informal cash payments to teachers and doctors have assumed such importance as to overshadow the significance of formal education and health institutions.

The informal economy within Vietnam's education system is known as 'extra study' (*hoc them*), an extensive system of after-hours teaching that runs in parallel with the state education system (see Figure 9.1). Almost exclusively, teaching in this private system is conducted by 'public' teachers. Classes are sometimes held in 'public' school facilities, but more often in the cramped quarters of teachers' homes, often given away by a tangle of 20 or 30 bicycles outside. To parents, the value of extra study lies in enhancing their children's performance on Vietnam's system of competitive entrance exams, which dictate whether students will be admitted to upper secondary school or college, and as 'public' or 'semi-public' students. Teachers value the opportunity to increase their income. Unsurprisingly, wealthier households are more able to afford extra study and extra study is more extensive in cities. Yet extra study is now common in rural areas, even in poor districts. In relatively wealthy households (especially in Ho Chi Minh City and Hanoi), it is not uncommon to spend hundreds of US dollars per year on 'extra study'.[18] In poor areas, 'extra study' is frequently a household's largest non-food expenditure.

The informal economy in the health system is more complicated, since the line between public and private is fuzzier still: informal transactions more often take place within the setting of state medical facilities. A 1996 report estimated that some 49 per cent of all private healthworkers and 83 per cent of all private physicians were government employees. The concern, and widely observed pattern, is that permitting public doctors to provide private services in public institutions produces incentives for doctors to minimise their time with public patients. The result is increasing absenteeism by public health service providers and a diminished sense of responsibility for their public patients. The informal economy in the health system compounds this problem. In principle, private doctors within public hospitals are supposed to follow a strict fee schedule set by the MoH. In practice, there is a wide disparity between official fees and household expenditures on doctors: the informal health economy involves patients passing *phong bi* to doctors, in addition to formal fees, so as to secure greater attention and more timely care.[19] One state official provides the following, describing the 'rules' of the informal health economy:

Figure 9.1 Accessing education. In contemporary Vietnam, gaining access to education services beyond the primary level depends increasingly on households' earnings and, in particular, their ability to maintain a variety of out-of-pocket expenditures, on everything from school supplies, to official 'contributions,' to fees for 'extra-study'. The cover from a popular satirical magazine shows the difficulty of getting to school (the school house appears in the upper right corner).

Source: *Tuoi Tre Cuoi*, September 1999.

'Hospital fee + envelope is the level which the "consumer" accepts to pay. "Heavy envelope" or "light" depends both on the financial capability of the patient and the quality of the service and fame of the provider' (Nguyen Hoang Anh 2000: 72).

While there is little systematic research on informal health payments, the World Bank observed a 14-fold gap between households' reported expenditure on fees on the one hand, and MoH receipts from medical fees on the other (World Bank

2001c). The presence of informal economies may help to explain this gap. In formal discussions, state officials insist that one may gain access to adequate education and health services without resorting to private payments. In informal discussions, most Vietnamese view informal payments as a matter of necessity.

The limits of exemptions and ameliorative programmes

Vietnam's leaders have recognised that the state's post-1989 education and health policies impose high costs, particularly on poor families.[20] Since 1989, they have sought to address the problem of education and health fees though the implementation of several well-publicised national programmes that exempt certain categories of households from formal fees. Eligible households include those falling below the state-set poverty line, and households with war invalids, orphans, or mothers of fallen soldiers. In practice, however, fee exemptions have never been particularly effective. As early as 1989, one newspaper account pointed out that reducing fees by 50 per cent or even 100 per cent does not provide sufficient help for a poor family, particularly when such exemptions seldom include medicines (Hang Chuc Nguyen 1989: 5). The costs of education and health were doubly burdensome for households in poorer rural areas, which often lacked even basic education and health infrastructure.

To address these issues, the VCP and the state began to design and implement various hunger eradication and poverty reduction (HEPR) schemes explicitly designed to ameliorate widening socio-economic disparities between high and low economic growth regions. In 1993, the Ministry of Labour, Invalids and Social Affairs (MoLISA) drafted Vietnam's first national poverty lines, which were to be used as means tests for targeting state aid to poor communities and households. But it was not until the Eighth Party Congress in 1996 that the Party outlined its HEPR objectives, which included infrastructure improvement in 1,300 (later raised to 1,715) of the nation's poorest communes, and expanding access to land and credit among the poor, as well as securing them free access to basic education and health services. It took the government two years to specify the institutional arrangements for these programmes' implementation, but by the end of 1998, the state had established HEPR boards in 6,958 communes (out of 7,518 at the time), and local authorities commenced poverty-mapping efforts – using government criteria to identify poor households in each commune. Yet across provinces, districts and communes, wide variation was reported in the efficacy of poverty mapping, and patronage was widely reported regarding the designation of poor communes and households (MoLISA 1999).

HEPR was designed to improve access to education and health services. The education provisions of the HEPR programmes were to eradicate illiteracy, exempt or reduce school fees and contributions for designated poor households, and to provide books and grant scholarships for the rural poor to attend upper secondary and higher education institutions in cities. For these activities the MoET needed to commit VND 834 billion over three years (HEPR 1999) an amount equal to roughly 2 per cent of the annual education budget.[21] Similarly, the HEPR programme's health component aimed to improve access to health services by providing fee exemptions for all 'starving' households and 80 per cent of government-certified 'poor' households, including the yearly distribution of medical insurance cards to the former. For these activities, the MoH had a budget of VND 800 billion, an amount equal to roughly 1.1 per cent of recurrent health expenditures over the same three years. In addition to the limited economic resources committed, the HEPR education and health measures have two additional problems: obtaining certification to secure fee exemptions is a difficult process, and in any case formal healthcare fees form only one element of the expenses involved in treatment.

Conclusion

Vietnam's transition from state socialism to a market economy produced rapid economic growth, coupled with significant if uneven improvement in living standards. Economic growth benefited the country's education and health systems, enabling expanded investments in education and health. Vietnamese today have unprecedented access to education and health services. Yet in the course of its market transition, Vietnam has seen fundamental changes in its institutions: an appreciation of these changes is essential for understanding the conduct and outcomes of education and health policy.

The state socialist regime was distinguished by the quasi-egalitarian principles and institutions that governed mass education and health provision. There was a wide gap between principle and practice, however. State socialism was a coercive system of class domination and under the state socialist regime, party members, state managers, state workers and urban populations enjoyed the best social services, while rural and politically marginal populations – such as those with associations to the former Saigon regime – were relegated to second-class status. For practical purposes, the end of the state-socialist regime came by 1979, when Vietnam's state socialist institutions began to crumble under the stresses and strains of postwar poverty, renewed war, and their own systemic inefficiencies.

The transitional regime saw the gradual demise of state socialist economic institutions, culminating in a fiscal crisis of the state that threatened the functioning of the education and health systems, nationally and at the grassroots. In the late 1980s, national and local arrangements for financing education and health sectors services nearly collapsed. Between 1987 and 1991, public use of education and health declined dramatically – enrollment gains in primary education stagnated, while enrollments in lower secondary and upper secondary education declined by upwards of 30 and 40 per cent respectively. Between 1987 and 1993, utilisation of outpatient state health services declined by 50 per cent. Declining utilisation of state education and health services owed significantly to the declining quality of services and to the state's introduction of fees in 1989, a measure that required the VCP to alter the country's 1982 constitution.

The rapid economic growth that Vietnam has experienced under the market regime has had clear benefits, yet the effects of economic growth on mass education and health provision have been complex and subject to sharp regional variation. While quantitative data indicate truly remarkable gains in access to education and health services, the distinctive feature of the market regime was the emergence of principles and institutions that effectively shifted the financial costs of education and health services from the state to individual consumers. In practice, the market regime combines state socialist and market principles and institutions. While the state provides a floor of basic services, such as primary education and preventive health care, higher levels of service provision are increasingly subject to market principles, whether through the introduction of formal fees for public services, the privatisation of services, or through informal cash payments made to nominally public education and health officials. Education and health policies continue to favour those in wealthier regions, while imposing proportionately higher costs on the poor. However noble in their principles, state policies designed to 'protect the poor' have been quite limited in scope and in their effects. Vietnam continues to ensure a degree of equity by providing all citizens access to basic education and health services. Increasingly, though, access to non-basic education and health services depends on household earnings and little cash-filled envelopes.

Notes

1 A much longer – and more extensively referenced – version of this chapter appeared in *American Asian Review*, 19 June 2003.
2 Nguyen Van Huong (1970: 11), cited in Bryant (1998: 247); Banister (1985).
3 General Statistics Office (1978), cited in Banister (1985).
4 Hoang Dinh Cau (1965: 42, 58), cited in Bryant (1998: 247).
5 Specifically, per capita outpatient consultations dropped from 2.10 in 1987, to 1.82 in 1988; then by some 35 per cent to 1.20 in 1989, before bottoming out at just 1.01 in 1990, and at 0.93 in 1993. But inpatient utilisation also dropped, from 105 admissions per 1,000 persons per year in 1987, to 79 in 1989, and 68 in 1990 (Ministry of Health, cited in World Bank 1993).
6 World Bank in Vietnam routinely uses the 80 per cent figure; data on education expenditures are less widely cited; the 70 per cent figure is an estimate based on a review of the Viet Nam Living Standards Survey (VNLSS) data and the author's own interviews.
7 Comparable figures for upper secondary education could not be located.
8 At the time, fees were set at the cash equivalent of 4 and 7 kg of rice per month per student for lower and upper secondary students respectively.
9 An AusAid report (AusAid 1997: 7) quotes an unnamed 1991 document stating that in 1990, 50 per cent of 139 pharmacists in northern Vietnam could not differentiate essential from non-essential drugs. Another survey of 1,833 patients in two Hanoi pharmacies in 1994 revealed that only 0.8 per cent had a medical prescription, while 94.9 per cent had already decided which drug they would purchase before reaching the pharmacy (World Bank 2001c: 109).
10 Tornquist (cited in World Bank 2001c) shows that between 1989 and 1997, the value of domestic drugs production in Vietnam increased from 777,000 to 107 million. By 1999 there were 18 central government pharmaceuticals factories – plus 126 at the

provincial level, nearly all state owned. The World Bank reported that by 2000 there were an estimated 20,000 drug retail outlets.

11 The Ministry of Health and the World Bank distinguish between the State Budget on Health and Total Public Spending on Health. The latter measure includes government use of user fees and funds from insurance.

12 Inflation for the years 1994, 1995, 1996, 1997 and 1998 ran at 14.7, 12.4, 4.5, 3.8 and 9.2 per cent. Source: Ministry of Finance.

13 In early 2003, drugs prices in Ho Chi Minh City soared by 60 per cent, as local pharmacies spontaneously (and illegally) raised prices far beyond new state-mandated prices designed to curtail the sale of counterfeit, smuggled and unregulated drugs. An account of this can be found in *Vietnam News*, available online at http//perso.wanadoo.Fr/Patrick.guenin/cantho/vnnews/melo.htm.

14 According to the National Institute of Nutrition, as cited in Koch and Nguyen (2001).

15 The expanded programme of immunisation (EPI) helped reduce the rate of polio from 2.6 per 100,000 persons in 1986 to 0.6 per 100,000 persons in 1996, diphtheria to 5 per cent of its 1986 levels, and has virtually eliminated neonatal tetanus (World Bank 2001c: 10).

16 Infant mortality stood at 36.7 per 1,000 live births according to the General Statistics Office 1999, and 30 per 1,000 according to the UN (2002).

17 The World Bank estimates indicate that between 1993 and 1998 national per capita expenditures grew 30 per cent faster in officially designated urban areas than in designated rural ones.

18 According to the 1998 VNLSS, extra study expenses, on average, comprised roughly 18 per cent of household education expenditures for lower secondary students and 28 per cent for upper secondary students. These figures are misleading. First, there is considerable evidence that extra study has increased since 1998. Second, average expenditures on tutoring blur the wide disparities in expenditure on extra study between rich and poor. From my own research in 2000, in central Vietnam's Quang Nam province, I observed many rural households expending VND 100,000 per month on extra study for secondary-school students, as compared with VND 17,000 for school fees.

19 The actual transaction is fascinating to observe: it is quick, occurs in a private setting, and is often acknowledged only momentarily and passively by the doctor. Precise monetary amounts are *never* discussed up front. One personal observation in a Ho Chi Minh City emergency room was illustrative: the patients stuffed a large wad of 50,000 dong notes into the gaping pocket of the doctor's white coat on the way from one examination room to another. The practice seems to give the patients greater peace of mind.

20 The Seventh Party Congress in 1991 explicitly recognised the problem of education and health access for the poor (HEPR 1999).

21 This figure was calculated by dividing the HEPR funds by the sum of the education budget for three years.

10 Centralism – the dilemma of educational reforms in Vietnam

Doan Hue Dung

This chapter explores the characteristics of centralism in educational management in Vietnam and reviews some of the salient effects of centralism on the outcomes of educational reforms in the country. Since the early 1990s the system of education in Vietnam has seen major changes in organisational structure, educational mission, curricula and the management of both finances and human resources. Even though these reforms have resulted in a rapid increase in numbers of students, numbers and types of educational institutions and courses of studies at all levels of education, the national education system seems to be facing a deterioration in quality. Most local newspapers do not hesitate to describe educational innovations in Vietnam as messy, confused and disappointing.

The chapter will analyse the effects of centralism on major aspects of educational reforms: curriculum, staff quality and educational growth. Highly centralised management and the state's limited capacity for educational planning and policy-making are considered the main drawbacks, undermining educational reforms and paving the way for the spread of nepotism, corruption and the stagnation of the national education system. The Vietnamese educational system is based upon fundamental principles of centralised state education such as strict central control over educational matters, uniform curriculum and civil servant status of teachers. But to what extent has the present centralised, command-based system responded to current demands for educational development in Vietnam?

The provision of education

The national education system comprises five levels: preschool education (5 years), primary education (5 years), secondary education (7 years), higher education (4 to 6 years), and postgraduate education. In addition, vocational education and training provides educational opportunities for those secondary school leavers who are unable to enter higher education. Table 10.1 gives a statistical summary of the position. While there is evidence that access to primary education is increasing, overall education attainment may be declining in Vietnam despite recent economic growth (Long *et al.* 2000: 137). Gabriel Kolko argues that Vietnam's education system is now in serious decline, characterised by dilapidated buildings, underpaid teachers, falling quality and *de facto* subsidies to better-off families through extensive

Table 10.1 Education in Vietnam, 1999

Levels	Student population	Teacher population	Number of schools/ institutions
Preschool (1996)	1,931,611	75,034	7,213
Primary	10,247,000	336,294	13,066
Secondary	7,225,000	250,896	10,220
Vocational	179,480	9,732	256
Higher education	716,389	24,080	190
Postgraduate	6,500		
Universities			66
Research institutes			62

Sources: MoET 5 January 2001; MoET 1999.

government support for higher education (Kolko 1997: 109–10).[1] While Kolko suggests that Vietnam's education system has embraced the market too eagerly, others argue that shortcomings arise largely from the government's failure to reform educational management structures so as to ensure better performance.

Centralised management mechanisms

The central government, through the Ministry of Education and Training (MoET) and its departments, formulates and adopts education policies. In effect, education reforms are based on the overall guidelines and agenda promulgated by the Central Committee and the Politbureau of the Vietnamese Communist Party (VCP). In other words, education policies are formulated, revised and updated in accordance with the state's general action plans defined at the VCP national congresses and the Vietnamese National Assembly manifestos every five years. In particular, the National Assembly also promulgates the laws on education and makes decisions concerning budgetary and strategic plans for educational development.

At the top of the hierarchy is the Minister, supported by one standing Vice-Minister and four other Vice-Ministers. There are four general ministerial departments – the Department of Personnel, Department of Financial Planning, Department of International Relations and the Department of Science and Technology – with power and control over all levels of the education system. Besides these, there are specific departments at the ministerial level, in charge of each provision of education. It is impossible to draw a precise chart to describe the managerial mechanisms because of the overlapping allocation of power and responsibilities among central departments and among other authority bodies in the hierarchy (see Figure 10.1). Currently, every general department is heavily involved in numerous activities taking place at all levels of the system. However, all decisions have to be made in consultation with several other departments. The process of decision-making and policy implementation is therefore inevitably time-consuming and usually generates bureaucracy. Like many other Vietnamese government organisations, MoET is often preoccupied with turf wars between different

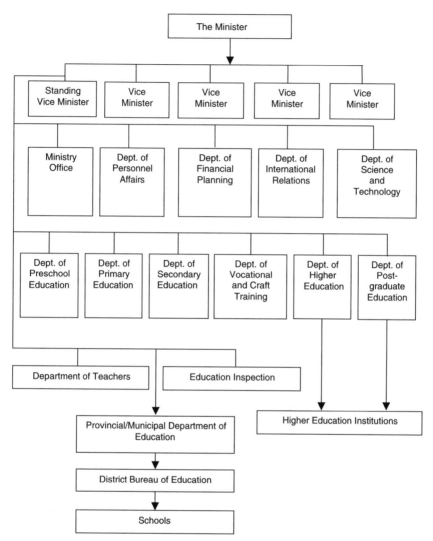

Figure 10.1 The structure of the national education system

departments, concerns which divert energy and resources away from boosting education attainment (Templer 1998: 148–9). In addition, the management frameworks at the regional level and institutional level fail to work efficiently because there are no precise and consistent rules on the delegation of power at each level. This is particularly striking in the management of the university system (Doan Hue Dung 2000: 37) and the vocational education and training sector (*Tuoi Tre*, 31 November 2000). The educational system in Vietnam strongly reflects the power structure of the social context – that is, the prevailing power structure of a highly centralised state.

Curriculum and quality controls

Each level of the education system receives a different degree of central control over the curriculum. The primary school and secondary school curricula are national and compulsory and, therefore, centrally controlled. Standard numbers of hours, content and textbooks are dictated by the MoET. Central control over the curriculum consequently enforces common practices and standards across the whole system, and is associated with the adoption of a national system of qualifications. Much of the emphasis is on rote learning; during a week of observation in a Vietnamese school, two Swedish education specialists noted that pupils did not ask teachers a single question about the content of their lessons (Rubin 1988: 51).

School performance is generally evaluated and ranked on the basis of the percentage of good students, grade-repeating and drop-out students. Therefore, schools are working under pressure to produce as many high-achieving students as possible. As a negative consequence, grades are given generously for all classroom activities, so that more than 90 per cent of students obtain good grades of nine and above. However, students' supposed 'high achievement' in terms of grades and the percentage of 'excellent' students can hardly reflect the real teaching and learning quality of the system. Rather, it testifies to many pervasive practices, such as 'extra study' by students who pay sizeable additional fees to their teachers for out-of-hours tuition (see Chapter 9 in this volume), and the widespread practice of 'learning' by memorising lesson samples that closely resemble final exams, so as to maximise student scores. In addition, there is aggressive competition to enter top schools, where places are very limited. Therefore, it has become a norm that parents need to pay substantial 'donations' as contributions towards school buildings, in order to secure admission for their children. In effect, low-level corruption pervades the relationships between providers of education and the end-users. These problems partly reflect the inefficiency of inspection mechanisms, and the ineffectiveness of assessment models.

Another integral element of the national curriculum is the implementation of uniform textbooks across the system. However, lesson contents have been criticised as irrelevant and unsuitable for a large number of students, partly due to the uneven quality of teachers. For students who live in rural and remote areas, geographical and cultural differences may also make it difficult for them to understand the concepts and ideas of people from other areas: the curriculum reflects a central state view that may differ substantially from their own experiences. There is currently no scope for 'localising' the curriculum to reflect the needs of, say, the Central Highlands. It has therefore been impossible to achieve common standards across the country (*Tuoi Tre*, 25 November 2000). The revision of textbooks for primary and secondary schools has also been a very complicated and time-consuming task. While teachers and parents have called for the urgent revision of teaching methods and lesson contents, the process of change is taking place at a very slow pace because it involves a large number of people at different levels of the hierarchy. A set of textbooks to be implemented nationwide to establish a uniform curriculum by 2003 has been in use as a pilot series since 1999. However, the books have been the subject of strong criticism from teachers and the wider public because of their factual as well as typographical mistakes.[2] By contrast, a new series of English language texts has been produced in collaboration with an American non-governmental organisation funded by a range of US corporate sponsors, including Coca-Cola – the books actually contain the sponsors' logos – and their introduction has been supported by a programme of retraining teachers to use more participatory language teaching methods (Lamb 2000). The ability of the MoET to ensure that these new books are adopted nationwide illustrates the potential advantages of centralised textbook control, an interesting example of collaboration between state, market and non-profit sectors.

In higher education, the undergraduate and postgraduate curricula also follow the uniform frameworks set by the MoET, which determine the total number of credits and the percentage of core courses, required courses and specialised courses for each field of study. Central control is placed particularly over required courses such as Marxist–Leninist political sciences and foreign languages, in terms of the number of hours and the teaching content. The contents of the remaining courses are generally decided at the institutional level. The major advantage of central control over the curriculum of higher education is its enforcement of a common structure of study programmes for each type of degree throughout the country. All postgraduate degrees have so far been authorised and conferred directly by the MoET.

In theory, such controls mean that quality is maintained and abuses are curtailed. Yet a 1998 report to the National Assembly highlighted widespread problems concerning the 'purchase' and 'sale' of examination marks, and the production of fake diplomas and certificates.[3] Over 14 per cent of student files checked by MoET contained irregularities. This suggests that a highly centralised and bureaucratised system does not itself ensure that quality is delivered, even at the most fundamental level of accurate documentation and records. Uproar broke out in December 2001, when extensive abuses of the enrollment system were uncovered at Dong Do College in Hanoi. Education Minister Nguyen Hien told the media, 'There are many causes behind (Dong Do) abuses, but I would like to single out the intention of some people to commercialise the education sector' (Tran Dinh Thanh Lam 2002). Education reform in Vietnam was characterised by a fundamental contradiction: a desire to bring the discipline of the market to bear upon an often ramshackle and corrupt state system, which was ill at ease with a serious allergy to the 'commercialisation' of education. Ultimately, the leadership believed that the state had greater discipline than the market – but this was a contentious assumption.

Reforms in curriculum areas in higher education and postgraduate education have faced many critical problems. The concepts of credit accumulation, modular structure and two-cycle curricula have been introduced; however, they are neither thoroughly understood nor willingly accepted by educational managers at the national and institutional level alike. Therefore, they have not been implemented properly. The curricula of postgraduate education have been under strong criticisms from participants and the wider public for their overemphasis on theoretical issues, overloading of courses, covering subjects irrelevant to learners' needs, and paying inadequate attention to self-study (Doan Hue Dung 2000: 37–44). Such problems testify to the continuing popularity of overseas study for wealthier students, and for those with the ability or connections to secure scholarships. Others turn to the growing private university sector, which includes provision offered collaboratively with international institutions. To consider possible changes in Vietnamese policies and practices, numerous meetings and conferences are held at all levels and the decision-making process remains tardy and bureaucratic. In many respects, the situation still resembles that described by David Marr in a widely cited essay on Vietnamese higher education first published in 1988. Marr noted that the system suffers from structural weaknesses of outdated curricula, compartmentalisation of knowledge and excessive central control. Marr observed: 'However, as many well-educated Vietnamese are coming to realise, it is relatively easy to identify particular development problems and propose solutions, but extremely difficult to accomplish changes amidst widespread institutional rigidity' (Marr 1988: 44).

Personnel

Staff management in Vietnamese education is highly centralised. Staff are incorporated into the civil service, which involves control of recruitment, promotion, dismissal and retirement. In effect, the state fixes salary scales, decides on the reward system, and controls the number of posts at the national, municipal and institutional levels. Policies and decisions on staff management and development are therefore formulated by MoET and implemented by institutions (in the case of higher education), or by municipal departments of education and schools. For instance, the number of permanent staff at each individual university is planned by the institution itself based on its operational needs and is subject to approval by MoET. Permanent staff at secondary and primary schools are managed by the Office for Education at the district level, and by the Department for Education at the city or provincial level.

The critical shortcoming of centralised management over personnel is the inflexibility and impracticality of many national policies, which are unsuitable for teachers in certain areas. What might be appropriate for implementation in big cities is not necessarily workable in rural areas and vice versa. There are huge gaps in educational attainment between different parts of the country: in 1992, illiteracy levels were 1.9 per cent in the Red River Delta, compared with 26.4 per cent in the Central Highlands (Long *et al.* 2000: 40). These discrepancies point to the short-sightedness of 'one-size-fits-all' policies imposed by the central state. For instance, the central regulations on civil status of teachers have created a dilemma in staff recruitment. According to this regulation, full-time teachers have to be of civil servant status, which requires a formal and competitive selection examination. This principle causes serious problems for regions where teachers are in short supply. It is reported that the system lacks 100,000 teachers, yet ironically, many graduates from teacher training institutions are not able to find employment, partly due to the restriction of this regulation (*Tuoi Tre*, 12 September 2000). This situation is also caused by the inflexible quota system at the central level that controls and restricts the number of teaching staff in each institution across the country, but fails to catch up with the real demands of the locality. If the system of employing teachers were decentralised, local schools and districts could hire trained teachers to fill vacancies more flexibly.

Other weaknesses of the current personnel management are caused by the principle whereby permanent staff members retain their positions until they reach retirement age, regardless of their performance. In other words, the current policies on staff incentives are based on tenure and seniority rather than performance. This is the main factor that makes government salaries for teachers extremely low. The current system of rewards and incentives for the academic profession in general carries more symbolic value than practical value. Though ranked as the sixth highest in the government salary scale, salaries of teachers and other educational personnel remain acutely low and do not keep pace with the rapid increases in living costs. The average monthly salary of permanent lecturers in 1997 was approximately VND 400,000 (equivalent to US $30) while the average basic living cost required for an individual was about VND 1,300,000 (Vu Trieu Minh 1997: 55). Unrealistically low salaries have the serious consequence that virtually all teachers need to find second jobs to supplement their income, and the quality of teaching is therefore unstable. For instance, a survey in 1991 found that around 50 per cent of Vietnamese teachers were involved in supplementary jobs that did not relate to their professions (UNESCO *et al.* 1992: 28). There is no reason to believe that the situation is any better today. A more recent statistic shows that 80 per cent of off-quota teachers in preschool education in rural areas, who are contracted by the local government, have a monthly salary lower than VND 144,000 (approximately US $10) (*Tuoi Tre*, 18 November 2000).

In higher education, the management of staff is based on a highly centralised structure. The mechanism operates at two levels: the personnel offices at individual institutions and the Department of Personnel Affairs at the MoET. The procedures for appointing senior lecturers, associate professors and professors, are initiated at the institutional level then confirmed through the professional fields concerned, and finally screened for approval at the ministerial level. Councils for academic title appointment are formed at every single level of administration throughout the appointment process. At the ministerial level, it is the National Council for Academic Appointment, the chairman of which is the MoET. The criteria for each academic title are uniform, and therefore often fail to match the actual capabilities of academics in different fields. The concentration of power at the centre is likely to facilitate the development of an authoritarian system of administration, especially while dealing with personnel matters.

The most serious weaknesses of staff management identified by the MoET were the lack of managerial competence at many levels of administration, and the unfavourable ratios of teaching staff to non-teaching staff. In fact, non-teaching personnel exceed teaching staff in many institutions (MoET 1999). The present function of the personnel management system is mainly to record staff profiles rather than to plan and monitor human resources. For instance, recent research by the writer into the employment of foreign-educated Vietnamese academics in higher education found that even though the process of sending academics to study abroad was monitored at the central level, the employment of the returnees took place at the institutional level. No link was made between the sending of academics abroad and assignment of posts on their return. As a consequence, only 37 per cent of the sample of 137 returnees surveyed were currently working in academic areas appropriate to their acquired skills and knowledge (Doan Hue Dung 2000: 228). Given these drawbacks arising from the inefficient mechanism of staff management, universities should have full autonomy regarding the employment of staff, while retraining and replacement of staff should become the shared responsibility of MoET and individual institutions. Otherwise, well-qualified academic staff will remain demotivated, seeking supplementary and more remunerative employment outside the university sector, instead of dedicating themselves to teaching and research activities (Doan Hue Dung 2000: 232).

Finance

Unlike the present situation in curriculum and personnel management, the degree of central control is lessened in financial management. The concept of 'socialisation' of education is widely interpreted as mobilising all potential sources of funding essential for educational growth.[4] The proportion of the state budget allocated for education has been increased from 5 to 9 per cent in the 1980s, from 10 to 12 per cent in the 1990s and reached 15 per cent of total state expenditures in 2001.

Based on sources of financial support, educational institutions and schools fall into three categories. First, public or state-run institutions are funded by the government. The majority of staff working in public institutions are government officials, or staff on permanent or long-term contracts. Around 85 per cent of students at state universities are fee-paying, while the remainder receive government scholarships (Doan Hue Dung 2000: 39). Pupils in state primary schools do not have to pay school fees, though secondary school students do (see Chapter 9 in this volume). Second, semi-public institutions are provided with rudimentary premises by the state. The managerial staff at semi-public universities are necessarily appointed by MoET, whereas at schools they are under the control of the local authority. All students and pupils at semi-public institutions are fee-paying. Third, 'people-founded' or private institutions are created and managed by a social organisation or individuals or groups of individuals, and excluded from state-funding schemes.

Though sources of funding for educational operations are diversified, the MoET and the local authorities preserve their autonomy in determining quotas of student enrollments for each institution. The quota set for upper secondary schools (grades 10 to 12) in Ho Chi Minh in 2001 was 52,137 students, among which 25,425 students were in public schools making up about 49 per cent; 20,760 in semi-public schools (40 per cent), and 5,952 in people-founded or private schools (11 per cent) (*Tuoi Tre*, 10 April 2001). The university system in 1999 had 171 state institutions, 3 semi-public and 16 people-founded institutions, serving around 716,839 students (MoET 2000a).

The state budget is able to cover from 26 to 65 per cent of the financial requirements of schools (Pham Minh Hac 1998: 182); therefore, schools are allowed to generate other sources of finance including parental contributions, teaching extra-curricular courses, and renting out classrooms in the evenings. However, central control over financial management and personnel is associated with the adoption of the central quota system for students and staff. Universities and schools are therefore unable to satisfy society's increasing demands for education. Only around 160,000 candidates out of nearly two million are selected to enter higher education at the university entrance exams every year. In other words, universities can accept less than 10 per cent of students who have the desire to study higher education. The chance to enroll in public schools is also very competitive because, due to the limited state budget, there is an increasing trend to convert public schools into semi-public schools. Central control restricts the capacity of local institutions to offer better services to the market-driven economy and society.

Conclusion

The most problematic characteristic of educational reforms in Vietnam is the remarkable inconsistency of educational policies and plans which are formulated at the central level but not successfully implemented across the system. In brief, school decentralisation and institutional autonomy arguments have been adopted more in rhetoric than in practice in Vietnam. However, centralised educational management is not appropriate and effective in many respects. Centralisation tends to turn each central unit into an authoritarian overseer of its assigned area, thus limiting suggestions and initiatives from others, especially those at lower levels. Actually, creativity usually comes from localities, particularly from the grassroots levels and from professionals, whose daily interactions with the real world of education ought to provide clear, precise and appropriate modifications for policy and planning. Overcentralisation at the national level hampers the development of the educational system by discouraging enthusiasm, initiatives and creativeness among both individual teachers and their institutions.

The dilemmas of educational reforms in Vietnam are intensified by two conflicting trends: preserving and enforcing central power on the one hand, and accepting the influencing power of market-driven ideas, practices and values on the other. There is an old Vietnamese saying that 'the emperor's writ stops at the village gate'; in the contemporary context, centralisation must be based on a degree of consensus, and requires co-ordination between central and local authorities. In many instances, such co-ordination does not actually exist. However, it is highly controversial to claim that decentralisation would immediately enhance the effectiveness of Vietnamese education. In fact, since decentralisation is a new concept in Vietnam, attitudes and practices will take time to change. In addition, both administrative and legal mechanisms have not been well-established to support social change. Moreover, great disparities among provinces are likely to result in further educational inequality. If decentralisation occurs unevenly in different areas, it tends to limit co-ordination and co-operation, and hinder reforms. Centralisation, to some extent, is still necessary. Thus, it is significant to define the division of power among different managerial levels for decision-making and for implementation. In other words, a combination of less centralisation and more decentralisation seems a practical and appropriate choice.

Notes

1 Kolko also asserts that student enrollments have declined, especially in upper secondary schools, a claim not supported by more recent data – see Chapter 9 in this volume.
2 See, for example 'Why errors found in Primary Six textbooks have not been corrected?' *Tuoi Tre*, 10 October 2000; 'The post-2000 textbooks: a great change in education?' *Tuoi Tre*, 16 January 2001; 'The new series of textbooks for primary school will still be implemented' *Tuoi Tre*, 7 April 2001.
3 Cited in *Vietnam 1998–1999* (1999) Hanoi: The Gioi Publishers, 63–5.
4 On the meaning of 'socialisation' in the Vietnamese context, see Chapter 9 in this volume.

11 An emerging civil society?

Local associations working on HIV/AIDS

Marie-Eve Blanc

Since the onset of *doi moi*, Vietnam has experienced remarkable social changes. The emergence of a market economy and the opening up of the society to globalisation, combined with substantial domestic migration, has created a host of new problems. Vietnam's development has been far from homogenous: some more remote regions were relatively unaffected by the process of economic change, yet regions and households have been increasingly differentiated, as the gap between rich and poor has widened. Socio-economic inequalities produced difficulties for many households, limiting access both to good primary healthcare and to educational opportunities. A widespread perception in Vietnam has been that socio-economic changes, combined with a liberalisation of the media, have opened the door for sexual emancipation, moral laxity and a range of associated problems. As a result, the state has used measures such as the 1993 Law on Publishing to maintain its control over domestic information flows.

One of the greatest problems of the early 1990s was the spread of HIV/AIDs (human immunodeficiency virus/acquired immune deficiency syndrome) from the South to the North, amounting effectively to a new 'war'. The first HIV case was discovered in Ho Chi Minh City in 1990. By November 1997 there was a big discrepancy in infection rates between North and South: 2,314 reported cases in Ho Chi Minh City and only 56 cases in Hanoi. Initially, the disease spread gradually from South to North, though recently drug trafficking across the Northern border between China and Vietnam has led to a 'second front' of HIV infection. By early July 2003, Vietnam had 67,000 recorded HIV carriers. This new war was replete with symbolism about the need to eradicate the negative dimensions of openness, and curtailing the abuses associated with the rise of capitalism. In combating HIV/AIDS, the emphasis was upon eradicating not simply the disease itself, but also the social problems associated with it, such as prostitution and drug abuse. These supposed consequences of *doi moi* caused political leaders to pay more attention to cultural changes, stepping up the repression of 'bad behaviour'. In reality, however, AIDS is not a political or ideological problem, but one rooted in economic and public health issues. Poor education and low incomes have played a crucial role in producing new modes of economic activity, such as the sex trade and drug trafficking.

Who is responsible for helping poor people deal with issues such as drug abuse and AIDS? In practice, access to health and education in Vietnam is crucially linked to the ability to pay: it is common, for example, for parents to offer 'presents' to their children's teachers to ensure that they receive sufficient attention in class, a form of low-level corruption widely mirrored in other interactions between the users of public services and those charged with providing them. Only those with money can readily obtain medicines, and those without regular employment do not have access to proper health insurance. Meanwhile, a new system of social insurance for all workers has been set up, but this does not include the cost of medicines or of services such as blood-testing, which is very important for providing access to better care for HIV patients. Social insurance cards can themselves form the basis of a form of discrimination, since doctors prefer patients with real money than card-carrying patients, for whose fees they must seek reimbursement from the state (Blanc 2003b: 11–16).

This gap between the needs of the poor and the provisions of the state has created the space for new organisations to emerge as campaigning organisations and service providers on issues such as AIDS. Since 1994, a growing number of clubs, small local non-governmental organisations (NGOs), community-based organisations (CBOs) and groups have emerged to participate in AIDS-related work. Yet such organisations have not been allowed to act independently: they have been obliged to register with one of the mass organisations linked to the Vietnamese Communist Party (VCP). Various bodies are linked to the 'umbrella' mass organisation, the Fatherland Front: the most prominent include the Peasants' Association, the General Confederation of Labour, the Women's Association and the Ho Chi Minh Communist Youth League (Kerkvliet 2001b: 246). These organisations are headed by leading figures in the VCP, at both national and local branch level. In this light, can civil society be said to be emerging in Vietnam? Many Vietnam specialists – both Vietnamese and non-Vietnamese – have long argued that Vietnamese society is characterised by a state-dominated order, in which there is no autonomous civil society. The Marxist–Leninist orthodoxies taught in all Vietnamese schools offer no place for a liberal concept such as civil society. In an important recent essay, Ben Kerkvliet cautions against assuming that civil society as understood in the West can be said to exist in Vietnam, since such a society 'requires an accommodating state – one that not only tolerates differences and criticisms, but helps to maintain institutions, laws and practices that make public debate possible without violent or silencing repercussions' (Kerkvliet 2001b: 241). Yet he also notes that civil society is a matter of degree, and argues against 'trying to distinguish between what is in the state and what is in society' (2001b: 268). Some analysts have suggested that degrees of civil society are indeed emerging in Vietnam, in certain realms, periods and places. Chris Dixon (Chapter 2 in this volume), for example, argues that tentative signs of the emergence of civil society may be seen in some areas of contemporary Vietnamese life.

What is the difference between a Vietnamese NGO and a mass organisation? Is creating an NGO simply a pragmatic ploy to attract foreign funding? Are CBOs really created and founded by ordinary citizens? Are these models of association borrowed from the West, or are they revivals of older Asian institutions? To examine these and related questions, this chapter will first try to understand what civil society means in the context of Vietnam. It will then look at the origins of local NGOs and other social institutions in Vietnam today, linking them to specific Asian associational practices involving a traditional management unit at the level of the village community. Second, it will propose a typology of these new organisations and link them to an emerging civil society. The following questions will be addressed: How far are these organisations really autonomous? How far are state–society relations shaped by what Kerkvliet terms a 'dominating state', some form of 'mobilisational corporatism', or a 'dialogical' rapport between societal groups and the state (2001b: 242–5)? Lastly, the potential influence of these organisations on the political life of the country will be outlined. Are they a revival of traditional institutions, or part of a new democratisation process?

Origins of civil society in Vietnam

What is civil society? This is a large question that can hardly be fully answered here, but Zunetta Liddell's definition is a good place to begin: 'free associations of citizens joined together to work for common concerns, or implement social, cultural, or political initiatives which complement, as well as compete, with the state' (1999: 54). Civil society is clearly separated from the body politic – and from politicians themselves. The concept became very fashionable during the last two decades of the twentieth century, when it became linked to several major global shifts, including: the collapse of the communist bloc, the 'third wave' of democratisation, the decline of the welfare state, and the globalisation of economies produced by widespread liberalisation (Etemadi 2000: 96–7). These changes reflected the failure of earlier modes of social organisation, and generated profound anxieties for many people around the world – not least in Vietnam. The policies of *doi moi* were effectively an acknowledgement that the communist system had failed to deliver the promised goods, both economically and politically. Yet could these failures by the state be remedied simply by 'renovating' existing state structures, or did *doi moi* imply the emergence of new countervailing social organisations, to mirror the emergence of new market forces in the economic sphere? How could the state grant space to new social forces, without risking a substantive loss of social control, and all the attendant potential political consequences? Anxieties generated by developments such as the 1997 Asian economic crisis readily manifested themselves in authoritarian reversions, of a kind seen in policies adopted in the late 1990s to contend with 'social evils' such as prostitution, drug abuse, gambling, karaoke, night clubs – and AIDS (see Templer 1999: 237–56). Such social evils were commonly constructed as direct outcomes of liberalisation and greater openness.

State versus village: Asian communitarianism or civil society?

Edna Co argues that one of the main characteristics of civil society is 'its autonomy and independence from the state' (1996: 192). She asserts that:

... it is the citizenry, and the traditional structures of power, which breathes life to civil society. Its power comes from the power of citizens and their movements, and not necessarily from the legitimate powers of the state, the economy, and politics.

(Co 1996: 192)

In the case of Vietnamese society, attention must be paid to the history of the state, and the role of traditional village structures. Traditionally, Vietnamese society was under the control of the state, and more autonomous activities were limited to the village area. In their traditional village organisation, the Vietnamese used to create associations for such purposes as temple building, organising festivals and creating community solidarity. Associations in pre-modern Vietnam – as in the wider Chinese world – were a tool for managing social space, and for defending the community when threatened with calamities such as invasion, war, famine or natural disasters. Under Chinese rule, the village was far from the capital and from the reach of the state. The relationship between the Vietnamese and the Chinese was a feudal one, akin to ties between vassal and suzerain. In accordance with ancient customary law, Vietnamese villagers retained their own organisations and a degree of autonomy. According to an ancient maxim, 'the Emperor's law surrenders to the village's custom' (*phep vua thua le lang*) (Nguyen Van Huyen 1994: 69).

The Vietnamese village (*lang*) was subdivided into three kinds of administrative or mutual benefit associations: *giap*, associations of male individuals from the same age group; *hoi* (literally, meeting or festival) or *tuong te hoi*, associations of individuals organised for a particular aim and sharing common funds; and *phuong*, associations of individuals from the same profession or from the same field of activity, engaged in mutual assurance activities. In some villages which lacked enough people to create a *phuong*, villagers established a *hoi bach nghe* (literally, hundred crafts association), with the same aim of mutual support (Toan Anh 1999: 90). Thus associations were not so much a source of countervailing power to challenge the state, as a tool for community management, organising economic resources and identifying the village as an associative system. Village-level associations remain to the present day a major dimension of social relations in Vietnam.

Village-level associations lacked official status, and remained independent of the official communal organisation, despite having an influence on the activities of the village. Male individuals – owing to the influence of Confucianism, women were largely excluded – were free either to join or to quit these associations. Historians have failed to find any reference to the activities of these associations in village customary law texts (*huong uoc*) (Nguyen Tu Chi 1993: 130). Since every association had its own rules, village society in pre-colonial Vietnam was characterised by real autonomy and a degree of political power. How can this independence be explained? Society was divided into small elements under the Confucian bureaucratic system, which concentrated its power into small areas and specific administrative entities, according to a pyramidal power organisation. This was a form of divide and rule: the state concentrated on the big picture, thereby tacitly granting a degree of autonomy and invisibility to associative structures at the lower levels. Thus the villagers partly bypassed the official structures of the communal village (*lang xa*), paying their taxes, but avoiding direct state control.

Superficially, the village associations may have appeared apolitical. Yet in both China and Vietnam, political associations have long resembled secret societies, since invisibility and secrecy were prerequisites in times of harsh control and repression by the state. A penchant for secrecy reflects Confucian ideas, which are profoundly anti-individualistic, emphasising communitarianism, mutual assistance, family ties and neighbourhood ties (Vandermeersch 1986: 162). Communitarianism presupposes that an individual as a social being is predetermined by his social relations. In other words, an individual exists and can develop his identity exclusively in relation to membership of a group. In Vietnamese secret societies, this group-based identity took the form of 'brotherhood' ties between members, bound by strict rules. This kind of associative life was quite beyond the jurisdiction of the state.

From colonialism to bureaucratic socialism

During the colonial period, Vietnamese associative practices were modified by the introduction of French rule, and by exposure to French society and ideas. In 1933, French legislation of 1901 concerning association and meeting rights was implemented in Indochina. This law sought to prevent anti-French political activity, and limited the aims of associations. At the same time, Vietnamese students, workers and sailors who travelled to France gained new ideas about democracy, trade unionism and building Western-style associations. They created a strong associative network in major French cities in the 1920s and 1930s, even publishing their own newspapers (Blanc 2003a). This exposure to French ideas of social organisation formed an important inspiration for the Vietnamese nationalist movement and anti-colonial struggle.

Influenced by such ideas, the VCP sought from the outset to employ social organisations as a pillar of its nation-building project, merging together the state apparatus with 'civil society' groups such as associations, in order to create a new nation 'with the people, for the people'. Civil society was integrated into the state through a pyramidal party organisation, a system both centralised and decentralised, reaching right from the capital city into the villages. Through this system of mass organisations, people were supposed to be able to participate in the political process and express themselves. The same system proved invaluable for reunifying the country after 1975. As Georges Boudarel has shown, this method was imported from China to Vietnam (*chinh huan*), and produced a large-scale bureaucratisation of the party, the state and every sector of society (Boudarel *et al.* 1983: 31–106). The lingering presence of neo-Confucianism in Vietnam despite Marxist ideology meant that this process of bureaucratisation was further enhanced: the VCP partially replicated precolonial modes of social organisation, emphasising legalism and rule-bound order. This pervasive legalism, compounded by the bureaucratised manner in which socialism was constructed, produced a heavy-handed and ineffective apparatus, under which grassroots voices could not easily be heard by those at the top. Attempts were made to address the problem in the 1970s by a form of decentralisation, emphasising the role of the districts (Werner 1988: 147–62). Ordinary Vietnamese found themselves required to implement a wide range of directives aimed at increasing agricultural productivity. Since membership of mass organisations was automatic, many supposed 'members' were uncommitted to their assigned roles: all women, for example, were members of the Women's Association, and all peasants were designated members of the Peasants' Association. By the early 1980s, Vietnam was facing severe economic problems resulting from excessive bureaucracy, and a need to promote individual economic initiatives.

Doi moi and social change

Since the implementation of *doi moi* in 1986, there has been a rapid growth in associative groups in every sector of society, including rural and sustainable development, the environment, minority issues, education, the empowerment of women and health. However, these groups have been formed under the jurisdiction of the mass organisations; there is no legal space for people to create an NGO independently from an institutional structure that is linked to the VCP or to Peoples' Committees at the local level. 1957 regulations barring the creation of independent groups have yet to be abrogated. Other laws passed in 1989 and 1990 sought to promote the associative sector, but with limited results (Sidel 1996: 300–1). The only exception remains the Vietnamese Red Cross, which nevertheless reproduces the four-level structure of a mass organisation (central, provincial, district and commune levels) and receives some funding from the government. A 1997 discussion aimed at revising the law on NGOs pointed out again that associations and clubs should belong to one of the mass organisations, or should operate under their umbrella.

More recently, the government has recognised the need for a new legal and policy framework for local associations and NGOs, specifically in supporting poverty reduction programmes. In this respect the 1999 Decree 177/CP on Social Funds, and the 2000 Law on Science and Technology (21/2000/Q10), are important steps in the direction of creating a new legal framework for associations and domestic NGOs. For the first time, scientific and technological research organisations, whether government or independent, are now granted autonomy in the development of ideas and research topics related to economic development and addressing social problems. Overseas Vietnamese communities have also been invited to participate in this area of research.

Media and newspapers remain under relatively strict control; most newspapers and journals are under the jurisdiction of one or other ministry or mass organisation. They have to request authorisation prior to publication, submitting the content of their articles to the Ministry of Culture and Information for approval. In 1999, the National Assembly passed amendments to the Press Law, making the Ministry of Culture and Information responsible for all media outlets, and for the Internet (Heng 2001: 217–20). Yet this restrictive legal framework does not mean that

Vietnamese news media ignore pressing social problems. The Ho Chi Minh City newspaper *Tuoi Tre*, for example, regularly carries critical coverage of social issues and corruption cases (for examples, see Gainsborough 2003: 83–90). Nevertheless, the media is always conscious of operating within tight boundaries; the authorities may license more open discussion of particular stories or issues, but this does not amount to a general lifting of controls (see Abuza 2001: 131–60). Censorship is not simply a matter of limiting coverage of sensitive political issues, but also includes moral censorship. In July 2003, an issue of *Sinh Vien* magazine – a popular publication of the Ho Chi Minh Youth Union – was banned because of a cover showing a wooden statue of a couple making love. This image was criticised for inappropriately encouraging young people to engage in early sexual activity.

Typology of civil organisations

What is an NGO in Vietnam? The term 'NGO' has grown increasingly popular during the post-*doi moi* period, denoting a modern organisation engaged in development activities. Yet defining the term precisely is more difficult in the Vietnamese context. Gerard Clarke has defined NGOs as 'private, non-profit, professional organisations with a distinctive legal character, concerned with public welfare goals' (1998: 2–3). Yet given the legal framework in Vietnam, it is not easy to consider NGOs separately from state or party organisations. While in most developing countries NGOs can offer livelihood alternatives for people who are unable to find positions in the traditional sector, the legal position of Vietnamese NGOs makes this difficult.

Where a Vietnamese NGO (VNGO) is linked to a governmental mass organisation, how does it differ from that mass organisation? The crucial difference is that VNGOs do not receive financial support from the government, but from foreign NGOs, United Nations (UN) agencies, or private donors. In some cases, VNGOs are not 'professional' groups as defined by Clarke, but CBOs, operating locally, and often with no full-time staff. International donors often prefer to support CBOs, since they meet their criteria for promoting 'bottom up' grassroots participation. Yet the bureaucratisation of the aid business in Vietnam means that not all funding reaches the intended recipients: all international aid is channelled through the Ministry of Investment and Planning, leading to considerable frustration on the part of donors.

Vietnamese CBOs seek to exploit the limited legal scope for autonomous associative activity as best they can. Since the early 1990s, most CBOs working on HIV/AIDS prevention have obtained permission from the VUSTA (Vietnamese Union of Scientists and Technicians Associations), which includes medical doctors' associations. Hanoi-based CBOs have generally registered at the Department of Sciences, Technologies and the Environment, which comes under the People's Committee. While some HIV/AIDS CBOs are founded by doctors, others are set up by social scientists and intellectuals, including retirees. Young doctors are typically involved in running private clinics, charging fees to better-off clients, but offering free services for the less well-off. Such clinics create employment for these doctors, since there are insufficient junior posts available in public hospitals: the result is an organisation from which everyone involved benefits. In Vietnam, patients suffering from sexually transmitted infections (STIs) are generally reluctant to attend public clinics because of cultural norms, not to mention the lack of confidentiality and personal attention available. In the more discreet setting of a private, humanitarian STI clinic, doctors can offer better treatment, as well as a range of preventive information and counselling.

In this respect, CBOs take advantage of windows of legal opportunity, notably the Party's Central Committee Decree No. 52-CT/TW of 11 March 1995, urging everybody to fight the AIDS epidemic (Blanc 2000: 177–82). Previously, preventive education programmes aimed at prostitutes or drug users were considered illegal, because of the illegal activities in which the target groups were engaged. For example, distributing condoms or clean syringes could be considered as encouraging negative behaviour, and state officials were obliged to act at all times in accordance with party ethics. Since they were not state officials, CBOs were able to carry out such programmes without breaking the law.

There are clear regional variations in CBO activity. In the North, especially in Hanoi, CBOs appear to be more developed, carrying out surveys openly, distributing preventive information, and starting to organise peer education training. They have less interest in taking care of AIDS patients, however, and often include HIV/AIDS within a broader programme of STI-related activity. In Ho Chi Minh City, by contrast, there is a greater tolerance of religion and a wide range of informal charity initiatives. Both Catholics and Buddhists are active in charity organisations that emphasise caring for the sick. Morbidity and mortality linked to AIDS has been more visible in the South. But at first the authorities were reluctant to allow such religious organisations to operate; only the mass organisations – already more active in the South – have the right to provide social assistance to the population. The government was afraid that the solidarity structures of the former Southern regime might be revived. In practice, however, mass organisation structures tend to be ineffective in poor areas, and in places where prostitution, drug addiction and delinquency occur. Usually the police are more active in such places, but this only makes the task of prevention or education more difficult. When a CBO starts to operate, it is always under strict police scrutiny. The overseas Vietnamese community plays a major role in fund-raising for CBOs in the South (Blanc 2003a: 277, 342). In part, this is because strengthening civil society in Vietnam seems an attractive project for those abroad who hope to stimulate democratic change within the country. Networks of overseas Vietnamese communities, often making use of the Internet, are crucial in ensuring the sustainability of these CBOs.

In Ho Chi Minh City, for example, CBOs direct their activities concerning sex education towards specific sectors of the populations, such as high-risk groups, homeless adolescents and street children. Unlike the mass organisations, they are able to establish close contact with slum-dwellers, adopting flexible ways of managing their organisations. They distance themselves from the state bureaucracy by avoiding daily meetings, saving time and keeping expenses to a minimum, partly by using very little office space. Templer discusses the 'rare energetic buzz' at the office of one such group in Saigon, 'a hothouse of degeneracy in the eyes of many Vietnamese' (1999: 238). They are typically based close to 'hot-spots' and red-light districts, have a good feel for the concerns of their target groups, and are well-placed to help solve pressing problems. Their previous experience with international NGOs is often invaluable. Many of them come from disadvantaged sections of the population – they may be former drug users or prostitutes themselves – and most were adolescents at the end of the war, an important generational issue in Vietnam. These CBOs use methods favoured by international NGOs, such as 'peer education', adapting them to local conditions. By contrast, youth clubs belonging to mass organisations such as the Youth League are less efficient, since despite recent efforts to assist street children, their main focus has always been children at school. There is usually a social gap between peer educators trained by the Youth League and young street children, making peer educational methods less effective.

In the South, alliances emerged between private charities and social workers; post-1975, social work emerged as a new profession (Nguyen Thi Oanh 1998), and a range of professional and private organisations were created after the onset of *doi moi*. The Vietnamese founders of CBOs in the South maintain good relations with international NGOs working in Southeast Asia on related issues. Many of them worked for foreign NGOs or for UN agencies such as the United Nations Children's Fund, the United Nations Development Programme or the World Health Organisation (WHO), gaining valuable experience before establishing local organisations. By contrast, NGO staff in the North more commonly began by working for one of the governmental mass organisations.

In 1997, the National AIDS Committee (NAC) estimated in a report that around 40 local non-profit organisations had been established in Vietnam since 1994 to work on HIV/AIDS prevention and care, some defining themselves as NGOs, and others as clubs or associations (Chung A. *et al.* 1997: 14). Some of these were newly created or had been initiated by the NAC, but all of them were working under the umbrella of a mass organisation. The majority were associations of medical doctors at provincial or district levels. These 'AIDS activists', and associations led by people living with HIV or AIDS (PLWHA), could engage in social mobilisation, but only at the district level, and mainly by assisting poor patients in hospitals or at home. They lacked sufficient resources or financial support to extend the scope of their activities. PLWHA groups often worked in large cities, working under the control of the district level health department.

As Janine Bardot demonstrated in the case of France (1999: 160), there are two patterns found in movements to combat AIDS: the 'mediators', and the 'victims'. The 'mediators' are commonly found in the VNGOs of Hanoi, which typically advocate general and medical approaches to the management of the epidemic. The 'victims' are far from the capital geographically, socially or politically, and are recruited from marginalised groups such as disadvantaged people, prostitutes, intra-venous drug users and homosexuals, who are members of CBOs. The Vietnamese HIV/AIDS movement is like a catalyst for social change. As Templer puts it,

'HIV presents Vietnam with an array of economic, political, social and moral issues that it has never dealt with before' (1999: 238). The division between North and South Vietnam on these issues is a striking problem, more than 25 years after reunification.

Concluding remarks: a democratisation process?

The development of NGOs in Vietnam is not homogenous, and is based upon different social groups in different parts of the country. In the North, mainly in Hanoi, these organisations spring mainly from the initiatives of intellectuals, scientists, doctors and local officials. This 'intellectual elite' is concerned mainly with development and improvements in social policy. In the South, especially in Ho Chi Minh City, people involved in CBOs come from different social strata: intellectuals, journalists, scientists and social workers are middle-class professionals. Their focus is more on the disempowered strata of society, with an emphasis on social service and social activism rather than policy research. Arguably, then, civil society is more developed in the South, and more open to different social strata. Could it be said that this is a more democratic civil society? The creation of domestic NGOs is based on the emergence of agents of change, based mainly on a new-born middle class which is playing a different role in building a new sort of society (Wischermann *et al.* 2002). The industrialisation of Vietnam is one major factor in this change, leading to the emergence of a new class of professionals in urban areas where individualism is more widespread.

The emergence of civil society groups linked to the struggle against AIDS has revealed social fractures. Where pressing economic, social and educational needs emerge, CBOs are most likely to provide an adequate response. When traditional family-based structures come under strain from critical problems such as AIDS, CBOs offer the basis for an alternative form of community and solidarity. This new mode of community strongly reflects social changes produced by a growing economic differentiation between rich and poor. CBOs have recently been gaining in self-confidence. For example, in November 2001 four delegations of PLWHA gathered in Hanoi for the first time, voicing concerns and making recommendations to the authorities and mass organisations. They called for an end to discrimination against HIV-positive people, and asked for support to build a better prevention network. These four delegations came from Hanoi, Ho Chi Minh City, Quang Ninh and Thanh Hoa – the latter are disadvantaged provinces badly affected by the epidemic. The meeting was held under the auspices of a VNGO known as the Centre of Public Health and Development (CEPHAD), with support from the WHO representative in Vietnam.

Despite their achievements, CBOs remain trapped in a shadowy realm between HIV/AIDS sufferers and the Vietnamese state. While CBOs are nominally state-approved, the value of their work has never been officially recognised. They are therefore unable to participate in developing new social or medical provisions for the needs of AIDS patients – a problem common to AIDS activist groups around the world (Epstein 1996), yet exacerbated by the structure of state–society relations in Vietnam, which provides no natural home for such a sphere of activity. Social discrimination could ultimately push the poorest and most disadvantaged PLWHA out of the AIDS-prevention and healthcare system. PLWHA associations now find the very basis of their citizenship put to the test: are their members real, active, engaged and useful citizens, or merely weak and disempowered patients? Issues such as HIV/AIDS raise difficult questions about what it means to be a Vietnamese citizen.

State officials in Vietnam are generally unsympathetic to associative culture. 'Statism' (Wischermann *et al.* 2002: 23) and Vietnamese state culture, stemming from Confucian formalism, are big obstacles to the democratisation process, and to the participation of domestic NGOs in social policy and other sectors. As shown by Thayer (1995), Vietnam is characterised by a mono-organisational model of state–society relations. In certain respects, Vietnamese NGOs and CBOs are working like villages in the past, managing their own problems, and finding their own solutions with help from the capital. David Koh (2001b: 282) is right to point out that people 'frequently breached the party-state's boundaries in several key socio-economic policy areas'. Solidarity exists in disadvantaged wards in large cities: urban people – themselves often ex-villagers – have been able to improvise their own associative lives, combining their own know-how and available means by mixing traditional *hoi* with Western-style NGO structures. Meetings can be held in parks, in streets or even on beaches, offering laboratories for experiments in local and grassroots democracy. Recently, the People's Committee of the Ho Chi Minh City granted the first ever official permit to a domestic NGO in the social work field. This might seem like a positive step, but this sort of permission could be a prelude to regulation or co-optation.

Nevertheless, Vietnamese NGOs and CBOs are playing an increasing part in the development of a fledgling civil society. To some extent, they draw upon a longstanding Vietnamese tradition of local-level associative structures operating beyond the reach of the state. So long as their concerns are localised, they pose little challenge to the existing order and may readily be tolerated. Their difficulties come when they seek to organise themselves into networks and alternative structures capable of lobbying the state for resources, or for substantive changes in social policy. Generational and geographical divides in Vietnam are highly salient in explaining the character of associational life. Associations working on HIV/AIDS assume different characters in different parts of the country, reflecting contrasting modes of social order that predate unification. Civil society is arguably more developed in the South, where a mode of activist citizenship is better established. In Hanoi, CBOs and NGOs typically have a more conservative orientation, and are less likely to challenge or subvert state-led programmes. Relatively few younger people are actively engaged in the process of building up voluntary associations, which are typically seen as a preserve of the elderly and the senior. Overall, foreign donors and international agencies are agreed that Vietnam needs more non-governmental bodies able to serve as real partners in policy building and imple-mentation. More than any other social problem, the HIV/AIDS issue is helping to prompt a rethinking of state–society relations and the nature of civil society in

Vietnam. While many continue to argue for the 'dominating state' view that 'pressure for political reform comes from within the Communist Party itself' (Abuza 2001: 179), there is evidence that some CBOs are struggling to create greater democratic space through issue-based grassroots work that confronts some of the fundamental divides in Vietnamese society.

12 Pursuing success in present-day Vietnam

Young graduates in Hanoi

Phuong An Nguyen

In Vietnam, people belonging to the 15–30 age group account for about 30 per cent of the population. Of this 30 per cent, university students and graduates account for a mere 2 per cent (Nguyen Van Trung 1996: 66–7). Although young people with university education make up a very small proportion of the youth population, university graduates are interesting subjects for research for two main reasons. Firstly, in the context of a modernising Vietnam, knowledge has been increasingly recognised as crucial to achieving the goal of modernisation. Thus people with higher education and knowledge, including university graduates, have been given greater attention by the state – as compared to the 'socialist' period before *doi moi*, when greater emphasis was placed upon peasant and worker youths. Hence there is now an increasing need to study young university graduates. Secondly, as university graduates tend to concentrate in large urban areas (simply due to the geographic locations of major universities in Vietnam), this segment of youth is particularly exposed to the ongoing economic changes and social transformations taking place in the country. Therefore, by studying graduates and their interactions with socio-economic developments in the country, we can gain valuable insights into the social transformations currently taking place in Vietnam.

With the aim of gaining further understanding of present-day Vietnamese society, I undertook research among young graduates in Hanoi. During 12 months of fieldwork in Hanoi in 2000, I conducted in-depth interviews with a total of 75 university graduates under the age of 30, of whom 38 were men and 37 women. Loosely structured interviews and participant observation were the main mode of investigation and data collection throughout my fieldwork. As a local young graduate myself, I was able readily to participate in this community to learn first-hand the ways in which these young Vietnamese themselves experience and interpret their lives. I also had countless casual conversations with people, young and old, whom I encountered in various contexts. It was difficult to quantify these informal conversations, because their duration varied: some lasted for only 20 minutes, but others were lengthy and involved. However, these informal conversations were valuable and they helped to provide me with background and insights into various social realities, spark ideas, or confirm my findings on certain aspects of social life.

Although conversations with young graduates often started on various issues and subjects, it soon became clear to me that most interviewees were greatly concerned with the matters of employment and career. This partly reflects the competitiveness of a labour market entered by more than 1.7 million new workers annually (*Youth in Vietnam* 2000: 17). It also reflects the fact that young graduates are anxious to achieve success in their career and profession. Based on this observation, and on information derived from interviews, this chapter will discuss the perceptions of 'success' in post-*doi moi* Vietnam, and examine ways in which these urban young graduates are attempting to achieve it.

Success as a key concept

My discussion on the shifts in the idea of 'success' and ways of achieving it in Vietnamese society starts with an assumption borrowed from psychology that all individuals have acquired a 'motive to achieve' and a 'motive to avoid failure'. In other words, all persons have some capacity for interest in achievement and some capacity for anxiety about failure. Both are expressed in any situation when it is apparent to the individual that his/her performance will be evaluated in reference to some standard (Atkinson 1974: 18). This is a useful starting point, because it provides the conceptual tool needed for analysing and explaining various patterns of behaviours, concerns and activities of young people throughout this research. That is to say, as Vietnamese young university graduates have a 'motive to achieve', their activities and behaviours are characterised by the struggle to *achieve* an end, and upon achieving this end they consider themselves, and are considered by their peers and their society as a whole, as being *successful*. Within this framework of motivation, 'motive to achieve' is the starting point, and 'success' is the important end, thus success implies actually achieving something that one aims for.

The notion of success was discussed as early as the sixth century BC, as seen through the writings of ancient Greeks such as Hesiod, Solon and Theognis (Pahl 1995: 25). In the context of Greek society in antiquity, new sources of wealth were permitting the emergence of prosperous landowners; the prevailing conception of success was associated with possession of great wealth. However, already at that time, there had been questions about whether great wealth on its own was sufficient for achieving 'true success' (see more on the origin of the notion of success in Pahl 1995: 25–31).

The rapid growth of modern industrial capitalism gave rise to a new, modern conception of success, and early writings on this new notion can be found in Weber's works. In *The Protestant Ethic and the Spirit of Capitalism* (1930/1995), Weber described modern capitalism as a social power that forces people to subject themselves to the social conditions it has created, regardless of whether or not they are willing (Mommsen 1989: 57). This is where the spirit of modern capitalism, the fierce competitive struggle, was set to work. Weber argued that 'the conditions of capitalist success were implacable: those who could not, or would not, accept them either went under or, at best, stayed where they were' (Pahl 1995: 22).

Early ideas of success had perhaps placed too much emphasis on a 'rather narrow male, elitist version of success', and primarily on the acquisition of wealth (Pahl 1995: 18). Since then, during the past century or so, the notion of success has been constantly evolving. There exist many variants of success, including fame, occupational success, possession of wealth, or even 'successful' marriage. Furthermore, notions of success differ greatly from one culture to another; people of differing cultures interpret 'success' differently. The idea of success is full of ambiguity, and there is no universally accepted definition for it. Hence, and more usefully for this, I will now discuss the notions of success in the specific context of Vietnam.

Notions of success in Vietnam prior to *doi moi*

In Vietnamese society prior to 1945, the sole path to success for men (not women) was through study in order to pass the mandarin examinations. Starting from the Tran dynasty (1225–1400), mandarin competitions, held at the Temple of Literature on a regular basis, were open to educated common men from all over the country. Passing the examinations meant much more than scholarly success, especially for ordinary men, as it would enable them to leave 'the ranks of the people to enter the mandarin "caste"' (Nguyen Khac Vien 1974: 26). Even after failing to become a mandarin, if one came back to village life as a Confucian scholar and a schoolteacher, one would be held in high esteem by all the villagers. Such prospects gave the incentive for many young men to study. As education became more popular with the opening of many private schools in almost all villages to train and prepare young men for the mandarin examinations, young men of a lower social background were then given the opportunity to compete for entry into the feudal class (Buttinger 1958: 289). Women, on the other hand, did not have access to study, nor could they sit the mandarin examinations: as a consequence, the dominant notion of success, chiefly associated with gaining social status by way of study, was solely restricted to men.

The idea of achieving success by means of study came into existence during the feudal period, and persisted until the end of French colonial rule in the mid-1950s, despite the fact that under French colonialism there was a sharp decline in the numbers of schools (Duiker 1976: 130). Education was not widespread and was by this time limited only to the urban middle class. However, the route to success was still widely perceived by the Vietnamese as through study. Tran Trong Kim, French-educated and a prominent writer, wrote in 1929 that

> Any one of these young people who obtained an education became a success. They all gained some position of status, never mind how, sufficient to win the respect of the general public … It is recognised that for making one's way in this world it could not be otherwise …
>
> (quoted in Jamieson 1993: 95)

After the French colonial period, the socialist state in northern Vietnam called for an era of 'building socialism in the North and liberalising the South'. It was around this time that a radical change in the notion of success occurred. As people became drawn into this national cause, the sense of 'individualism' and the associated notion of 'individual success' greatly declined. A new collective notion of success was conceived and widely disseminated, with novels and songs serving as highly effective means to communicate the idea to the masses (Jamieson 1993: 222). In the wartime period of 1954–75, the collective notion of success meant collective action and collective strength to achieve the 'great victory' of reunification. With the onset of peacetime after reunification in 1975, this notion was reinterpreted to refer to the eradication of private ownership and building socialism in the entire country. As there was virtually no private ownership, it was impossible to become individually rich. Individual success stories were stories of farmers and workers, in co-operatives and factories, with high production records.

However, another route to success remained accessible to the masses in peacetime socialist Vietnam: study. Bright young men and women, who passed university entrance examinations with high results and had the right political credentials, would be sent abroad, mainly to universities in the Union of Soviet Socialist Republics (USSR) and Eastern Europe. As with the mandarins of the past, families of the young people who were sent abroad to study took great pride in their academic achievements. Many of the students returning from studying in Eastern Europe and other socialist countries went on to hold key positions in the government. In other words, they achieved to some extent professional success as individuals – and by extension on behalf of their families – but they had to put this 'personal' achievement to the service of the greater success of the collectivity. As they were sent abroad by 'the people', represented by the socialist state, they were told that they were the best seeds, and their efforts at study were to contribute to the cause of socialism.

In sum, success was a rather restricted notion. There existed no socialist conception of 'individual success' in the sense of choosing one's own route in the course of life to achieve one's own personal goals. Personal achievements would not have been perceived nor recognised as success unless they categorically contributed to the cause of socialism. In the centrally planned and subsidised system, where the state possessed control over the distribution and circulation of goods and daily life necessities for the people, the notion and the measure of success were amongst those many things – from food and essential goods, jobs, housing to ideology – distributed by the state.

Success in a market economy: another cycle unfolds?

By the late 1980s when *doi moi* was launched, a top priority for the Vietnamese leadership was to overcome economic stagnation and achieve growth. Market-oriented policies have since abolished the state's subsidy system (*bao cap*), allowed private ownership of business and production, liberalised internal and external trade, and encouraged foreign investment and business. As the goal of *doi moi* set out by the state and the Party is '*Dan giau, nuoc manh, xa hoi cong bang van minh*' (Wealthy people, strong country, equal and civilised society), people were encouraged to engage individually in economic activities. To a certain extent, such a call for 'wealthy people, strong country' resembles China's Deng Xiaoping announcement in the early 1980s that 'to get rich is glorious'. With this slogan, he issued 'a rallying cry to Chinese youth as alluring as the refrain of any pop ballad' (Tesoro 2000: 36). In Vietnam since *doi moi* the power of wealth has been similarly legitimised, and even glorified. By the 1990s, not only had people's anxieties about getting rich and staying rich been allayed, but also the dream of getting rich had become a common goal.

Consequently, young people seem to realise that achieving individual success by way of becoming wealthy professionals fits well with the overall national objectives. Ngoc Anh (male, 28) is a graduate of Russian language from the former Hanoi Foreign Language Teachers Training University (now part of Hanoi National University). In early 2000 he started his own advertising firm by borrowing money from his cousins: during his first year in business he billed his clients a total of US $200,000 and broke even. In September of the same year, the *Asian Wall Street Journal*, reporting on Vietnam's advertising industry, cited Ngoc Anh's firm as a prime example for the nascent but expanding market-driven industry in the country under reformation. His eight-person agency was described in the article as 'resourceful, young and energetic'; it might still do smaller jobs for the time being, but aspired to take on more prestigious and creative projects from big clients and enter into a partnership with a big foreign agency (Flagg 2000).

I met successful Ngoc Anh one evening in a café on Ly Thuong Kiet Street, a street café in the French quarter of Hanoi frequented by 'yuppies' (young, upwardly mobile professional people) – assuming such a term can be relevant in Vietnam. Casually dressed in baggy trousers and a check shirt, he had just emerged from work. But even in the café, he was still busy talking business with clients on the phone. In between two telephone conversations, he told me: 'My clients are mainly foreigners, since only foreign firms could afford the kind and quality of service I'm offering. At the moment, I'm preparing to open an office in Ho Chi Minh City as well.' For Ngoc Anh, creative advertising has long been a passion. Several years back whilst he was working in different jobs for a number of different foreign firms in Hanoi, he had already focused on learning the skills and expertise of public relations and advertising, and establishing contacts with a view to setting up his own firm one day. Today, he is the director and owner of a business, employer to a handful of other youths, and a business partner in a number of large foreign companies. He is also fluent in English, and has travelled extensively abroad on business.

Among my interviewees, Quoc and Phuoc are other examples of young graduates seeking to get rich by setting up their own businesses. They are both 26 years of age, come from poor families in suburban villages, and moved to Hanoi to attend university. Upon graduation they both remained in the capital city and worked for a foreign company for three years. It was at this company that they became friends. Together they decided to quit the firm, borrowed money from friends and family relatives, and set up a company of their own to manufacture bamboo and lacquerware products. They work so hard that they 'have no idea what Saturdays and Sundays are'. After over a year in business, they now employ 40 workers, and have a modern production workshop in a hi-tech industrial park adjacent to Hanoi. Their products are exported to Europe and the United States of America. They also told me of their plans to market their products on the Internet so as to reach more clients directly and to expand their production further.

The number of success stories similar to those of Ngoc Anh, Quoc and Phuoc is still small: only four of my 75 interviewees were self-employed. However, their successes are recognised and admired by the wider youth as well as by society at large: in the national media there have recently been more and more stories of *cac doanh nghiep tre* (young enterprises), featuring young men and women, who succeeded in their entrepreneurial endeavours, and many of whom come from poor family backgrounds. Their successes are significant especially in a context where self-employment is still a new concept and practice, made possible only since *doi moi* and the introduction of a multisector market economy, and where there is a widely held belief that the power of wealth is a prerequisite for seizing business opportunities. Trinh Duy Luan (2000: 42) noted that in today's society, only those already advantaged possess the prerequisites to be able to become affluent groups: hence the already well-off will become even richer. Many young people also seem to share this belief that wealth is the key to success in the market economy. When asked to identify 'factors that determine failure or success of business', 62 per cent of all youths in the 1995 national survey consider capital as the decisive factor, by far the highest rating compared to other factors such as experience (35 per cent), occupational skills (34 per cent), education (31 per cent), and opportunity (24 per cent) (Thai Duy Tuyen 1995: 121). In this context, the successes of *cac doanh nghiep tre* are admired by other youths, because although these entrepreneurs did not possess the power of wealth to start with, they dared to set up their own businesses. Through determination, knowledge and hard work, they have been able to capitalise on the opening up of the country and eventually become successful.

Many other graduates might not be up to establishing their own businesses, but seek professional and financial success through other routes. Take Le (female, 26) for example. She started her job at an American law firm in 1995 as an interpreter and secretary, with a starting net salary of US $200 per month.

> The reason for my choice of the firm was not because of money, but because I was hoping for a chance to actually learn a profession, and that I liked law. During the first years I worked as a secretary, but I had also asked to be sent to an accounting course ... It was a short course and soon after finishing it, I was assigned to be in charge of the secretarial, translation work and the accounting work for the whole office ... In 1996, I applied for a course to read for a law degree. Classes were everyday after work and I did it for three years ... I've now taken up the position of a lawyer. My current [net] salary is 1,000 [US] dollars per month, and more importantly I like this job.
>
> (Le, interviewed in Hanoi, August 2000)

She also said that compared with some 16 ex-classmates of hers from university, she was one of the highest earners. Her willingness to tell her story, combined with the pride in her voice, showed that she saw herself as having achieved success in both financial and professional terms. To her, hard work and further training after university had been her route to career success.

In-depth interviews with other graduates show that further study is widely seen as the route to success, even for those who have already achieved certain successes in business and career. Ngoc Anh, for example, is still anxious about obtaining further training and sees it as essential for further achievements:

> I need further training for skills and knowledge of business management, so an MBA [Master of Business Administration] is necessary. But not an MBA from a home university. What I need is real knowledge and that can only be attained at a university overseas. The only problem is that my business is still new, so I'm sort of stuck here. I don't have the heart to leave it to go to university abroad. I'd have to wait for a while until everything is up and running smoothly, then I can leave business to someone else to take care of it for me, and go for a year or so to study.
>
> (Ngoc Anh, interviewed in Hanoi, November 2000)

Nowadays, further study after graduating from university has indeed been a very popular phenomenon amongst Vietnamese youths. Often such further training or *hoc them*[1] is for the purpose of getting a job, or for career advancement. In this research, as many as 34 people have either already attained or been attending a course leading to a second bachelor's or a postgraduate degree. Ten other people said they would soon attend a course for an additional bachelor's degree. All these 44 people stated that they undertake *hoc them* in order to improve their employment and career prospects. Results from the 1995 nationwide survey also confirmed that youths today tend to take up further training not for academic purposes, but primarily because of employment and career considerations. Of the 1,542 young men and women under 30 years who were asked to identify their motives of *hoc them*, 59 per cent of all said that they undertake further training in order to make it easier to find a job, 37 per cent mentioned the goal of achieving career success, and 15 per cent said they undertake further training in order to change occupation. For university graduate interviewees in this nationwide survey, these percentages are as high as 84, 58 and 16 per cent respectively (Thai Duy Tuyen 1995: 124).

On the one hand, the widespread phenomenon of young people's *hoc them* shows that university graduates today have a clearer understanding of the importance of education for success. Learning for new skills and higher qualifications increased the competitiveness of the graduate in a market economy. On the other hand, it reflects the inability of local universities to turn out qualified graduates to meet the demands of the job market. Whilst the nation develops and modernises, and the demands of employers are growing, university training remains rigid and unrealistic. A professor from Hanoi National University told me that at present universities were subject to the government's prescribed curriculum and so no universities were able to provide tailor-made degree courses adjusted to the needs of the market. According to him, Ministry of Education regulations require all students to do compulsory subjects such as physical education, national defence education, political economy, philosophical thoughts of Marxism–Leninism, the science of socialism, the history of the VCP, and Ho Chi Minh thought. The teaching of these many compulsory subjects takes up to 49 per cent of the 210-credit curriculum, leaving specialised subjects accounting for 25 per cent, employment-related skills (such as research methods, English, and information technology (IT)) accounting for 21 per cent, and the final dissertation accounting for only 5 per cent. He said that his students do not receive enough relevant training to prepare themselves for the job market, and the teaching staff of the department share the view on the need to reduce the number and extent of compulsory subjects in the curriculum.[2] Before the system of higher education receives a real shake-up, *hoc them* by the individual youth remains a micro-level solution to a macro-level problem.

Further training can range from simply learning a foreign language and computer skills, to re-skilling for a whole new profession and attending higher education at postgraduate level. In a globalising Vietnam, computer skills and English are among the four most popular subjects that youths undertake *hoc them*, with the other two being economics and law. Graduates whom I spoke to are of the view that in the market economy those with a good command of English and/ or with qualifications in the areas of IT, trade and law are in great demand. Evening classes at universities such as *Dai hoc Kinh te Quoc dan* (National University of Economics), *Dai hoc Ngoai Thuong* (University of Foreign Trade), *Dai hoc Luat* (University of Law) and *Dai hoc Ngoai ngu* (University of Foreign Languages) are packed with young graduates reading for a second degree in one of these subject areas.

Whilst many youths attend classes after work, further training can also be undertaken through work. There are four major business sectors in which my interviewees work. These are the state sector (including work for the government and in state-owned enterprises), the foreign/joint-venture sector, local private businesses and self-employment. Often young graduates cited further education, or chances of it, as a major reason for their selecting work in one employment sector rather than another. The qualifications and knowledge gained would in turn help to advance their career.

Each employment sector provides its own opportunities for the young graduate to learn. Many people choose to work in the state sector for opportunities for a scholarship to study abroad. My interviewees unanimously stated that going overseas for higher education has always been a major aspiration. Nilan (1999: 360) even asserts that studying abroad has become a 'key objective' of 'middle-class' educated youths. Degrees gained abroad are widely regarded as passports to active participation in the country's process of integration into the outside world. However, the high tuition fees and the general costs of living overseas have made it a dream hard to realise for the majority of Vietnamese youths. The best chance for young graduates who cannot afford overseas education is to station themselves in government offices, preferably in research institutes, ministries or large governmental organisations, and keep applying for various scholarship schemes until one is granted (Nguyen Phuong An 2002: 233). Scholarships are available in the state sector thanks to various co-operative programmes, both governmental and institutional, and the government's recent policy to fund overseas postgraduate programmes for young officials. During the 1990s some 14,000 people were granted scholarships as part of co-operative programmes and aid agreements with foreign countries, and the government also uses its own budget to send 350 'young scientists' annually to study overseas during the period 1999 to 2005 (*Vietnam News*, 1 September 1999). However, these scholarships are restricted to employees on the state payroll (*Vietnam Economic Times*, 10 May 2001). As a result, for many young graduates, employment in the state sector with a scholarship opportunity in sight has become a viable path towards realising their aspirations in education and training.

In the non-state employment sector, there are not so many opportunities available for overseas scholarships. However, it does not mean that young graduates do not have occasions to learn. Outside the state sector, young employees can search for challenging jobs, where they not only can test their abilities, but also learn new skills (Nguyen Phuong An 2002). Normally these are practical skills such as foreign languages, IT, communication and management skills. They learn these skills through work and practice in their daily jobs. Although this type of practical training does not lead to degrees, young graduates can start learning as soon as they begin their employment, instead of having to wait for their applications for a scholarship to be successful as in the case of employment in the state sector. Being equipped with these skills means that young graduates are becoming more professional and subsequently enjoying a greater earning capacity. As Vietnam opens its doors and integrates with the outside world, these pragmatic skills and knowledge are indispensable and increasingly demanded by employers, yet they have not been sufficiently taught in university courses or most government offices.

There exists a slight difference in the routes of success for employees in the state and the non-state sectors. In the state sector, gaining a scholarship to study abroad is widely seen as a primary goal and a first step towards success. In the non-state sector, on the other hand, making money and becoming rich are equally important as learning professional knowledge and skills. In other words, the route to professional success in the non-state sector is through simultaneously achieving both financial and professional gains, but in the state sector, it is often the case that qualifications and knowledge lead to success later in one's career.

Personal success and beyond

This chapter has focused on young graduates' concern to achieve success in terms of career and wealth. However, this does by no means connote that these young people overlook achievements in the family and domestic sphere. Further data from my research (Nguyen Phuong An 2003) shows that although young graduates are very much concerned about success in terms of career and finance, they are also concerned about achieving harmony and happiness in various interpersonal relationships, particularly relationships with parents and love relationships. They carry on the traditions of maintaining strong links with parents and the family, respecting older people, and obeying parents' opinions with regard to a 'compatible' marriage. Their notion of success in life would be incomplete and imbalanced if it contained only professional and financial gains, and lacked aspects of family success. Data from my interviews suggest that amid social change, young graduates regard ingredients for success in family life as still including 'traditional' corner-stones such as filial piety through respectful, harmonious and loving relationships with the parents and finding a 'compatible' spouse – a crucial element both for marital success and for fulfilling filial piety. These underpin the emphasis on the institution of the family and its values.

Indeed, there is for them a wide range of aspects incorporated in the making of a successful life. A young man, for example, may strive for potential professional success by acquiring a foreign degree. His parents might boast of his academic and professional achievements, but at the same time they feel ashamed of the fact that he was going out with a girl that they deemed 'incompatible' for him. They might also long for him to get married because they would want grandchildren. On the other hand, his partner may not be too happy either, because she might find him too 'flirtatious' and not committed enough to their relationship. At the same time, she herself might have completed university, or even postgraduate studies, and wanted to delay marriage to achieve professional success. However, her parents or even her partner might be of a different view. What should she do to achieve her own ideas of success? There also exist questions such as how other portions of the Vietnamese youth population perceive 'success'.

These and many similar questions points to the fact that discussion of young people's perception of 'success' is not simple, inasmuch as *doi moi* has brought about a diverse and complex reality, and Vietnamese youth is 'no longer a monotonous, rigid, and uniformly moulded group as in the central planning time, but they now comprise diversified and energetic groups, which are becoming increasingly complex and difficult to recognise' (Dang Canh Khanh 1996: 23).

Conclusion

Though it seems that the perception of 'achieving through learning' goes back as far as the feudal society in the thirteenth century, the notion of success has clearly evolved through different periods in Vietnamese history. Before the establishment of a socialist state, only men had access to studies and mandarin examinations. Success was then a gendered notion, and essentially was directed at gaining the status of a mandarin. Subsequently, during the colonial period, despite the diminishing education system, success continued to be perceived as something to be achieved through learning.

Under the socialist regime, women were regarded as equal to men. Everybody could be successful as long as (s)he contributed to the collective and the general cause of building socialism. Now in the market economy, success is no longer an across-the-board notion defined by the socialist state. That is to say, success prior to the 1990s was a 'nationalised' notion, but in the *doi moi* era it has been 'privatised'.

As seen through the stories of my interviewees, young people today work hard and compete not because the state tells them to do so, but rather because of their own desired goals. Furthermore, data I collected from the field do not indicate that young people distinguish between the notions of such professional and financial success for men and women. Young women can dream as ambitiously as young men, and – as in the socialist period – can achieve the same success.

Vietnam has rapidly transformed from *bao cap* – a fully subsidised and centrally planned system in which the state ensured the provision of everything, including goods, services, jobs, housing, education and ideology – to a system in which private ownership is allowed and market mechanisms operate. When the state's provision have ceased to exist, and when the conditions of a market economy are competitive, the individual is expected to exert personal efforts to survive and acquire what (s)he desires. To a certain extent, young graduates' focus on professional and financial success amid the country's transition to a market economy is similar to Weber's description of the achievement of 'capitalist success' as discussed earlier in this chapter. Given the society's greater emphasis on the power of wealth and the competitive job market created since *doi moi*, young graduates have no choice but to work hard and be professional in order to stay employed and earn money.

Nevertheless, it is interesting to note that achieving one's own desired goal in present-day Vietnam does not mean obtaining success for merely 'oneself'. Today we regularly hear of terms such as a 'knowledge-based economy' and 'learning society', showing the government's emphasis on promoting knowledge and technology as the cornerstone of its modernising policy. Parallel to such emphasis, the Vietnamese government widely disseminates the slogan 'wealthy people, powerful country', while the media extoll success stories of 'young entrepreneurs'. These positions demonstrate the leadership's commitment to integrate with the 'world community' via knowledge and economic integration. Therefore, although there has been no specific appeal for young people to become individually rich, it is clear that personal success achieved in terms of profession and wealth is acknowledged as directly contributing to the present-day national cause of development and integration into the global economy. As an interviewee specifically puts it: 'It does not matter what you do, as long as you are becoming rich; not only are you admired and respected by others, but also you are contributing to, and helping to increase, the national GDP [gross domestic product]'. Such an attitude is very much a residual influence of the pre-*doi moi* socialist ideology.

On this latter point, it is possible to conclude that the attitudinal shift towards individual success as demonstrated by the case of young graduates in Hanoi reflects a multilayered and complex socio-economic reality brought about by *doi moi*. On the one hand, there is a 'capitalist' mentality of achieving professional and financial successes through the individual's hard work and efforts. On the other hand, there remains in today's attitude towards success an influence of socialist ideology: as the individual is to contribute towards the nation's good, becoming individually rich and successful is seen as a way of contributing to national prosperity. Additionally, there is the preservation of the nation's long tradition of bending over backwards to attain knowledge, as these young graduates regard learning as the route to professional and financial successes. What we see from this study of young graduates is the palimpsest of a Vietnamese society where the legacies of 'traditional' feudal past, the orientation of socialist ideology, and the essence of a market economy are all at work at the same time.

Notes

1 The literal translation of the term *hoc them* is 'supplementary learning'. However, the term contains various nuances, and when used amongst young graduates it refers to further training, or the participation of a youth in either full-time or part-time education further to their attaining a university degree and entering employment.
2 Fieldwork interview in Hanoi, February 2000.

Part IV
Foreign relations

Vietnam's external relations

Exports:	$14.3 billion (f.o.b* 2000)
Major exports commodities:	Crude oil, marine products, rice, coffee, rubber, tea, garments, shoes
Major exports partners:	Japan 18.1%, China 10.6%, Australia 8.8%, Singapore 6.1%, Taiwan 5.2%, Germany 5.1%, US 5.1% (2000)
Imports:	$15.2 billion (CIF*, including foreign aid in goods 2000)
Major imports commodities:	Machinery and equipment, petroleum products, fertiliser, steel products, raw cotton, grain, cement, motorcycles
Major imports partners:	Singapore 17.7%, Japan 14.4%, Taiwan 12.1%, South Korea 11.1%, China 9.1%, Thailand 5.2%, Hong Kong 3.9% (2000)
Foreign direct investment (FDI):	$750 million (2002)
Major FDI nations:	Singapore, Taiwan, Japan, South Korea, Hong Kong, France, Virgin Islands, The Netherlands, Russia, UK
FDI implementation ratio:	83.8% (2000)
Debt (external):	$13.2 billion (2000)
Economic aid (recipient):	$2.1 billion in credits and grants pledged by international donors for 2000
Number of countries enjoying diplomatic relations:	164 (2003)
Joining major international organisations:	UN (1977), ASEAN (1995), APEC (1998)
Territorial disputes involved:	Maritime boundary with Cambodia; the Spratly Islands with China, Malaysia, Philippines, Taiwan, and possibly Brunei; maritime boundary with China in the Gulf of Tonkin; the Paracel Islands with China and Taiwan; demarcation of boundaries with Laos; demarcation of the land boundary with China

Note * f.o.b: free on board; CIF: cost, insurance and freight
Sources: CIA (2002) *The World Factbook 2002*, Washington, DC: CIA; ADB (2001) *Key Indicators 2001: Growth and Change in Asia and the Pacific*; *VVG Economic Indicators, August 2003*, available online at http://www.vvg-vietnam.com/economics_cvr.htm#Rates; *Vietnam Economic Times*, available online at http://www.vneconomy.com.vn.

13 Rethinking foreign investment in Vietnam

Fuzzy figures and sentiment swings

Nick Freeman and Curt Nestor

There is a consensus that foreign direct investment (FDI) has played an important role in the economic development of Vietnam during the last decade. Although foreign-invested companies employ less than 1 per cent of the total workforce in Vietnam, they cumulatively account for around 27 per cent of the country's (non-oil) exports, 35 per cent of total industrial output, represent almost 13 per cent of Vietnam's gross domestic product (GDP), and contribute around 25 per cent of all tax revenues.[1] Nonetheless, there seems to be some disagreement on the actual size of FDI inflows that the country has received. Estimates given by international organisations – such as the International Monetary Fund (IMF), World Bank and Asian Development Bank (ADB) – are often different from the corresponding figures published by Vietnamese national authorities. This chapter explores this issue, and provides reasons for the discrepancies in reported FDI data.

One point on which all the FDI figures agree is that Vietnam witnessed a substantial rise in FDI inflows during the first half of the 1990s, and a contraction of inflows during the latter half of the 1990s. This chapter also aims to identify the factors behind this rise and fall in new FDI inflows. Although the Asian regional crisis of 1997–8 undoubtedly contributed to the contraction in FDI inflows, the first indications of a downturn in foreign investor sentiment pre-dated the crisis by more than a year.

Different conceptual applications and estimates of FDI

The successful attraction and rapid increase of inward FDI is generally considered as a leading example of the economic transformation that occurred in Vietnam during the 1990s. However, there is a quite significant lack of congruence in estimates of the actual size of these flows, as reported by various domestic sources and international institutions. For example, *The Economist* reported that FDI in Vietnam in 1996 reached US $8.3 billion (8 January 2000: 74, 76) whereas the World Bank and the Asian Development Bank estimated FDI in Vietnam at slightly more than US $1.8 billion during the same year (World Bank *et al.* 2000d, Table 3.1: 141, and ADB 2000, Table 8: 23). What is the cause of these so obviously contradictory data? Actually, the different values may in a sense be considered equally correct, as the figures reflect two different aspects of FDI: the former refer to the *approved* amount of FDI and the latter to the *disbursed* FDI during the year. In this case, it is simply a matter of poorly defined data; a problem that is all too common for FDI data in Vietnam.[2] Failure to distinguish between approved and disbursed FDI capital may lead to grossly erroneous inferences regarding the actual situation of foreign investment flows and stock in Vietnam.

Conceptual applications

Thus, a better understanding of the concept of FDI and its application in the case of Vietnam needs to be developed. This is *not* a problem confined solely to Vietnam, but also applies to a number of other developing countries, as well as some developed ones. There are currently two widely accepted definitions of FDI provided by the IMF (1993) and the Organisation for Economic Co-operation and Development (OECD 1996). These definitions are broadly compatible and are hereinafter referred to in the singular as the IMF/OECD definition of FDI. According to the IMF and OECD, the concept of FDI refers to an international investment that reflects a lasting interest and control of a resident entity in one economy (foreign direct investor or parent company in the home country) in an enterprise located in another economy (FDI enterprise in the host country). A minimum level of 10 per cent equity ownership of an enterprise is suggested to separate FDI from other forms of international investment, such as portfolio investment. The capital flows associated with an FDI undertaking comprise three major components: equity capital, reinvested earnings, and inter-company debt – that is, loans extended by the parent company to the FDI enterprise. As defined by the IMF/OECD, *FDI capital flows reflect only financing mobilised directly by the foreign investor*, thus excluding other possible financial sources, such as commercial bank loans.

Most countries collect data on FDI, essentially as a requirement for balance-of-payments (BoP) purposes. IMF member states are requested to report this type of data for publication. However, there are still a number of countries unable to report data on all three components, primarily due to constraints in data collection and reporting procedures. Numerous shortcomings of recorded FDI statistics are widely acknowledged, and there are a number of reasons for these apparent deviations.[3]

Apart from FDI statistics compiled for BoP purposes, some countries also compile another set of data on *approval* or *notification* basis, as opposed to actual FDI flows. The two sets of FDI data, approved capital and disbursement, are normally never equal and cannot be used synonymously. For various reasons, some FDI projects never materialise. Furthermore, approved investment capital indicates intentions based on total project cost estimates. The intentions, as well as the capability, of the foreign investor may very well change after the initial approval, resulting in expanded or contracted operations, or a total withdrawal. While this type of data does serve as a 'barometer' of investment intentions, it is the least satisfactory measure at hand. Research from various countries indicates that only a fraction of *approved* FDI is actually disbursed, ranging from less than one-tenth to approximately half the approved amount (see, for example, Alvstam 1993; Japan

External Trade Organization [JETRO] 1999; Lall 1993). Hence data on approved FDI and disbursements cannot be used interchangeably. Nor can approvals be used as a proxy for disbursed capital, since this implies an improbable conformity in the ratio of disbursements across industries.

For the most part, FDI data are national data, created by aggregating project data reported to host governments. National governments in turn report the aggregate data to the IMF and other international organisations involved in the compilation of such statistics. Thus, the accuracy of FDI statistics published by international organisations is heavily reliant upon the quality of data supplied by national governments. Various aspects of the conceptual application of FDI discussed here are highly relevant to the case of Vietnam.

Sources of Vietnamese FDI data

Any researcher interested in compiling FDI data in Vietnam based on secondary sources will soon find it a frustrating task to track down relevant sources, as they are often not widely known or easily accessed. Since Vietnam is a non-reporting member of the IMF, Vietnamese FDI data are not included in the IMF Balance of Payments Statistical Yearbooks.[4] Aggregate data may be obtained from annual publications such as the United Nations Conference on Trade and Development (UNCTAD) *World Investment Report* (for example, UNCTAD 2000a) or *World Investment Directory* (UNCTAD 2000b). There are several special reports on the Vietnamese economy published by international organisations, such as the World Bank, IMF and ADB (see, for example, World Bank *et al.* 2000d; IMF 2000; ADB 2000), providing various data on FDI in Vietnam. A number of these reports have recently been made available on these organisations' respective websites. FDI statistics are also published on a regular basis in the *Vietnam Statistical Yearbook* (see, for example, General Statistics Office 2001) and in the domestic English language press, such as the bi-weekly *Vietnam Investment Review* (VIR) and the monthly magazine *Vietnam Economic Times* (VET). Furthermore, FDI data are frequently published in Vietnamese press outlets such as *Dau tu* and *Thoi bao Kinh te* (non-identical sister publications of VIR and VET respectively).

A number of government organisations also publish directories of FDI projects (see, for example, Ministry of Planning and Investment [MPI] 1996; MPI 1996–2000; Vietnam Trade Information Centre 1998), usually detailing the name and address of the company, capital investment, scope of activity and similar information. The major drawback of these sources is that the information only refers to approval data when the investment licenses were issued, and do not cover subsequent amendments and changes. Furthermore, the directories are not complete; a large number of projects located in industrial zones and investment licenses issued by local authorities are not included. Several government-based websites in Vietnam – perhaps most comprehensively that of Ho Chi Minh City[5] – now also provide information on FDI projects.

Together, these sources offer vastly differing information on the capital value of Vietnam's FDI, often with little or no definitional clarity. Different publications offer alternative measures of FDI, though most sources indicate the MPI as the original source of the information. A special section within the MPI is in charge of FDI application and screening procedures, as well as monitoring the implementation of licensed projects. The authority to issue FDI licences has since 1997 been gradually decentralised to the provincial level – including export processing and industrial zones – with certain restrictions on business scope and total project value. By the end of 2000, some 50 different agencies from central to local level had approved and issued licences to foreign investors. However, the MPI still retains the central function of collecting and processing mandatory activity reports submitted by all foreign invested projects, and so remains the key FDI data source.

Vietnamese estimates of inward FDI

In Vietnam, approved FDI has long loomed largest, while data on actual disbursement has in general been scarcer. However, only disbursed FDI can exercise a real impact on the economy, and this type of data has been more generally available in recent years. The aggregate values shown in Table 13.1 represent one estimate of total approved and disbursed FDI during the period 1988–2000. According to this source of information, Vietnam attracted 3,223 foreign invested enterprises with total investment commitments reaching US $44.3 billion, of which US $19.1 billion had been disbursed over the period. This is an example of the more comprehensive kind of FDI data presentation that can be found in Vietnamese publications today. The data exhibit a fairly symmetrical pattern; the reasons for the shape of this pattern are discussed later.

However, based on the IMF/OECD definition, does this set of data provide a relevant picture of current FDI in Vietnam? As shown below, a careful dissection of the various FDI capital components, partly based on additional information provided by the same source, yields different interpretations of available data.[6] The total approved capital is based on project cost estimates comprising equity capital and loans. In this case, the share of equity capital and loans are not known. However, other sources indicate that these are roughly equal (see, for example, General Statistics Office 2001). The total capital also includes increases to the initially registered capital values of individual projects (US $38.4 billion) amounting to US $5.9 billion. The composition of equity capital and loans of the disbursed capital is also unknown.

Genuine inward FDI flows, conforming to the IMF/OECD definition, only comprise the foreign equity contribution and loans directly provided by the parent company. Accordingly, the Law on Foreign Investment in Vietnam defines FDI as 'the bringing of capital into Vietnam in the form of money or any other asset by foreign investors for the purpose of carrying on activities in accordance with the provisions of this Law' (Article 2). However, in spite of this rather clear-cut definition, most Vietnamese sources of FDI data typically comprise the total capital – in other words, including the Vietnamese equity capital contribution and total loan component – when producing FDI statistics on approval basis, as well as estimates of actual disbursements.

With regard to *approved* FDI capital, the total amount includes the Vietnamese equity capital contribution which typically consists of the value of land use rights, existing buildings and equipment and, to a limited extent, cash. These are items that by definition cannot be considered as *foreign* (direct) investment, but rather as domestic investment, or values pertaining to the existing domestic capital stock. This implies that the total stock of FDI capital on approval basis needs to be reduced by the value of the Vietnamese share of the equity capital. The problem is that aggregated FDI data do not allow for this. Previously, the Vietnamese equity share was estimated at 20–5 per cent of total approved capital (Nestor 1997; United Nations Development Programme [UNDP] 2001b). Given the increasing number of wholly foreign-owned enterprises during the latter half of the 1990s, the average share of the Vietnamese contribution in total FDI approvals has shrunk to 10 per cent over the examined period (Nestor forthcoming). In addition, more than 600 investment licenses valued at US $7.6 billion were revoked over the period. Thus, subtracting the value of cancelled projects and the Vietnamese equity capital contribution, estimated at 10 per cent, yields US $33.1 billion of remaining 'genuine' potential FDI capital at the end of 2000.

Consequently, in order to arrive at a more accurate assessment of the magnitude of FDI inflows that conforms to international standards, the total *disbursed* FDI capital needs to be adjusted accordingly. The Vietnamese share was limited to US $2.2 billion, equivalent to slightly more than 11 per cent of total disbursements during the period. The remaining capital, US $16.9 billion, represents the foreign equity capital including reinvested earnings and total loans. However, this amount also includes an unknown proportion of disbursed capital relating to cancelled projects, probably exceeding US $1 billion, consisting mainly of foreign equity, and to a lesser extent of loans. In principle, foreign investors are entitled to repatriate remaining equity capital after fulfilling their financial obligations in Vietnam, although no empirical data are available to show that such transactions have actually been made. Accordingly, total disbursements over the period should be revised downwards to less than US $16 billion.

In summary, the value of total FDI approvals during the period 1988–2000 has been reduced by about 25 per cent, and total disbursements by more than 16 per cent. However, these estimates do not conform to the IMF/OECD definition of FDI. The type of aggregate data on which the analysis here is based does not allow for a distinction in the size of total loans, let alone the composition of loans provided by the parent company and loans obtained from banks.

Furthermore, foreign investors are frequently accused of overvaluing machinery and equipment as part of their equity contribution in joint ventures with Vietnamese parties. Based on the experience of FDI disbursements in China, UNDP (2001b) estimates that overstated values may correspond to as much as 12 per cent of total approved FDI capital. Other Vietnamese sources indicate even higher levels of over-reporting (see, for example, Vo and Ngo 2000). The UNDP estimate implies further reduction of approved FDI capital and disbursements by about US $4 and $2 billion respectively; however, such a reduction is not attempted here.

As a measure to gauge the actual level of FDI implementation in Vietnam, the ratio between disbursed and approved FDI capital levels is often calculated (see, for example, World Bank 1997a and Webster 1999). Again, available data only allow us to do this while including the Vietnamese share of the equity capital.

The average FDI implementation ratio for the entire period reached over 40 per cent (Table 13.1), in line with previous studies (JETRO 1999; Lall 1993). The annual ratio increased rapidly to 80–90 per cent towards the end of the period, as a result of the sharply reduced levels of new capital commitments compared to relatively high disbursement levels. The cumulative FDI implementation ratio peaked in 1994, indicating that cumulative new capital commitments grew faster than disbursements during the remaining period.

However, measures such as the FDI implementation ratio are only indicative, and should be interpreted with caution. Outcomes vary, depending on the composition of imputed data. For example, deducting the capital of cancelled projects from new commitments during 1999 and 2000 would yield annual implementation ratios exceeding 100 per cent, since disbursements were larger than net commitments.

Estimates of inward FDI by international organisations

To illustrate the problem of differing data estimates further, a selection of FDI data for the period 1995–9 was compiled from recent publications by several international organisations, as well as the English-language local press (Table 13.2). The selection represents the most readily accessible sources, likely to be widely cited internationally.

Comparing the cumulative totals of disbursed FDI of the different datasets for the period 1995–9 reveals wide discrepancies, ranging from the World Bank estimate of approximately US $7.6 billion[7] to more than US $12 billion based on a domestic source. Most notably, the World Bank, IMF and, to a lesser extent, ADB data for 1998 and 1999 substantially deviate from the figures provided by other sources. This suggests some shared methods and sources used by these three organisations.

For approval data, the information provided by the IMF, VIR and VET is more homogenous for the period as well as individual years, with the exception of data reported by VIR for 1997. Total capital for the period averaged about US $25 billion and superseded US $29 billion when including capital increases. In terms of approved FDI capital versus disbursements during the period, the choice of dataset yields different results. The different sources diverge into two groups regarding the FDI implementation ratio: the World Bank, ADB and IMF suggest a rather low implementation level of 25–30 per cent; while the MPI, UNCTAD and VET present a much higher implementation level of 40–8 per cent.

The discrepancies in reported data may arise from the use of different sources, as well as conceptual variations when measuring FDI capital flows. VET, VIR and IMF refer to the MPI as the original source for data on approvals. The World Bank, ADB and IMF refer to local sources of information regarding data on

Table 13.1 Vietnam FDI implementation ratio, 1988–2000 (US $million)

	Total	1988–91	1992	1993	1994	1995	1996	1997	1998	1999	2000
Approved capital	44,345	2,815	2,077	2,829	4,262	7,915	9,396	5,796	4,755	2,114	2,386
Disbursements	19,082	478	542	1,097	2,213	2,761	2,837	3,032	2,189	1,933	2,000
Annual ratio[a] %	43.0	17.0	26.1	38.8	51.9	34.9	30.2	52.3	46.0	91.4	83.8
Cumulative ratio[b] %			14.0	19.6	28.9	21.6	14.6	13.7	8.9	7.8	7.9

Source: *Vietnam Economic Times* (www.vneconomy.com.vn). Calculations made by author.

Notes
Approved FDI capital and FDI disbursements includes foreign and Vietnamese equity capital and total debt financing.
a Yearly disbursement divided by yearly registered capital including capital increases, a 'flow' measure.
b Yearly disbursement divided by the cumulated 'stock' of undisbursed capital commitment including capital increases from previous years plus registered capital commitment of the current year.

Table 13.2 Estimates of inward FDI capital in Vietnam, 1995–9 (US $million)

	1995	1996	1997	1998	1999	Cumulative total 1995–9
World Bank disbursed capital	2,236	1,838	2,003	800*	700*	7,577
ADB disbursed capital	2,276	1,812	2,074	1,041	961	8,164
IMF disbursed capital	2,276	1,813	2,074	800	700*	7,663
MPI (quoted by IMF) disbursed capital	3,048	3,032	2,336	1,806	1,474	11,696
UNCTAD disbursed capital	2,349	2,455	2,745	1,972	1,609	11,130
VET disbursed capital	2,671	2,646	3,250	1,956	1,536	12,059
IMF Approvals	6,608	8,640	4,654	3,897	1,563	25,362
VIR Approvals	6,616	8,538	4,010	4,059	1,535	24,758
including increased capital	7,928	9,262	5,110	4,828	2,089	29,217
VET Approvals	6,607	8,640	4,654	3,897	1,548	25,346
including increased capital	7,915	9,396	5,796	4,773	2,114	29,994

Sources: World Bank et al. (2000d, Table 3.1: 141) based on data provided by Vietnamese authorities and World Bank staff estimates; ADB (2000, Table 8: 23) based on data provided by State Bank of Vietnam and staff estimates; IMF (2000, Table 28–9: 31f) based on data provided by MPI, State Bank of Vietnam and staff estimates; UNCTAD (2000a, Table B.1: 286) based on data provided by MPI; VET (No. 79, September 2000: 34) based on data provided by MPI; VIR (various issues 1996–2000) based on data provided by the MPI.

Note: * Preliminary

disbursements: the MPI, the State Bank of Vietnam (SBV), or the vague term 'Vietnamese authorities'. Furthermore, the data provided by the World Bank, ADB and IMF were supplemented by unspecified 'staff estimates'. The three organisations have permanent representations in Vietnam and their reports on the Vietnamese economy are published on a regular basis. They rely to a large extent on the General Statistical Office, MPI, Ministry of Finance and SBV for most of the data inputs in these reports. The various agencies apparently make use of similar sources, but nevertheless arrive at different conclusions on the size of FDI capital inflows to Vietnam.

To what extent, then, does the conceptual application of FDI measures contribute to the different estimates? UNCTAD (2000a) actually provides a definition of FDI based on the IMF/OECD recommendations. FDI inflows reported by UNCTAD are based on data provided by 'national official sources', most probably the MPI, and the accuracy of the data has been verified and confirmed in a communiqué to UNCTAD. Nevertheless, reported values are significantly higher than those reported by the World Bank, ADB and IMF. The FDI data provided by the World Bank and ADB are included in tables presenting BoP statistics; they thus presumably comply with the IMF/OECD definition of FDI, as no further information is provided. Careful scrutiny of the footnotes in the IMF (2000) report reveals that staff estimates of total disbursements are based on data supplied by the SBV on foreign equity and foreign borrowings by joint ventures. Furthermore, the staff estimates for 1998 and 1999 are also based on other (undisclosed) indicators of investment flows. MPI disbursements data, quoted by the IMF, are based on total disbursements net of the Vietnamese equity contributions, and include loans to some extent. The IMF also provides a note of caution that the data are subject to extensive revision.

Disbursement data reported by SBV and MPI are obviously different: the SBV's values are less than 60 per cent of those provided by the MPI. The reasons for this were further elaborated in a previous report by the IMF (1999). FDI data provided by the MPI are based on comprehensive periodical reports submitted by individual foreign invested enterprises. On the other hand, the SBV monitors only the loan component of FDI inflows, as registered by the foreign invested enterprises. The IMF deemed MPI data biased upwards and the SBV data underreported, and adjusted the total loan component of FDI-related loans by the end of 1998 to US $4.1 billion. Furthermore, the footnote to IMF approval data (IMF 2000) indicates that the data derived from the MPI includes investments by domestic joint venture partners. The same presumably applies to the quite similar MPI-derived approval data of VET and VIR, although this is not indicated.

Despite widespread acceptance of the IMF/OECD definition of FDI, none of the estimates presented above seems fully to comply with this definition. Basically, Vietnamese estimates of FDI exceed those provided by the World Bank, ADB and IMF due to the inclusion of the domestic equity share. Conversely, FDI data reported by the three international organisations may be underestimated, as the extent to which FDI-related loans are underreported is not known. This also implies that the current Vietnamese debt burden may be larger than suggested, which would lead to higher repayment requirements in the near future.

The case of Vietnam clearly illustrates the existing limitations in the measurement of international FDI capital, revealing conceptual and methodological problems that are also prevalent in a number of other countries. Such limitations must be properly acknowledged in the future studies of FDI in Vietnam, especially studies based on approval data. However, the current situation offers little comfort to bewildered researchers lost in the Vietnamese jungle of differing FDI measures and data.

The rise and fall of foreign investor sentiment

However Vietnam's FDI is defined and measured, the 1990s saw remarkable shifts in the level of investment. Put simply, FDI inflows steadily increased during the first half of the decade, before contracting in the latter half, congruent with a rise and fall in foreign investor sentiment towards the country. The inflection point at which inflows stopped rising, and began to turn down, was roughly 1995–6, in the year leading up to the Eighth Party Congress. With the benefit of hindsight, it is clear that the foreign investor community in Vietnam 'got ahead of itself' during the initial years of market entry, anticipating a pace of economic and business liberalisation – and resulting economic growth – that ultimately did not materialise (Freeman 1998: 58–9). For those foreign investors whose business models were predicated on high, straight-line economic growth rates and significant strides in business liberalisation, operational losses were incurred, prompting many to scale down their Vietnam operations; some actually withdrew from the country altogether. The 'fallout' from the regional financial crisis of 1997–8 only served to exacerbate this trend.

Vietnam's response to this downturn in FDI inflows was fairly slow in coming, largely incremental in scale, and generally lacking in imagination. Not only did these initiatives fail to address the fundamental difficulties faced by foreign investors in Vietnam, they also did not excite the interest – or stimulate the creative juices – of potential new investors. These changes also failed to take account of changing business and investment patterns in Asia, notably with regard to cross-border merger and acquisition activity, and the rise of cross-border production networks in the region.

The rise of sentiment and FDI inflows

Having promulgated its first foreign investment law in late 1987, by the early 1990s Vietnam was gaining a reputation as one of the most prospective markets in Asia and the emerging market universe (Hiebert 1991: 62–5). In some ways, the prevailing US trade and investment embargo added to the allure of a country that had previously been off-limits to all foreign capital beyond the socialist bloc (Freeman 1993: 13–22). European and Australian firms took full advantage of a rare chance to invest in a country where their US competitors were excluded. A little later, Japanese and other East Asian companies followed in their wake. By

February 1994, when US corporates were given the green light by Washington to make a belated entry into Vietnam, a relatively substantial foreign business community was already active in the country. Foreign investment sentiment towards Vietnam was arguably at its zenith in the 12 months following the lifting of the US investment embargo.[8]

To some extent at least, there was also a sectoral pattern to the FDI inflows of the early 1990s. Foreign oil and gas firms made some of the first inroads into Vietnam, signing production-sharing contracts to explore Vietnam's offshore acreage for hydrocarbons. Australian mining firms were also fairly quick to explore for commercially viable mineral deposits in onshore Vietnam. Hospitality companies entered Vietnam to open new hotels, primarily to cater for the influx of foreign business delegations and 'early bird' investors. Then came foreign banks, law firms and consulting companies, to provide support services for the burgeoning foreign investment community. A proportion of this initial FDI activity could be termed 'default FDI': investment activity that almost automatically enters when a new market opens, and which is not particularly sensitive to the relative merits of the host country's FDI regime. This sort of FDI activity can also be driven as much by 'push factors' in the home countries of foreign investors, or the dynamics of the industry in which they operate, as by intrinsic 'pull factors' of the host country itself.

Foreign investment activity in the manufacturing sector, and some agricultural processing, followed the first waves of Vietnamese FDI waves, and grew considerably in the years that followed. The primary orientation was towards labour-intensive activities, such as garments and footwear, with much of the investment capital sourced from East Asian countries. Output from such manufacturing activity by foreign-invested firms now represents a considerable proportion of Vietnam's total export earnings.

A critical factor in the sequencing of FDI into Vietnam has been the anticipated rates of return associated with individual projects, and business sectors as a whole. This explains in part why FDI activity in the hospitality sector (where rates of return can be relatively high) was vigorous in the early 1990s, whereas FDI activity in what is arguably the Vietnamese economy's most important sector, agriculture, has been fairly disappointing. The anticipated rates of return for the latter were generally not commensurate with the perceived risk of committing capital to a country like Vietnam. Another important determinant in Vietnam's FDI profile has been the MPI and its predecessor, the State Committee for Co-operation and Investment. During the 1990s, the MPI gradually relaxed some of the FDI regulations, and allowed foreign capital to flow into sectors previously closed to non-domestic businesses, as part of general business liberalisation efforts towards the private sector (both foreign and domestic). The MPI has also adopted a more relaxed view towards granting licences for wholly foreign-owned FDI projects. The pace of this liberalisation process in recent years has partly been in response to the decline in FDI inflows witnessed during the latter half of the 1990s, and attempts by Hanoi to buoy foreign investment activity by opening up sectors that were previously off-limits to foreign capital.

The sorts of general 'pull factors' that attracted foreign investors to Vietnam – and were recited, almost mantra-like, during the early 1990s – included: the country's large market of over 70 million consumers, the country's anticipated natural resource wealth, and a large and relatively well-educated workforce that also showed indications of a strong work ethic. Located in a region with an impressive record in hosting FDI, Vietnam was also able to leverage off the goodwill that pertained towards Southeast Asia in the late 1980s and early 1990s. It should also be noted that the timing of Vietnam's opening to foreign capital was very propitious, coinciding nicely with a 'bull run' in foreign investment activity (both portfolio and direct) in emerging and transitional economies. As a transitional economy, located in Southeast Asia, Vietnam was at the nexus of the emerging markets boom of the early 1990s.

Indeed, foreign investor appetite towards Vietnam became excessive in the early 1990s, with too many foreign investors avidly chasing too little business. Initially, at least, this did not seem to matter, as investors spoke about the need to establish a presence in the fledgling market, and a willingness to incur losses in the short and medium term, in anticipation of substantial profits in the long term. Some foreign investors may have entered Vietnam relatively early in order to ensure that they did not become excluded at a later date. Indeed, Vietnam pandered to this 'first come, first served' perception, intimating that only a fixed number of foreign investment licences would be issued in certain business sectors. In sum, the general tone was of great bravado (on both sides), in conformity with the 'up-beat' perceptions of Vietnam during the first half of the 1990s.[9] Along with this bravado came a willingness by foreign investors to endure the difficulties of operating in a transitional economy undergoing radical change, including: excessive bureaucracy and delays; high levels of corruption; inadequate physical infra-structure; an opaque business environment; excessive interference in business activity; and high charges (including dual pricing) for some utilities and services.

In retrospect, positive foreign investor sentiment towards Vietnam probably peaked about a year after the lifting of the US investment embargo in 1994. In some business sectors, such as banking and offshore hydrocarbons, Vietnam had deliberately held back some licences for US firms, while in numerous other sectors, American companies attempted to catch up with their respective Asian and European competitors. But even as US investors began to establish a bridgehead in Vietnam, some of the earlier foreign investors from Europe, Australia and Asia were already revising down their expectations of what could be achieved in Vietnam, and tailoring their operations accordingly. By 1996, US firms were also adopting a more reserved stance, learning from the mistakes of their predecessors.

The decline of sentiment and FDI inflows

After official FDI inflow figures peaked in 1996, the following three years saw a consistent contraction in Vietnam's foreign investment approvals. Indeed, FDI approvals shrank to a level in 1999 where overseas development aid (ODA) pledges actually began to exceed foreign investment pledges.[10] Even though Vietnam continued to show relatively good macro-economic indicators after 1995, and was one of the few East Asian countries to record positive GDP growth throughout the Asian crisis period, a view developed in the foreign investment community that Vietnam's economic reform process had markedly slowed during the lengthy run-up to the Eighth Party Congress of mid-1996, and immediately afterwards. As a destination for foreign capital, Vietnam had clearly lost its initial lustre.[11]

Given earlier euphoria, it was no surprise that the 'sentiment pendulum' would swing in the opposite direction, once a more sober assessment of Vietnam's potential as an FDI host became apparent. Although foreign investors would insist that their own decisions to enter and withdraw from Vietnam were based on sound fundamental factors, a degree of herd instinct can be discerned in their movements. It is undoubtedly true that too many firms in certain business sectors entered Vietnam, which did not have an economy big enough to support so many enterprises in the same line of business.[12] In some other business sectors, such as hydrocarbons and mineral exploration, it was to be expected that only those firms that found commercially viable reserves would continue operations, and that the rest would depart. Consequently, a general 'shake out' of the foreign investor community was almost inevitable.

The MPI has had a tendency to massage the official figures for FDI. For example, in recent years the Ministry has licensed a number of large-scale FDI projects in the last month (and even final days) of the calendar year.[13] While some of these FDI large projects licensed in the tail-end of each year could be regarded as legitimate projects that will ultimately become tangible realities, some other project proposals have been much more open to doubt. A couple of large property projects licensed in late 1996, for example, seem very unlikely to be realised, and only served to widen the large margin that exists between the official statistics for licensed and pledged FDI, and foreign investment actually disbursed and committed.[14] If one discounts these two large property projects approved at the end of 1996, then 1995 was the zenith for foreign investment inflow pledges. While such substantial discrepancies are to be expected in a country that has only recently opened its doors to foreign capital, after a while this margin can become a credibility gap for a host country if it does not begin to contract.

It would be useful if there were ways to measure foreign investor sentiment towards Vietnam. One measure might be the performance of Vietnam's Brady bonds, but these were only issued in March 1998, and are not an ideal proxy for FDI sentiment. A slightly better (but still not ideal) proxy would be the half-dozen listed country funds that have pertained to Vietnam. Launched between 1991 and 1995, these country funds took a number of years to develop portfolios of direct investments in Vietnam and, as a result, they tended to hold a substantial quantity of cash (or cash equivalents) in their portfolios during the early 1990s.[15] Yet despite their substantial cash holdings, the share prices of these funds all traded at substantial premia to their net asset values (NAVs) in the years leading up to the US investment embargo being lifted, and particularly in the period immediately afterwards. Investors in the funds, it seems, were willing to pay a premium to hold shares in Vietnam-oriented country funds, even though they were heavily 'cashed up'. This paradox can only be accounted for by the high degree of positive investor sentiment towards Vietnam at the time. But tellingly, the share prices of these funds all declined into deep discount territory after 1996. Indeed, at one point in early 1998, the Vietnam country funds registered the steepest discounts to NAV of any country funds in the entire emerging markets universe.[16] What makes this decline even more remarkable was that, by the latter part of the 1990s, these country funds had built up portfolios that contained actual investments in Vietnam, and were no longer just holding cash or cash equivalents. Yet some funds were being priced by the market at levels equivalent to their cash holdings alone, suggesting that investors in the funds valued their actual investments in Vietnam at virtually nil.

Reviving sentiment and FDI inflows

> The large [FDI] inflows of the mid-1990s must not be understood as normal. Vietnam's attractiveness has sunk in recent years as other countries have become more attractive, and the high costs of doing business in Vietnam ... have become evident.
>
> (World Bank *et al.* 2000d: 10)

There are some initial indications that the contraction in Vietnam's FDI inflows *may* have hit their nadir around 2000, as the signing of a trade deal with the US in July 2000 and a number of other positive developments are beginning to revive foreign investor sentiment towards the country.[17] (The extent of this improvement in sentiment is a little hard to gauge, however, as the global backdrop for FDI has been so poor.) Could it be that another rethink of the merits of Vietnam as an FDI host is now underway amongst the foreign investor community? Vietnam's official FDI inflow *pledges* in 2000 were up on 1999, albeit thanks in large part to the US $1.1 billion Nam Con Son gas project, which was approved in mid-December 2000. (Indeed, if the Nam Con Son project is excluded from the aggregate FDI inflow pledges – of US $1.97 billion – for 2000, foreign investment actually declined by 43 per cent from the previous year.)[18] Crucially, an upturn in sentiment does not mean that an increase in foreign investment activity is a foregone conclusion, or that it can be sustained in the long term.

The external environment is much less conducive to new FDI activity in Vietnam than during the early 1990s. In particular, the attractions of the Southeast Asian region as a destination for foreign investment have been significantly dented by the Asian financial crisis, recent political instability, and the subsequent 'fallout'. FDI activity in the region has also morphed in recent years, away from the more conventional foreign investment activity that Vietnam is most familiar with (that is, creating new production capacity in 'greenfield projects'), and more towards cross-border mergers and acquisition activity (in other words, acquiring existing capacity), of which Vietnam has much less experience. Critically, China's entry into the World Trade Organisation is also serving to exacerbate a growing trend in the 1990s, of FDI inflows being 'diverted' away from Southeast Asia and towards China.

Although some fairly substantial improvements have been made to Vietnam's foreign investment law – notably in 1996 and 2000 – these changes in the foreign investment law have been partly 'drowned out' by the plethora of minor revisions made to the decrees and implementing regulations that envelope the foreign investment law. The constant 'white noise' of regulatory changes and revisions can be counterproductive when it means that slightly more substantial improvements in the foreign investment law get overlooked. A foreign investment regime that appears to be continually changing, and increasingly complex in terms of the (sometimes contradictory) regulations that are introduced and revised, will deter potential investors.[19] The numerous revisions made to the FDI legal regime have also failed to tackle some of the main difficulties that foreign investors encounter in Vietnam, such as the interrelated problems of bureaucracy and corruption, the inadequacies of the country's physical infrastructure, various financing and taxation issues, and the high operating costs of conducting business. Attempts by Vietnam's policy-makers to tackle these sorts of disincentives to FDI have been mixed, even though these are probably the main factors that drove the downward revision in investor sentiment. As UNCTAD has noted, with most host countries now offering liberal foreign investment laws, the benefits to be derived from making further revisions can result in diminishing returns (UNCTAD 1998: xxvi–xxvii).[20]

A more robust relationship between foreign investors and the growing number of local private enterprises should be encouraged. Paralleling their marginalisation from bank credit, local private sector firms have also found it very difficult to establish joint ventures with foreign investors, and vice versa.[21] In addition to establishing equity relationships with foreign investors, there is scope for local firms to establish alliances and other forms of business relationships with foreign firms, notably in the field of subcontracting work and the burgeoning trend in international production networks (IPNs).

Finally, the IMF has been critical of what it regards as the imbalanced sectoral composition of Vietnam's FDI stock during the 1990s, noting that a substantial proportion of FDI has been oriented towards import-substituting and non-tradable industries (such as property construction and telecommunications) where the country enjoys relatively few comparative advantages. The IMF argues that Vietnam should have focused on FDI in export-oriented manufacturing and in low-cost and labour-intensive industries where it has a comparative advantage. Whilst a valid point, an assumption is made that Vietnam's policy-makers are able to dictate the kinds of FDI that flows into the country (IMF 1999: 10–21). But, as noted above, FDI inflows have been driven as much by push factors in the home country or industry of the foreign investors. Looking at Vietnam today, it is sometimes hard to imagine how unprepared the country was to host foreign capital in the mid–late 1980s, and some of the developments required to attract export-oriented and labour-intensive FDI have necessitated some foreign investment in non-tradable sectors.

Conclusion

By any standard, FDI capital inflows to Vietnam have been instrumental for economic development during the 1990s. Data on FDI are available on approval and disbursement basis, where the former seems to be the most readily available measure. However, various estimates of actual disbursements convey an ambivalent impression of the size of these flows. In general, estimates by domestic Vietnamese sources are substantially higher than the corresponding estimates provided by international organisations such as the World Bank, IMF and ADB. The trends of the estimates are similarly downward. However, the estimated level of the contraction differ with increasingly large discrepancies towards the end of the period. Many of the gaps between reported data are apparently due to different coverage of the various components included in the concept of FDI, and none of the estimates seem fully to comply with recommendations by the IMF and OECD. The present situation poses numerous difficulties in the analysis of FDI in Vietnam, as the composition of available data is often not properly defined and, at times, data on an approval basis is confused with data on actual disbursement.

In the mid-1990s, foreign investors revised down their perceptions of Vietnam as a host country for their capital, explaining in large part the contraction in FDI inflows to the country during the latter part of the decade. Crucially, there seemed to be insufficient examples of foreign investors who had been successful in Vietnam to provide an attractive demonstration effect. Ironically, the US investment embargo probably served to extend the sense of excitement towards Vietnam, as it staggered the entry of foreign investors in the country. Had the US embargo been lifted much earlier, it is conceivable that foreign investor sentiment towards Vietnam would have cooled much earlier and, as a result, FDI inflows would have peaked well before 1995. The contraction in FDI flows that Vietnam experienced in the latter half of the 1990s partly coincided with Southeast Asia's economic downturn. But the regional economic downturn was not the primary cause for the contraction in Vietnam's FDI inflows, as evidenced by the fact that inflows peaked roughly two years before the commencement of the Asian financial crisis.

Looking ahead, a general revival in the Asian regional economies will not automatically result in an increase in FDI inflows for Vietnam. There is clearly the need for Vietnam to improve its domestic business environment, in order to provide a more conducive host country platform for foreign capital. Most elements of a business liberalisation programme are already identified in a series of external agreements that Vietnam has committed itself to, including: the Bilateral Trading Agreement with the US, the most recent IMF loan programme, and the ASEAN Investment Area (AIA).[22] In fact, these agreements provide a roadmap for business liberalisation in Vietnam over the next decade, the fruits of which may assist in reviving FDI inflows to the country.

Notes

1 See *Vietnam Investment Review*, 16–21 January 2001: 9. The foreign investor community – spanning 2,620 projects – employed 349,000 people in 2000, generated revenues of US $6.5 billion, and contributed US $280 million in taxes. If one includes crude oil exports, Vietnam's FDI community now produces 48 per cent of the country's total exports. See *India Times*, 16 January 2001.

2 See Rivard and Khanh Hoang Ta 2000: 12 for other recent examples.

3 See UNCTAD (2000a, Annex B, Table 1: 269–71) for a list of countries where at least one component of FDI inflows is not available from the IMF. See also IMF (2000) for a detailed account of the state of FDI data collection and reporting routines in a number of countries.

4 However, a Vietnam country page was included for the first time in International Financial Statistics in June 2001 after years of discussions with the IMF (see IMF Public Information Notice (PIN) No. 99/46, June 8, 1999 and PIN No. 00/55 August 4, 2000).

5 See http://www.hcminvest.gov.vn.

6 The IMF/OECD definition of FDI only refers to capital *disbursements*. The same definition is here extended to apply to FDI capital *approvals*.

7 This estimated value of FDI is provided in a joint publication by the World Bank, ADB and UNDP (2000d). However, the FDI section was written by World Bank staff.

8 On reactions, see Hiebert and Awanohara 1994: 14–17.

9 A December 1995 front page article in *The Asian Wall Street Journal* evokes the upbeat mood at that time amongst foreign investors (Chua and Lehner 1995: 1, 12). The article begins: 'Call it taking a very, very long-term view. Call it suspension of disbelief. For Vietnam, foreign investors will jump through hoops, it seems.'

10 In 1996, FDI inflow pledges exceeded ODA pledges by more than three-fold, but by 1999, ODA pledges exceeded FDI pledges by around 45 per cent.

11 For a sample of business media coverage of Vietnam during this period of souring business sentiment, see Marshall 1998: 1, 5.

12 For example, roughly 11,500 vehicles were sold in Vietnam in 1994, of which 4,000 were cars. Yet by late 1995, 10 automotive assembly plants had been licensed (cumulatively pledging to invest US $648 million), with an aggregate production capacity of 120,000 vehicles. See Thornton 1995.

13 It should be recognised that foreign investors are also prone to inflating FDI figures. Conversely, a substantial number of very small-scale foreign investment projects, such as those enacted by the 'Viet Kieu' community, are not registered in the official FDI figures.

14 One of the property projects was a US $1 billion real estate development near Ho Chi Minh City, and the other was a US $2.1 billion mixed development project in Hanoi. Both received their investment licences on 30 December 1996, and the former had its licence revoked in November 1998. Another project, a US $1.3 billion joint venture with a Russian company to build an oil refinery in central Vietnam, was approved on 28 December 1998. However, the Russian partner decided to withdraw from the project in early 2003.

15 The first listed Vietnam country fund – the Vietnam Fund – was successfully launched in 1991, with five following in 1993–5. These included: Beta Viet Nam Fund, Lazard Vietnam Fund (now defunct), Vietnam Enterprise Investments Ltd, Templeton Vietnam Opportunities Fund (subsequently reconstituted as Templeton Vietnam and Southeast Asia Fund), and the Vietnam Frontier Fund.

16 See *GEMS Weekly*, ING Barings (London), 20 February 1998: 16.

17 Other positive developments have included: the opening of a securities market in Ho Chi Minh City in July 2000; the resumption of IMF lending announced in April 2001; the upgrading of Moody's sovereign rating outlook for Vietnam from negative

to stable (also in April 2001); roughly a doubling in the number of newly registered local companies, as a direct result of improvements in the business environment stemming from the introduction of the Enterprise Law; and positive media reaction to the change in the VCP leadership at the Ninth Party Congress (April 2001).

18   The World Bank estimates that actual FDI *disbursements* continued to decline in 2000, from US $700 million in 1999 to US $600 million.

19   One foreign law firm depicted Vietnam's FDI legal regime thus: 'The proposed amendments to the foreign investment law, like drafts of most new legislation in Vietnam has followed the world of particle physics. Subatomic particles are described using esoteric mathematics and are detected only through analysis of the cryptic curling and branching paths of bubbles they leave behind as they disintegrate.' *Indochina Notes*, Freshfields, April 2000: 1.

20   UNCTAD notes that there has been 'a relative loss in effectiveness of FDI policies in the competition for investment: adequate core FDI policies are now simply taken for granted' (UNCTAD 1998: xxvi–xxvii).

21   In the period between 1991 and 1998, less than 2 per cent of the total FDI capital inflows approved were for joint venture projects with local private firms. This compares with 64.6 per cent for joint venture projects with local state enterprises, and 21.5 per cent for 100 per cent foreign-owned projects. See IMF 1999: 16.

22   In early April 2001, the IMF approved a US $368 million Poverty Reduction and Growth Facility loan. Under the AIA, Vietnam is committed to providing national treatment to ASEAN investors by 2010, and national treatment to all overseas investors by 2020.

14 Recent changes in Vietnam's foreign policy

Implications for Vietnam–ASEAN relations

Jörn Dosch and Ta Minh Tuan

In December 1986, Vietnam's foreign policy took a new course when the Sixth National Congress of the Vietnamese Communist Party (VCP) adopted a strategy of *doi moi*, or renovation. Although the new approach was primarily directed towards reform and liberalisation of the national economy, it had decisive implications for Vietnam's foreign policy outlook. The political elite concluded that the international isolation of Vietnam following its occupation of Cambodia in 1979 had significantly contributed to the country's deep socio-economic crisis. The success of *doi moi* would largely depend on a radical change in foreign policy.

Politburo Resolution No. 13 of May 1988 outlined a policy of 'diversification' (*da dang hoa*) and 'multilateralisation' (*da phuong hoa*) of Vietnam's foreign relations. These guidelines were further developed when the Seventh Congress of the VCP solemnly declared in 1991: 'Vietnam wishes to befriend all countries in the world community' (Communist Party of Vietnam 1991: 43). The primary objectives of the new foreign policy can be summarised as follows:

* to break up the state of economic embargo and diplomatic isolation and to secure a peaceful and stable international environment for 'socialist con- struction';
* to boost foreign economic activity, including the attraction of foreign direct investment (FDI) and overseas development aid (ODA), and the acceleration of foreign trade;
* to integrate Vietnam into regional and international organisations.

This so-called *new outlook* resulted in a rapid expansion of diplomatic relations. While in 1989 Vietnam had official ties with only 23 non-communist states (Thayer 1997b: 365), 11 years later the government had established diplomatic relations with 167 countries (Le Kha Phieu 2000: 24), including all major powers and most international organisations. Vietnam's unconditional retreat from Laos and Cambodia and the government's constructive role in the process of settling the Cambodian conflict, both central elements of the new outlook, paved the way for improved relations with China, the country's main adversary in the 1980s. In November 1991 the two governments normalised their ties. But it was Vietnam's admission into the Association of Southeast Asian Nations (ASEAN) in 1995 that most clearly symbolised the new direction in foreign policy. ASEAN membership has often been described as one of Hanoi's most important achievements since the end of the Cold War. In 1998 Vietnam hosted a summit meeting of the organisation's heads of government, followed in July 2001 by the annual series of ASEAN conferences, including, for example, the Foreign Ministers' Meeting and the ASEAN Regional Forum (ARF).

ASEAN is an important but not sole pillar of Vietnam's post-Cold War foreign policy. Together, multilateral activities at the global, regional and sub-regional levels, such as co-operation within the Greater Mekong Sub-Region (GMS), ASEAN Free Trade Area (AFTA), the Asia Pacific Economic Co-operation Forum (APEC) or the Asia–Europe Meeting (ASEM), and normalised bilateral relations with the United States of America (USA) and regional powers, are expected to contribute to a secure international environment. This would no longer require Vietnam to use its resources primarily to maintain a strong defence infrastructure. The first part of the chapter begins with a general outline of changes in Vietnam's foreign policy in the *doi moi* period. We will analyse the results of the post-1988 approach, asking how far the new strategy has been effective, and has met initial expectations. We assume that changes like the marginalisation of ideology in foreign relations have opened new opportunities to broaden and diversify external contacts. In the second part, we will assess the implications of Vietnam's new foreign policy outlook for the country's relations with ASEAN as a crucial part of the government's foreign relations. We do not apply any particular international relations theory because the mainstream approaches have yet convincingly to demonstrate their usefulness in explaining regionalism and foreign relations patterns in Southeast Asia (for a discussion see Nguyen Vu Tung 2002). Our study is rather grounded in the tradition of general foreign policy analysis.

Essential changes in Vietnam's foreign policy

Following the reunification of 1976, the social, political and economic situation in Vietnam underwent a total change. However, the outlooks and aspirations of Vietnam's leaders remained the same. Although the Vietnamese already wanted a peaceful reconstruction of their war-torn homeland, their desire could not be fulfilled because of Vietnam's intervention in Cambodia in 1979. The West considered Vietnamese actions as 'aggression', while for ASEAN countries, Vietnam had become a threat to their security and to regional stability. As a result, Vietnam's prestige was severely damaged, and it faced diplomatic isolation. In the same year, Vietnam suffered a large-scale Chinese invasion that further drained its manpower and scarce material resources. The war ended shortly afterwards, but friendly and peaceful relations between the two countries had already been lost. Under such circumstances, Vietnam adopted a 'one-sided tilt' foreign policy (*nhat bien dao*). It now completely leaned towards the Union of Soviet Socialist Republics (USSR). It was soon clear that the dream of national liberation and unity did not bring about the expected results.

Confronted with mounting international pressure and a deep internal socio-economic crisis, Vietnam decided to change its foreign policy. Now it needed peace more than ever. When *doi moi* was inaugurated in 1986, the Vietnamese leaders initiated a new 'peace of co-operation' policy, reflecting an apparent realisation that only co-operation and equality in international relations could bring about lasting peace and stability. As the aim of *doi moi* is economic development, Hanoi had to abandon a communist revolutionary course. Vietnam completed the withdrawal of its troops from Cambodia in September 1989 and from Laos before 1990, then signed the Paris Peace Accords on Cambodia in 1991. After 1988, Vietnam no longer regarded China as an imminent and dangerous enemy, and the USA as a fundamental and long-term foe. Hanoi normalised its relations with Beijing and Washington in 1991 and1995 respectively. Vietnam's insistence that ASEAN was a hostile 'NATO-type' (North Atlantic Treaty Organisation) organisation was dropped in official propaganda, as was the contrast between 'capitalist ASEAN' and 'socialist Indochina'. To build trust amongst its neighbours, Vietnam acceded to the Treaty of Amity and Co-operation in Southeast Asia in 1992, and finally joined ASEAN in 1995.

In the post-Cambodia era, Vietnam advocates the settlement of all disputes by peaceful negotiations. Vietnam concluded with the Philippines a code of conduct in their disputed sea zones. In 1997 Vietnam reached agreement with Thailand on their sovereign claims to overlapping areas in the Gulf of Thailand. Vietnam also signed a land border treaty with China in 1999, and another treaty on the demarcation of the Gulf of Tonkin in 2000. Although the latter has not yet been completely implemented, these treaties have narrowed down the scope of China–Vietnam territorial disputes relating to the Paracel and Spratly archipelagos. At a regional level, Vietnam has co-operated with the ASEAN countries to resolve issues pertaining to peace and security in Southeast Asia. Vietnam signed the declaration on the Southeast Asian Nuclear Weapons-Free Zone (SEANWFZ) in 1995. At the international level, as a new member of the United Nations (UN) Conference on Disarmament at Geneva, Vietnam contributed to the conclusion of the Comprehensive Test Ban Treaty (CTBT) and hence to efforts to abolish all weapons of mass destruction. Vietnam actively joined the campaign for a treaty banning the use of land mines. These moves amounted to an entirely new 'peace policy'.

Perhaps the most dramatic change in Vietnam's foreign policy is the marginalisation of ideology. In a communist system, ideological factors usually play a significant role in the policy-making process. Prior to *doi moi*, Vietnamese foreign policy was based mainly on ideological considerations. Policy-makers perceived world politics as a 'struggle between capitalism and socialism', to decide 'who will win' (*ai thang ai*). Everything that was happening in the world was naturally linked to the 'revolutionary course'. This made Vietnam's foreign policy very narrow, limiting Vietnam's close relations to states with similar ideological values of 'opposition to capitalism'. This was related to a certain presupposition shared by the Vietnamese people and politicians alike that socialism was entirely good and capitalism was bad. Ideologically motivated foreign policy contributed in part to the isolation of Vietnam in the world. Thus, until the 1980s, Vietnam gave its support to all Soviet political moves and declared unity with the USSR the cornerstone of its foreign policy.

When the communist regimes in Europe began to collapse, Vietnamese leaders, however, concluded that ideological factors would no longer guide international affairs. But they did not evaluate whether their ideology was right or wrong. The Communist Party has probably learnt something in this respect from China's experiments. From 1988 to 1991, the relationship with the USSR ceased to be the cornerstone. To integrate itself into a restructured post-Cold War world, Vietnam had to go along with emerging trends in international relations, namely peaceful co-operation and economic development. Therefore, foreign policy had to be 'untied' (*coi troi*), meaning that the old ideological rhetoric about 'two camps' (*hai phe*) and 'three revolutionary currents' (*ba dong thac cach mang*) had to be dropped. From the 1990s, these phrases were rarely found in the vocabulary of Vietnamese foreign policy. Instead, new terms appeared, such as 'international economic integration' (*hoi nhap kinh te quoc te*), 'interdependence' (*su phu thuoc lan nhau*), 'region-alisation' (*khu vuc hoa*), and 'globalisation' (*toan cau hoa*). Even notions of 'socialism' and 'capitalism' (as they are used and understood in Vietnam) were radically modified. Vietnamese politicians acknowledged that 'socialism has been driven into temporary regression' (Communist Party of Vietnam 1996: 33). Only a small number of communist countries remain, each pursuing its own way. There is no longer a communist bloc, and Vietnam has no military allies. Accordingly, the sharp differentiation between friends and foes has disappeared.

Since 1990, Hanoi's leaders have started to claim that, 'the present enemy of Vietnam is poverty and backwardness, and the friend of Vietnam is everybody who is willing to co-operate with and help us to push back (*day lui*) poverty and backwardness' (Tran Quang Co 1995: 108). Friends are those who 'do not nurture an intention to interfere in Vietnam's internal affairs and territorial sovereignty' (Tran Bach Dang 2000: 8). This indicates that Vietnam is prepared to move beyond the bitter past and look to the future in its relations with former enemies. However, Vietnamese policy-makers have stressed that friendship must be based on a common goal of 'promoting peace, independence and development'.

One may wonder if the Vietnamese leadership is in search of a new ideology. As they are ideologically minded, they need some fresh political values that can serve as substitute for the orthodox Marxist–Leninist ideology, which has failed in Vietnam, and which they are trying to play down. The process is nevertheless gradual. Quick abandonment of the communist ideology could provoke a con-fidence crisis in Vietnam. Most Vietnamese people have grown used to propaganda about the 'building of socialism' closely linked with ideas of the nation. They have pursued such goals all their lives. This is especially true for the older generation that fought bravely and shed its blood in successive wars. If Vietnam's leaders suddenly declare that they will give up utopian ideals of socialism, millions of Vietnamese people will not know what to believe in. This could result in political instability. Therefore, in recent years Vietnamese politicians have attempted to propagate the slogan: 'a prosperous people, a strong country, and a just, democratic and civilised society' (Communist Party of

Vietnam 2001: 32). At the same time, industrialisation and modernisation of Vietnam's economy have been vigorously promoted. These developmentalist objectives seem to have become the new ideological values of the VCP. In fact, they accord with the interests of the Vietnamese people, and have thus received wide support. But not all agree. It can hardly be ignored that some conservative circles remain afraid of overly radical reforms. These actors, especially the military, fear that a wide opening to the outside world could create a fertile soil for 'hostile forces' to attempt a 'peaceful evolution'. Their warnings that national economic independence and sovereignty could be undermined may complicate any further marginalisation of ideology. In addition, the inertia of the political structure and of a bureaucratic system still organised along orthodox Marxist–Leninist lines has limited the efficient conduct of policy.

So far, however, the marginalisation of ideology in foreign relations has opened opportunities to broaden contacts with new partners. In addition to inter-governmental relations, a new approach to foreign political parties and international non-governmental organisations (NGOs) has been implemented. The VCP itself has forged closer ties with many ruling parties, workers' and socialist parties and other so-called progressive forces across the globe. Most recently, representatives of 35 foreign political parties participated in the Ninth Congress of the VCP in April 2001. 'People-to-people' contacts, or 'track-two diplomacy' as often termed by foreign scholars, have been encouraged as well, mostly through mass organisations such as the Trade Federation, the Women's Union, the Youth League, the Veterans' Association, and Vietnam Union of Friendship Organisations.[1] Relationships with foreign NGOs have attracted growing attention. This 'track-two diplomacy' has had considerable success. There are currently about 500 foreign NGOs operating in Vietnam. NGOs have made important contributions to the socio-economic development of the country in fields such as healthcare, education, hunger eradication, and poverty alleviation, particularly in rural areas. Between 1991 and 2000, total NGO aid to Vietnam reached US $624 million (Uy Ban Cong Tac Ve Cac To Chuc Phi Chinh Phu Nuoc Ngoai 2002: 16). These contacts have enlarged the scope of foreign relations, thereby breaking the monopoly of the Ministry of Foreign Affairs and the Commission of External Affairs of the Communist Party in foreign policy matters. Now not only government bodies but also individual Vietnamese citizens have far fewer difficulties in establishing direct relations with foreign counterparts. This implies that the state's former absolute control over the conduct of foreign relations is slipping.

The declining role of ideology has required a reconsideration of national interests. Before *doi moi*, Vietnamese politicians used to claim that Vietnam's revolutionary cause was an inseparable part of the 'world revolution' (*cach mang the gioi*). They tried to 'export revolution' (*xuat khau cach mang*) to other countries, such as Laos, Cambodia and Thailand, in an effort to contribute to the creation of a 'world revolution'. In doing so, they seemed to put the interests of the 'international communist movement' above Vietnam's national interests. When Vietnam invaded Cambodia, according to the official justification Vietnam's military presence there was to fulfill its 'international obligations' (*nghia vu quoc te*). Ironically, the decade-long isolation of Vietnam was the immediate outcome of its operations in Cambodia. This isolation was inimical to and actually harmed Vietnam's national interests.

With a new foreign policy, Vietnam's commitments (as popularly seen in Vietnam) or Vietnam's ambition of sub-regional domination (as portrayed by many foreign scholars in Laos and Cambodia) were changed in line with national interests. This was possible only after the shift of Vietnam's leadership in 1986 which was headed by Nguyen Van Linh, who was more realistic and pragmatic than Le Duan. Vietnamese troops were pulled out from these two countries. Vietnam had ceased to regard the fulfilment of 'international obligations' in the spirit of 'proletarian internationalism' (*chu nghia quoc te vo san*) as a strategic task. Such obligations were now limited to 'forms and at degrees corresponding to Vietnam's condition and the norms of international relations' (Nguyen Manh Cam 1991: 2). To replace the old slogan, Vietnam has adopted a new one from ASEAN, namely 'unity in diversity' (*thong nhat trong da dang*), in which diversity was accepted by Hanoi between 1976 and 1986. In 1992 Vietnamese leaders announced that the determination 'successfully to build socialism in Vietnam' would be a contribution to the international communist and workers' movement, and a way of fulfilling 'international obligations' (see Ban Tu Tuong Van Hoa Trung Vong 1992: 11). Perhaps this was an attempt to find a substitute for 'the struggle for communism'. However, from a practical perspective, the old ideological priorities in Vietnam's foreign policy were completely dropped. Vietnam's current national interests are fundamentally redefined as peace, economic development and the vague ideal of 'socialist construction'.

Another important change of Vietnam's foreign policy is the introduction of a new concept of 'security'. Earlier, Vietnamese policy-makers perceived security as guaranteed by a distant patron and by a well-guarded national border. Vietnam expected its alliance with the USSR to ensure security. But the alliance failed to realise this goal. Despite its ailing economy, Vietnam had to maintain the fifth largest army in the world (Thayer 1997a: 1) because of the government's role in Cambodia, China's heavy military pressure on Vietnam's northern border and China's ongoing threat to teach Vietnam a second lesson. In 1988, Hanoi's leaders concluded that security could be achieved not only by military might, but also by economic and political means. In this view, the security of a country may be assured when it is located within a common regional and global security system. On the other hand, economic weaknesses, economic blockades and political isolation will become sources of insecurity. The political elite has argued that with a strong economy, downsized but able national defence and broad international relations, Vietnam would be more capable of preserving security and national independence (see Nguyen Van Phiet, Major-General, 1992).

Based on this new concept, policy-makers outlined a fresh security strategy for Vietnam. Hanoi cut its main military forces by half in 1993 (Thayer 1997a: 4). In 1989, most of the troops withdrawn from Cambodia were immediately discharged. Overall, Vietnam's defence share of gross national product declined from 19.4 per cent in 1985 to 3.1 per cent in 1999 and is now comparable with the average for

Southeast Asian countries (United States Pacific Command 2002: 30). Furthermore, Vietnam has reached an agreement with Russia on the latter's complete departure from Cam Ranh Bay by the end of 2004. Concurrently, it has embarked on a programme of modernisation designed to develop 'a regular and modern' armed force, particularly in terms of combat efficiency and armaments. This is expected to help protect Vietnam's border security more effectively from external threats.

Vietnam has increasingly valued the preservation of national security by diplomatic means. This change is very significant in that it has transformed the old methods Vietnam employed to protect its security: the use of military force, and reliance on foreign patronage. The calculation is that the more friendly relations with various foreign countries Vietnam can cultivate, the more support Vietnam can get. Evidently, expanded relations with more new partners and friends creates greater scope for co-operation and more intertwined interests. In some cases, Vietnam's security interests coincide with the interests of other countries. For example, Vietnam's concerns about China's quiet military advancement in the South China Sea are shared by some other ASEAN states. Vietnam and other ASEAN states have been trying to reach with China a code of conduct in the South China Sea. In the ARF, Vietnam is also proactive in stimulating security dialogue.

For the past 10 years, economic policy has become an inseparable part of foreign policy. In terms of economic development, Vietnam has lagged behind its neighbours. The VCP has repeatedly warned that Vietnam's economy could face dangers of falling even further behind. As Vietnam has become more open to the outside world, people have gained more access to information about the rapid development of other East and Southeast Asian economies. The Vietnamese can now compare their economic situation with those of neighbouring countries. Why Vietnam did so well in wartime – defeating such powerful enemies as France and the USA – but has performed so poorly in peacetime, continues to be an unanswered question for millions of Vietnamese people. Their relative poverty more than 25 years after reunification has hurt the pride of the nation.

Today 'economic diplomacy' (*ngoai giao kinh te*) is the most important task of the Ministry of Foreign Affairs. In fact, 'Vietnam perceives that as a developing country, the threat of lagging behind in economic development is the greatest threat to Vietnam's national security' (Pham Cao Phong 2002: 3). According to foreign policy-makers, diplomatic activities need to focus on the following areas:

- To contribute to the process of integrating Vietnam into the regional and world economy;
- To promote foreign trade, especially finding new markets and expanding old ones to increase export of commodities, services and labour;
- To attract FDI and other international investments;
- To campaign for ODA, other economic assistance and settlement of Vietnam's foreign debt;
- To promote tourism and technology transfer;
- To mobilise the contributions of the overseas Vietnamese community for the development of the country (Bo Ngoai Giao 2000: 3–7).

Obviously, these tasks are almost entirely new. Before *doi moi*, 'economic factors' in Vietnamese foreign policy were mentioned. Vietnam used to 'beg for aid' (*di xin vien tro*) from the communist bloc, primarily from the USSR. Foreign trade was of little importance, as there was no need to compensate or pay for goods received. This made Vietnam's economy extremely inactive and inefficient. Since 1991, Vietnam has reformed its economy and started to trade with the outside world; economic reform has become an imperative and a 'one-way ticket' for the Communist Party. Kent Bolton even argued that the VCP has begun a process whereby its own legitimacy will be based – and presumably therefore evaluated – in terms of its economic performance rather than more abstract ideological factors (Bolton 1999: 192). Indeed, economic factors weigh heavily in Vietnam's foreign policy orientation, and have played a direct role in the development of bilateral relations (Thayer and Amer 1999: 220).

Therefore, it is not difficult to understand why foreign policy has assumed such new tasks. The leadership has embraced international economic integration, and affirmed that Vietnam must join the 'economic race' (*chay dua kinh te*), and cannot stand outside the process of globalisation and regionalisation. Vietnam has become linked closely with developed economies of East Asia, such as Japan, Taiwan, Hong Kong, South Korea and Singapore. Economic questions are a central element affecting Vietnam's relations with the European Union (EU) and the USA. It seems that Vietnam's economic development still relies much on foreign investments and markets, notwithstanding Vietnamese leaders' calls for 'bringing into play the inner strength' (*phat huy noi luc*) of the nation.

Given the growing role of trade diplomacy in Vietnam's foreign policy and the increasing importance of 'economic security' within the concept of national security (Pahm Cao Phong 2002: 3), Vietnam's membership of ASEAN prominently reflects economic interests among other central strategic issues. ASEAN membership seems to be both the materialisation and institutional cornerstone of Vietnam's post-1988 foreign policy. ASEAN has provided a suitable framework for the implementation of the two core elements in this respect: diversification and multilateralisation of the country's foreign relations. However, while the process of foreign policy-making in general has become more open and inclusive, resulting in a growing non-governmental impact, Vietnam's ASEAN policy is still almost exclusively an arena for state actors. Then again, this does not seem to be a specific feature of Vietnamese foreign policy, but can be observed in most ASEAN member states.

Vietnam's interests and role in ASEAN

The following analysis will be guided by two arguments. First, as far as Vietnam's *interests* in ASEAN are concerned, state actors prefer a status quo organisation that clings to its traditional principles, and strongly object to any initiative which could be interpreted as a move towards supra-nationality. ASEAN is perceived as an institutionalised framework of inter-governmental co-operation, suitable firstly to further Hanoi's overall strategy of diversifying its international relations, secondly to bridge the old Cold War gap between Vietnam and the USA, China and Japan, and thirdly to contribute to the nation's economic development. Second, officially state actors do not aim at playing any open leadership role in ASEAN, arguing that a low profile better suits Vietnam's overall interests. At the same time, as the most advanced among the new member states admitted since the mid-1990s, Vietnam has adopted the role of an informal spokesman for this group, which includes Burma, Laos and Cambodia. At the same time, Vietnam has been the leading force in working towards bridging the ASEAN–China gap.

Does Vietnam play any constructive role in ASEAN as a result of the government's new foreign policy strategy? The Voice of Vietnam radio station insists that it does. 'As the host and chair of the ASEAN Standing Committee in the 2000–1 term, Vietnam has made significant contributions to the success of ASEAN' (BBC Worldwide Monitoring, 31 July 2001). However, the annual series of ASEAN meetings held in July 2001 in Hanoi rather emphasised ASEAN's post-1997 identity crisis. Apart from a vague agreement to work towards bridging the development gap between the impoverished and richer member nations, ASEAN failed to produce new initiatives. Most observers complained about the lack of progress, or even labelled the meeting series a non-event. According to a report by the organisation's outspoken Secretary General Rudolfo Severino, 'ASEAN has slipped into its worst times both in reality and in perception'.[2] Can Vietnam be blamed for this state of affairs? Obviously previous ASEAN chairs had been more active in trying to adjust to the structural changes in the Asia-Pacific. The 1998 ASEAN Ministerial Meeting (AMM) in Manila was characterised by the group's most lively debate ever, which resulted in the groundbreaking decision to review ASEAN's cardinal principal of strict consensus-building and non-interference. Two years later in Singapore the Foreign Ministers agreed to institutionalise this new concept of 'enhanced interaction' by establishing the ASEAN Troika. Partly modelled on the EU Troika, the mechanism should enable the organisation's sitting chair to formally consult with his immediate predecessor and successor to tackle specific problems with regional implications.

Against the background of previous meetings and from the perspective of a neutral observer, the Hanoi AMM might be seen as a step back as the organisation reiterated its firm commitments to decision-making based on consensus and non-interference. However, the original and long-undisputed concept of a non-interventionist ASEAN is more in line with Vietnam's national interest than any attempts to establish elements of supra-nationality. Therefore, the Vietnamese Foreign Ministry's strategy to foster the traditional ASEAN way rather than following up on 'engagement' and other post-1997 initiatives seemed to be a rational decision. Vietnam has slowed down the pace of intra-regional integration, with respect to both economic and political co-operation, in order to reduce the danger of external interference with its domestic affairs and any outside attempts to undermine its sovereignty.

The government's reaction to September 11 and the subsequent 'war on terrorism' declared by the USA has been in line with this general foreign policy strategy. On the one hand, Vietnam has co-operated with the USA and ASEAN on the issue of anti-terrorist measures. The government agreed to monitor all transactions via the banking system in order to detect possible money transfers to terrorist groups, and promised to share with the USA any intelligence on possible terrorist organisations. Most importantly, Vietnam signed the 2002 'US–ASEAN Joint Declaration for Co-operation to Combat International Terrorism', when US Secretary of State Colin Powell met ASEAN foreign ministers. On the other hand, the Vietnamese government made clear that 'anti-terrorist fights should be carried out in the spirit of respecting independence, sovereignty and national independence'.[3]

A multilevel foreign policy aiming at a stable and peaceful regional order is perceived as the precondition for Vietnam's re-emergence as a respected figure on the chessboard of international relations and – perhaps even more important – the country's successful economic development towards the self-proclaimed goal of basically reaching NIC-status (newly industrialised country) by 2020.[4] Although other governments in Southeast Asia think along similar strategic lines, elsewhere in the region the importance of long-term security is not as overemphasised as in the case of Vietnam. The founding members of ASEAN were already well integrated within the regional and global environment and not forced to come to terms with former enemies, a challenge faced by Vietnam when the Cold War came to an end.

Despite Hanoi's clear hints in 1990–2 that Vietnam was ready for ASEAN membership, the strictly anti-communist association was not yet prepared to admit Vietnam. Although Vietnam 'began actively working on improving relations with the ASEAN members' (Amer 1999: 1,041), signed the ASEAN Treaty of Amity and Co-operation (the organisation's code of conduct) and was subsequently granted observer status in 1992, full membership was not on the short-term agenda. All over the region, senior government officials and observers alike predicted a long transitional period of five to 10 years (see Dosch 1997 for details). However, given Vietnam's rapid and successful process of redirecting its foreign policy on the one hand, and changing perceptions and interests among the old ASEAN members on the other, the country's full membership became feasible much sooner than expected. Most important was a convergence of key security interests. Both Vietnam and ASEAN perceived the need to engage Beijing while at the same time holding on to the strategic option of 'preventive containment towards China' (Rüland 1999: 338, 343).[5] Either way, an enlarged ASEAN was expected to be more capable of dealing with the task. Although officially the Chinese government welcomed Vietnam's admission in 1995 as a contribution to regional stability, it had earlier tried to discourage its neighbour from joining the organisation. Prior to Vietnam's admission, a group of Chinese academics from think tanks and research institutes urged the government in Hanoi not to proceed with the quest for membership, as a Vietnamese participant of the meeting recalled (personal interview, Hanoi, June 2001).

After Vietnam had joined ASEAN, reconciling the dual interests of bridging the gap between itself and the leading extra-regional powers, while at the same time trying to minimise extra-regional influence, have been a tightrope walk. In other words, it has been Vietnam's primary strategic interest within ASEAN to foster its international position and status, *as well as* to secure its national and political integrity by means of regional reassurance and support. This approach is best demonstrated with regard to Vietnam–US relations. Vietnamese government officials and observers from academia confirm that ASEAN membership and the institutional framework provided by the organisation have helped the government to normalise relations with the Cold War enemy.

Most neutral observers agree that Vietnam's admission into ASEAN has enhanced its bargaining position with other states. As a member of the regional organisation, Vietnam became strategically more important to its former Cold War adversaries China and the USA (see, for example, Thayer 1997b: 367). Although one cannot empirically verify that ASEAN membership was the cause for the rapid improvements in Hanoi's relations with Beijing and Washington (because it is impossible to know what would have happened in a 'no-ASEAN scenario'), a significant impact of the 'ASEAN factor' is nevertheless very likely. In both cases the speed of rapprochement has been impressive. As for US–Vietnam links, the formal normalisation of relations took place in July 1995, a few days before Vietnam's admission into ASEAN. In July 2000, Hanoi and Washington signed a Bilateral Trade Agreement (BTA) under which Vietnam will enjoy normal trade relations with the USA and vice versa. After Bill Clinton's landmark October 2000 presidential visit to Vietnam, in July 2001 Secretary of State Colin Powell met Vietnamese Prime Minister Phan Van Khai and VCP General Secretary Nong Duc Manh during the ASEAN Meetings in Hanoi. The latter event shows the importance of ASEAN as a framework for bilateral side-meetings, which often attract more attention and produce more immediate results than the formal multilateral gatherings.

As far as intra-regional relations are concerned, Vietnam's most important goal is to improve relations with Thailand, its traditional rival to the West and competitor for a pre-eminent power position in mainland Southeast Asia. A desire to ground the potentially conflictual Vietnam–Thailand relationship within the institutionalised framework of ASEAN co-operation has been in accord with two distinct features of the association. These are: ASEAN's status as a security community whose members refrain from using military force against other members; and ASEAN's role as an interpersonal network supporting border-crossing contacts at a range of governmental and non-governmental levels (see Dosch and Mols 1998 for a more detailed discussion).

ASEAN network membership has made it easier to strengthen links with Indonesia, the only ASEAN state that had maintained a generally sympathetic attitude towards Vietnam throughout the Cold War. Even during times of diametrically opposed ideological outlooks, the Indonesian political elite had cultivated a myth of brotherhood in their perceptions of – and attitudes towards – Vietnam. According to this view, Indonesia and Vietnam stood out from the other Southeast Asian nations because of their respective anti-colonial struggles. Unlike other young nations in the region, Indonesia and Vietnam fought for national independence immediately after World War II. Although the Vietnamese elite has never really reciprocated this sentiment of quasi-familial ties, the Indonesian perception has naturally been appreciated in Hanoi. Not surprisingly, Indonesia was also the driving force behind Vietnam's quick integration into ASEAN, while Thailand initially tried to delay the process in order to prevent a possible Hanoi–Jakarta axis.[6] Bangkok's fears of joint Indonesian–Vietnamese efforts to balance, if not contain, Thailand have proved unfounded, however.

ASEAN membership not only provided Vietnam with the opportunity of regular contacts with the leading global and regional powers, but also gave instant access to a wide range of treaties and organisations, such as the ASEAN–Japan Forum and the EU–ASEAN Co-operation Agreement. In sum, it seems safe to conclude that ASEAN membership has positively affected Vietnam's efforts to normalise, diversify and improve its foreign relations, thereby contributing to a more stable and secure regional environment. Not surprisingly, Vietnam's political elite has expressed satisfaction with the results of ASEAN membership. As Minister for Foreign Affairs Nguyen Dy Nien put it: 'Vietnam's entry into ASEAN has made a significant contribution to implementing the State and Party's foreign policy of independence, sovereignty, diversification and multilateralisation' (Nguyen Dy Nien 2000: 7, 9).

Along with its pursuit of strategic and political objectives, Vietnam has viewed ASEAN 'as a means to accelerate economic reform, modernisation and convergence with this dynamic region' (Gates 2000: 7). However, whereas Hanoi's strategic interests have generally been straightforward, at first glance it can be difficult to distinguish genuine economic interests from mere political rhetoric. In a general sense ASEAN membership has certainly been 'profitable to the industrialisation and modernisation of the Socialist Republic of Vietnam' (Nguyen Duy Quy 2000: 16). For example, intra-regional investment has significantly increased since Vietnam joined the organisation. By 2000, registered capital from other ASEAN countries accounted for US $9.2 billion, 320 per cent more than in 1995. The quickly improved Vietnam–Japan relations, symbolised by a massive 250 per cent increase of Japanese ODA in 1995, totalling US $600 million, has also partly been attributed to Vietnam's admission to ASEAN (Nguyen Duy Quy 2000: 15).[7] Last but not least, Vietnam's formal commitment to AFTA seems to have had a positive effect on state agencies. David Truong observes: 'The Ministry of Trade has managed rapidly to exploit new trade relations and increase its overall effectiveness in regulating market and trade distortions' (Truong 1998: 336). Overall, however, a general lack of effective co-ordination among state bodies within the bureaucracy and the prevailing pattern of institutional particularism are still visible features of Vietnam's political system.

More appealing is the argument that Vietnam's participation in AFTA and other schemes of economic co-operation such as the ASEAN Investment Area (AIA) and ASEAN Industrial Co-operation (AICO) 'paved the way for Vietnam's participation in other co-operation mechanisms and organisations such as APEC, WTO [World Trade Organisation] …' (Nguyen Dy Nien 2000: 7). In fact, one of Hanoi's core interests in joining ASEAN was to use the association as a vehicle for fast-track access to other organisations – a strategy that has proved successful. It is safe to assume that without ASEAN membership Vietnam would have been unable to join APEC as early as 1998, and might not have succeeded in obtaining observer status at the WTO.

This example again demonstrates the importance of ASEAN membership as a central element of Vietnam's overall foreign policy strategy of normalising and diversifying foreign relations and integrating itself in the regional and global post-Cold War order as quickly as possible. But what role has Vietnam played within ASEAN itself, to further its various interests? On the one hand, any Vietnamese leadership ambitions in ASEAN, or attempts to fill the 'guidance vacuum' caused by Indonesia's post-crisis inability to resume its traditional role as the organisation's *primus inter pares*, are categorically denied in Hanoi. On the other hand, national analysts usually claim that Vietnam has played a distinct role in three areas: China–ASEAN relations, integrating new ASEAN members, and preserving the 'ASEAN way'.

Bridging the ASEAN–China gap

The integration of China's arch-rival into ASEAN increased the group's strategic importance to Beijing. To some extent, Vietnam's admission transformed bilateral Sino–Vietnamese disputes into multilateral problems involving China and ASEAN as a group (see Thayer 1997b: 367). Most importantly, the enlargement of ASEAN meant that the association now included all of China's adversaries in the conflict about overlapping territorial claims in the South China Sea, especially with respect to the Spratly Islands. It increased both Vietnam's and ASEAN's bargaining position with China. Furthermore, since 1995 Vietnam has worked towards a more united ASEAN position *vis-à-vis* Beijing by constantly trying to convince its fellow members that a joint approach was crucial in order to get any Chinese concessions with respect to the residual conflicts (Will 1999: 306). This task has never been an easy one, given the multitude of different national China strategies and policies within the group. At least Vietnam's efforts seem to have resulted in general agreement that 'ASEAN's solidarity requires a common opposition to any use of force by the PRC [People's Republic of China]' (Umbach 2000: 175). More specifically, Vietnam has played an instrumental role in the ASEAN–China negotiations on a code of conduct for the South China Sea.

Integrating Burma, Laos and Cambodia into ASEAN

Soon after Vietnam had joined ASEAN, Hanoi started lobbying for the admission of the three remaining Southeast Asian states, Burma, Laos and Cambodia. The motivation was obvious: a further widening of ASEAN would help consolidate Vietnam's post-Cold War position in Indochina, strengthening Vietnam's regional role within an accepted, institutional framework. Additionally, to secure the maximum assistance from the original ASEAN members for modernising its economy, Vietnam needed the support of broadly 'like-minded' states faced with similar economic challenges. When Vietnam hosted the sixth ASEAN summit in

1998, Foreign Minister Nguyen Manh Cam used this opportunity to push for Cambodia's immediate admission into ASEAN. The Heads of Government, however, postponed Cambodian membership due to its unstable and conflict-ridden domestic situation. Eventually, Cambodia joined ASEAN as its tenth member in April 1999, at a ceremony in Hanoi. Since the completion of ASEAN–10, Vietnam has actively aimed at reducing the economic gap between the old and new members. Vietnam's efforts resulted in the *Hanoi Declaration On Narrowing Development Gap For Closer ASEAN Integration*, which was signed in July 2001. Since most of the original members have been reluctant to agree on any specific multi-lateral programmes that would go beyond already existing bilateral activities, the document remains vague. Paragraph 1 of the Declaration states,

> We shall devote special efforts and resources to promoting the development of the newer Member Countries of ASEAN (Cambodia, Laos, Burma, and Vietnam or CLMV) with priority given to infrastructure, human resource development, and information and communication technology.
>
> (ASEAN 2001b)

More important than the wording, however, is the declaration's de facto official acknowledgement of the existence of two sub-groups within ASEAN. As far as political relations within ASEAN are concerned, Vietnam has been more supportive – or, seen from a different perspective, less critical – of Burma than other ASEAN states, in order to foster sub-regional solidarity among the new members.

Keeping the traditional 'ASEAN way' alive

Vietnam has been keen to block any attempts at watering down key norms and principles such as consensus building and non-interference. In 1998, when Thailand's Foreign Minister Surin Pitsuwan proposed replacing the group's non-interference policy with 'flexible engagement' – drawing on then Malaysian Deputy Prime Mninister Anwar Ibrahim's call for a new policy of 'constructive intervention' (Anwar 1997) – only the Philippines supported it. But the concept, which was later renamed 'enhanced interaction', gained ground. Two years later in Bangkok the foreign ministers formally approved Thailand's proposal for an ASEAN troika. However, the implementation of this concept, which would represent a quantum leap in regional integration, has been held back by the increasingly assertive new ASEAN members. Vietnam and Burma are the most vocal, and the least keen on speedy integration. According to a source close to the Vietnamese government,

> Vietnam is keen to keep the status quo of traditional ASEAN principles and wants to slow down the process of any development towards active engagement. Vietnam will stay with this approach for at least the next five to 10 years.
>
> (Personal interview in Hanoi, June 2001)

In fact, Vietnam used the opportunity of hosting the 2001 ASEAN meeting series to water down the initiatives of previous chairmen. The Joint Communiqué of the 34th ASEAN Ministerial Meeting does not make a single reference to flexible engagement, enhanced interaction or the Troika (see ASEAN 2001c). Accordingly, the ARF meeting stressed the importance of more confidence-building measures rather than graduating to preventive diplomacy, the second phase of a gradual three-stage evolution of establishing trust among its members. The three-step approach (with conflict resolution as the ultimate goal) was agreed upon following the first meeting of the forum in 1994. Vietnam's interest in slowing down the ARF process is especially reflected in paragraph 4 of the Chairman's Statement:

> The Ministers reaffirmed that the ARF will continue to develop at a pace comfortable to all ARF participants and emphasised the importance of ARF making decisions by consensus and on the basis of non-interference into one another's internal affairs.
>
> (ASEAN 2001a)

It would be factually unsound, however, to put the blame for ASEAN's blocked institutional evolution on Vietnam alone. Other members such as Burma, Laos or Malaysia have been reluctant to share the enthusiasm for reform expressed by Thailand, the Philippines and, periodically, Singapore.

Conclusion

We have tried to shed some light on the structural changes in Vietnam's foreign policy which date back to the early days of the *doi moi* process and especially gained momentum after Politburo Resolution No. 13 of May 1988, which outlined a new approach of 'diversification' and 'multilateralisation' of the country's foreign affairs. The 'new outlook', as the concept has been dubbed, was mainly the result of lessons learnt from the foreign policy failures of the Cold War days: Vietnam's intervention in Cambodia, over-reliance on the USSR and general isolationism. Despite the fact that parts of the old Marxist–Leninist political elite have not completely lost their impact on foreign policy-making – particularly those aspects related to national security – the de-ideologisation of foreign policy is the most decisive element of Vietnam's changed approach towards the outside world.

Major achievements of the post-1988 foreign policy era, both in terms of structures and actors, may be summarised as follows:

- The rapid multiplication of diplomatic relations with other states, most importantly the USA;
- The ongoing dialogue between China and ASEAN on conflicting territorial claims and other bilateral relations blackspots;
- A shift from a narrowly 'hard (military) security' defined foreign policy strategy to a significantly more open and multidimensional approach, including trade diplomacy as a feature of growing importance;

- Vietnam's 1995 admission into ASEAN, which was achieved much earlier than originally expected.

ASEAN could be described as Vietnam's foreign policy arena in miniature, because most of Hanoi's new foreign policy interests and goals are reflected in its approach towards the organisation, including:

- The diversification of Vietnam's international relations;
- Closing the old Cold War gap between Vietnam and the USA, China and Japan;
- Strengthening bilateral ties within the immediate regional neighbourhood;
- Improved relations with Thailand, perceived as Vietnam's long-term regional adversary;
- Improved relations with Indonesia, one of the only non-communist states that has traditionally adopted a sympathetic view *vis-à-vis* Hanoi;
- Exploring suitable and effective means of contributing to the nation's economic development.

Although Vietnam has consciously refrained from playing any open leadership role in ASEAN, realising that a low-key approach would suit its interests better in the wake of fresh international memories of Vietnam's former hegemonic role in Indochina, Hanoi has put its mark on ASEAN affairs in three key areas:

- ASEAN's improving relations with China;
- Efforts to narrow the development gap between the six original members of ASEAN and the new, post-1995 members: Burma, Cambodia, Laos and Vietnam;
- Vocally supporting the organisation's traditional key values: consensus building and strict non-interference.

The question remains whether Vietnam can manage to have its cake and eat it, for which read: making maximum use of the organisation as a vehicle for the achievement of vital foreign policy goals, while at the same time opposing any attempts towards speeding up ASEAN's institutional evolution.

Acknowledgements

The authors wish to thank Professor Krzysztof Gawlikowski, Dr Liselotte Odgaard and Dr Martin Gainsborough for their valuable comments on parts of earlier drafts of this chapter. Research for this chapter was partly supported by a British Academy grant.

Notes

1 Although there is no absolutely independent or non-state organisation in Vietnam, the role that many organisations play is similar to that of NGOs. Therefore in Vietnam a common understanding is that these quasi-NGOs engage in track-two diplomacy.

2 As quoted by Singapore's Foreign Minister S. Jayakumar (see Channel NewsAsia, 27 July 2001, 'ASEAN to act to improve "disarray" image').

3 As cited in Xinhua General News Service, 'Vietnam says anti-terrorist measures should be in line with UN Charter', 5 December 2002.

4 The official announcement of the VCP is 'to basically turn Vietnam into a modern-oriented industrialised country by 2020' (Communist Party of Vietnam 2001: 35). The common understanding is to lay the basic foundations for Vietnam to become an NIC without necessarily reaching NIC status by 2020. In Vietnamese the word *basic* is rather vague. Therefore the VCP uses this word to err on the side of caution.

5 A diffuse China threat was not the only reason for Vietnam's quick integration into ASEAN. Both ASEAN-6 and Vietnam saw the enlargement as a significant contribution to the strengthening of Southeast Asia's position in the conflict over 'Western liberalism versus Asian value-relativism' (Rüland 1999: 342). According to Hanoi's perception, a firm and successfully communicated East Asian standpoint in the debate reduced the threat of external Western pressure on Vietnam's domestic political order, thereby making a decisive contribution to national security.

6 Personal interviews with government officials and academics in Thailand and other ASEAN states, conducted in 1999.

7 For a detailed discussion of the impact of the 1997–8 Asian crisis on Vietnam's political and economic integration into Southeast Asia and the world, see Grossheim and Houben 2001.

Bibliography

Abuza, Zachary (2001) *Renovating Politics in Contemporary Vietnam*, Boulder, CO: Lynne Rienner.
Abuza, Zachary (2002) 'The lessons of Le Kha Phieu: changing rules in Vietnamese politics', *Contemporary Southeast Asia*, 24, 1: 121–45.
ADB (2000) *Country Economic Review – Socialist Republic of Vietnam*, Manila: Asian Development Bank.
Alvstam, Claes G. (1993) 'The impact of foreign direct investment on the geographical pattern of foreign trade flows in Pacific Asia with special reference to Taiwan', in Chris Dixon and David Drakakis-Smith (eds) *Economic and Social Development in Pacific Asia*, London: Routledge, 63–84.
Amer, Ramses (1999) 'Conflict management and constructive engagement in ASEAN's expansion', *Third World Quarterly*, 20, 5: 1,031–48.
Anwar Ibrahim (1997) 'Crisis prevention', *Newsweek*, 21 July.
ASEAN (2001a) 'Chairman's statement: the Eighth Meeting of the ASEAN Regional Forum', Hanoi, 25 July (http://www.aseansec.org/print.asp?file=/amm/hanoi05.htm).
ASEAN (2001b) *Hanoi Declaration on Narrowing Development Gap for Closer ASEAN Cooperation* (http://www.aseansec.org/print.asp?file=/amm/hanoi02.htm).
ASEAN (2001c) *Joint Communique of the 34th ASEAN Ministerial Meeting*, Hanoi, 23–24 July 2001 (http://www.aseansec.org/print.asp?file=/amm/hanoi04.htm).
Atkinson, John W. (1974) 'The mainsprings of achievement-oriented activity', in John W. Atkinson and Joel O. Raynor (eds) *Motivation and Achievement*, New York: John Wiley and Sons, 13–41.
AusAid (1997) *Vietnam's Health Sector*, unpublished brief, Hanoi: AusAid.
Bach Tan Sinh (1995) *Environmental Policy in Vietnam: Conflicting Interests in Quang Ninh Province – Coal Mining, Tourism and Livelihoods*, Hanoi: Ministry of Science and Technology.
Ban Nghien Cuu Lich Su Dang (1982) *Nhung Su Kien Lich Su Dang Bo Ha Noi [Events in the History of the Hanoi Party Committee]*, Hanoi: Hanoi Publishers.
Ban Tu Tuong Van Hoa Trung Vong (1992) *Thoi Cuoc Hien Nay Va Nhiem Vu Cua Chung Ta [Current situation and our task]*, Hanoi: Tu Tuong Van Hoa Publishers.
Banister, Judith (1985) *The Population of Vietnam*, International Population Reports, Series P-95, 77, Washington, DC: US Bureau of Census.
Barbot, Janine (1999) 'L'engagement dans l'arène médiatique. Les associations de lutte contre le sida', *Réseaux* n° 95, CENT/Hermès Sciences Publications, 156–96.
Beresford, Melanie (1987) 'Vietnam: Northernizing the South or Southernizing the North?' *Contemporary Southeast Asia*, 8: 261–75.
Beresford, Melanie (1988) *Vietnam: Politics, Economics and Society*, London: Pinter.

Beresford, Melanie (1989) *National Unification and Economic Development in Vietnam*, London: Macmillan.

Beresford, Melanie (1993) 'The political economy of dismantling the "bureaucratic" centralism and subsidy system in Vietnam', in Kevin Hewison, Richard Robison and Garry Rodan (eds) *Southeast Asia in the 1990s: Authoritarianism, Democracy, and Capitalism*, St Leonards: Allen and Unwin, 215–36.

Beresford, Melanie (1997) 'Vietnam: the transition from central planning', in Gary Rodan, Kevin Hewison and Richard Robison (eds) *The Political Economy of South-East Asia: An Introduction*, Melbourne and Oxford: Oxford University Press, 179–204.

Beresford, Melanie and Fraser, Lyn (1992) 'Political economy of environment in Vietnam', *Journal of Contemporary Asia*, 22: 3–19.

Beresford, Melanie and McFarlane, B. (1995) 'Regional inequality and regionalism in Vietnam and China', *Journal of Contemporary Asia*, 25: 50–72.

Bhaduri, A. (1982) 'Agricultural co-operatives and peasant participation in the Socialist Republic of Vietnam', in A. Bhaduri and A. Rahman (eds) *Studies in Rural Participation*, Geneva: International Labour Organisation, 34–57.

Blanc, Marie-Eve (2000) 'Campagne de prévention de l'épidémie de Sida au Vietnam : représentation des risques, institutionnalisation de la prévention et enjeux socio-politiques' in Marie-Eve Blanc *et al.* (eds) *Sociétés Asiatiques face au Sida*, Paris: Coll. Recherches Asiatiques, L'Harmattan, 171–92.

Blanc, Marie-Eve (2003a) *La pratique associative vietnamienne: tradition et modernité*, Villeneuve d'Ascq: ANRT–Presses Universitaires du Septentrion.

Blanc, Marie-Eve (2003b) *Continuité des soins et réseaux sociaux au Vietnam*, Rapport pour le GIP ESTHER, Paris.

Bo Ngoai Giao [Ministry of Foreign Affairs] (2000) 'Cong tac ngoai giao phuc vu kinh te trong giai doan hien nay' [Diplomatic activity serves economics in the present period], *Tai Lieu Tham Khao*, June: 3–7.

Bolton, Kent (1999) 'Domestic sources of Vietnam's foreign policy', in Carlyle A. Thayer and Ramses Amer (eds) *Vietnamese Foreign Policy in Transition*, Singapore: Institute of Southeast Asian Studies, 170–201.

Boudarel, Georges (1980) 'Influences and idiosyncracies in the line and practice of the Vietnam Communist Party', in William Turley (ed.) *Vietnamese Communism in Comparative Perspective*, Boulder, CO: Westview Press, 137–69.

Boudarel, Georges *et al.* (1983) *La bureaucratie au Vietnam*, Vietnam Asie Débat 1, Paris: L'Harmattan.

Boyd, Susan (1997) 'Vietnam since the Eighth Party Congress: What does it mean for Australian business?' in Adam Fforde (ed.) *Doi Moi: ANU Ten Years After the 1986 Party Congress*, Canberra: ANU Political and Social Change Monograph 24.

Breslin, Shaun (1999) 'China: developmental state or dysfunctional development', *Third World Quarterly*, 17: 689–706.

Brocheux, Pierre (1994) 'Vietnam: une sortie à petits pas', in Jean-Luc Domenach and François Godement (eds) *Communismes D'asie: Mort ou Métamorphose?* Bruxelles: Editions Complexe, 71–89.

Bryant, John (1998) 'Demographic change in north Vietnam', *Population and Development Review*, 24, 2: 235–69.

Bui Dinh Khoi (2000) 'Bao chi cho nong dan con nhieu bat cap' [Problems with newspapers for peasants], *Nong Thon Moi*, 47, June: 20.

Bui Tuyet Mai (ed.) (1999) *Les Muong au Vietnam* [The Muong in Vietnam], Hanoi: Cultural Publishing House.

Business Monitor International (1994) *Vietnam 1994*, London: BMI.

Business Monitor International (1999) *Vietnam 1999*, London: BMI.

Business Monitor International (2002) 'An economic downturn, of sorts', *South East Asia Monitor*, February.

Buttinger, Joseph (1958) *The Smaller Dragon: A Political History of Vietnam*, New York: Frederick A. Praeger.

Chaliand, Gerard (1969) *The Peasants of North Vietnam*, Harmondsworth: Penguin.

Chua, Reginald and Urban C. Lehner (1995) 'Investors go the extra mile to get a foot in Vietnam', *The Asian Wall Street Journal*, 15–16 December.

Chung A, Phan Huy Dung, Dang Van Khoat and Bui Hien (1997) *Joint Action and Social Mobilisation for HIV/AIDS Education, Prevention and Treatment in Vietnam*, Hanoi: National AIDS Committee.

CIEM (1997) *Vietnam's Economy in 1996*, Hanoi: National Political Publishers.

CIEM (2002) *Vietnam's Economy in 2001*, Hanoi: National Political Publishers.

Clarke, Gerard (1998) *The Politics of NGOs in South-East Asia. Participation and Protest in the Philippines*, London, New York: Routledge.

Co, Edna A. (1996) 'Reinterpreting civil society: the context of the Philippine NGO movement', in Alan G. Alegre (ed.) *Trends and Traditions, Challenges and Choices: A Strategic Study of Philippine NGOs*, Quezon City: Ateneo Center for Social Policy and Public Affairs, Philippines-Canada Human Resource Development Program, 190–205.

Cohen, Margot (2001a) 'Vietnam: thunder from the Highlands', *Far Eastern Economic Review*, 1 March.

Cohen, Margot (2001b) 'Vietnam: have your state and eat it', *Far Eastern Economic Review*, 22 March.

Cohen, Margot (2001c) 'Vietnam: safety valve of the people', *Far Eastern Economic Review*, 3 May.

Communist Party of Vietnam (1991) *Seventh National Congress: Documents*, Hanoi: The Gioi Publishers.

Communist Party of Vietnam (1995) *Eighth Plenum of the Central Committee: Documents*, Hanoi: The Gioi Publishers.

Communist Party of Vietnam (1996) *Eighth National Congress: Documents*, Hanoi: The Gioi Publishers, 33–44.

Communist Party of Vietnam (2001) *Ninth National Congress: Documents*, Hanoi: The Gioi Publishers, 29–34.

Council of Ministers (1981) 'On functions, tasks and institutions of the commune authorities', Decision No. 112-HDBT, Hanoi: Official Gazette, 15 October.

Crawford, Gordon (1995) *Promoting Democracy, Human Rights and Good Governance Through Development Aid: A Comparative Study of the Policies of Four Northern Donors*, Leeds: Centre for Democratisation Studies, University of Leeds.

Dang Canh Khanh (1996) 'Khi thanh nien tro thanh doi tuong nghien cuu khoa hoc' [When youth becomes a subject of science research], in Dang Canh Khanh, Pham Bang, Duong Tu Dam and Le Xuan Hoan (eds) *Nghien cuu thanh nien: Ly luan va Thuc tien [Studying Youth: Theory and Practice]*, Hanoi: Thanh Nien Publishers.

Dang Huu Thu (1993) *Than The Va Su Nghiep Nha Cach Mang Nguyen The Truyen [The Life and Times of the Revolutionary Nguyen The Truyen]*, Melun: 5 Boulevard des Carmes.

Dang Phong and Beresford, Melanie (1998) *Authority Relations and Economic Decision-Making in Vietnam: An Historical Perspective*, Copenhagen: Nordic Institute of Asian Studies.

Dao Huy Giam (2000) 'Joining AFTA. Swim without life vest', *Quoc Te* [International Affairs Review, Vietnam], August: 27.

Dao The Tuan (1995) 'The peasant household economy and social change', in Benedict J. Tria Kerkvliet and Doug J. Porter (eds) *Vietnam's Rural Transformation*, Boulder, CO: Westview Press, 139–63.

Dau Hoan Do, SIDA Vietnam and GCOP Vietnam (1999*) A Study on the Implementation of Grassroot Democracy*, unpublished report, Hanoi: SIDA.

Dixon, Chris (2000) 'State versus capital: the regulation of the Vietnamese foreign sector', *Singapore Journal of Tropical Geography*, 21: 295–315.

Dixon, Chris and Kilgour, Andrea (2002) 'State, capital and resistance to globalisation in the Vietnamese transitional economy', *Environment and Planning A*, 34: 599–618.

Doan Hue Dung (2000) 'Foreign-trained academics and the development of Vietnamese higher education', unpublished PhD thesis, University of Nottingham.

Dodsworth, John R., Erich Spitaller, Michael Braulke, Keon Hyok Lee, Kenneth Miranda, Christian Mulder, Hisanobu Shishido and Krishna Srinivasan (eds) (1996) *Vietnam's Transition to a Market Economy*, IMF Occasional Paper 135, Washington, DC: International Monetary Fund.

Dollar, David (1999) 'The transformation of Vietnam's economy: sustaining growth in the twenty-first century', in Jennie I. Litvack and Dennis A. Rondinelli (eds) *Market Reform in Vietnam: Building Institutions for Development*, Westport, CT: Quorum.

Dosch, Jörn (1997) *Die ASEAN: Bilanz eines Erfolges [ASEAN: Evaluating the Success]*, Hamburg: Abera.

Dosch, Jörn and Manfred Mols (1998) '30 years of ASEAN – achievements and prospects', *The Pacific Review*, 11, 2: 167–82.

Duckett, Jane (1998) *The Entrepreneurial State in China*, London and New York: Routledge.

Duiker, William J. (1976) *The Rise of Nationalism in Vietnam: 1900–41*, Ithaca, NY: Cornell University Press.

Duiker, William (2000) *Ho Chi Minh: A Life*, New York: Hyperion.

Ehrenberg, John (1992) *The Dictatorship of the Proletariat: Marxism's Theory of Socialist Democracy*, London and New York: Routledge.

Ehrenberg, John (1999) *Civil Society: The Critical History of an Idea*, New York: New York University Press.

Epstein, Steven (1996) *Impure Science, Aids, Activism and the Politics of Knowledge*, Berkeley, CA: University of California Press.

Epstein, Steven (2001) *Le virus est-il bien la cause du sida? Histoire du sida 1*, Paris: Les empêcheurs de penser en rond, 276.

Etemadi, Nasser (2000) 'Limites et actualité du concept de société civile', *L'Homme et la Société*, n°136–7, April–September, 95–110.

European Bank for Reconstruction and Development (2000) *Transition Report*, London: European Bank for Reconstruction and Development.

Fforde, Adam (1995) *Vietnam Economic Commentary and Analysis*, no. 7, November, Canberra: ADUKI.

Fforde, Adam (2001a) *Aduki Newsletter*, January (http://www.aduki.com.au).

Fforde, Adam (2001b) *Vietnam: Economic Commentary and Analysis* (http://www.aduki.com.au).

Fforde, Adam (2001c) 'Light within the ASEAN gloom? The Vietnamese economy since the first Asian economic crisis (1997) and in the light of the 2001 downturn', paper presented at the Vietnam Update 2001, Singapore, 19–20 November.

Fforde, Adam and Anthony Goldstone (1995) *Vietnam to 2005: Advancing on All Fronts*, London: Economist Intelligence Unit.

Fforde, Adam and Steve Seneque (1995) 'The economy and the countryside: the relevance of rural development policies', in Benedict J. Tria Kerkvliet and Doug J. Porter (eds) *Vietnam's Rural Transformation*, Boulder, CO: Westview Press, 97–138.

Fforde, Adam and Stefan de Vylder (1996) *From Plan to Market: The Economic Transition in Vietnam*, Boulder, CO: Westview Press.

Flagg, Michael (2000) 'Vietnam ad firms start on billboards, aspire to big-time', *Asian Wall Street Journal*, 8 September.

Food and Agriculture Organisation, Regional Office for Asia and The Pacific (2001) *Report of the Expert Consultation on Lychee Production in the Asia-Pacific Region*, Bangkok, May (http://www.fao.org/docrep/003/x6907e/x6907e00.htm).

Forsyth, Tim (1997) 'Industrialisation in Vietnam: social change and environment in transitional developing countries', in Richard M. Auty and Katrina Brown (eds) *Approaches to Sustainable Development*, London: Pinter, 247–67.

Freeman, Nick J. (1993) 'US sanctions against Vietnam: international business and development repercussions', *Columbia Journal of World Business*, 28, 2: 13–22.

Freeman, Nick J. (1998) 'Bust or boom?' *The Vietnam Business Journal*, June: 58–9.

Funston, John (2000) 'ASEAN and the principle of non-intervention – practice and prospects', *Trends in Southeast Asia*, Singapore: Institute of Southeast Asian Studies, 5, March.

Gaddis, John Lewis (1997) *We Now Know: Rethinking Cold War History*, Oxford: Clarendon Press.

Gainsborough, Martin (2001) 'The centre strikes back: big corruption cases and the politics of economic decentralisation in Vietnam', paper presented to the EUROSEAS Conference, London, 7 September.

Gainsborough, Martin (2002) 'Political change in Vietnam: in search of the middle-class challenge to the state', *Asian Survey*, 42: 694–707.

Gainsborough, Martin (2003) *Changing Political Economy of Vietnam: The Case of Ho Chi Minh City*, London and New York: RoutledgeCurzon.

Galal, Ahmed, Leroy Jones, Pankaj Tandon and Ingo Vogelsang (eds) (1994) *Welfare Consequences of Selling Public Enterprises*, New York: World Bank and Oxford University Press.

GAO (1999) *Vietnam Economic Data – Assessment of Availability and Quality*, report to Congressional Requesters, United States General Accounting Office, GAO/NSIAD–99–109.

Gaspard, Thu Trang (1992) *Ho Chi Minh à Paris*, Paris: L'Harmattan.

Gates, Carolyn L. (2000) 'Vietnam's economic transformation and convergence with the dynamic ASEAN economies', *Comparative Economic Studies*, 42: 7–43.

Gates, Carolyn L. and Mya Than (2001) 'ASEAN enlargement: an introductory overview', in Carolyn L. Gates and Mya Than (eds) *ASEAN Enlargement, Impacts and Implications*, Singapore: Institute of Southeast Asian Studies, 1–25.

General Statistics Office (1978) *30 Nam Phat Trien Kinh Te Va Van Hoa Cua Nuoc Viet Nam Dan Chu Cong Hoa [30 Years of Economic and Cultural Development of the Democratic Republic of Vietnam]*, Hanoi: Statistical Publishing House.

General Statistics Office (1994) *Vietnam Living Standards Survey, 1992–1993*, Hanoi: Statistical Publishing House.

General Statistics Office (1999) *Vietnam Living Standards Survey, 1997–1998*, Hanoi: Statistical Publishing House.

General Statistics Office (2001) *Viet Nam Nien Giam Thong Ke – Vietnam Statistical Yearbook 2000* [bilingual], Hanoi: Statistical Publishing House.

General Statistics Office (2002a) *Statistical Yearbook*, Hanoi: Statistical Publishing House.

General Statistics Office (2002b) *So Lieu Dan So Va Kinh Te Xa Hoi, 1975–2000 [Population and Socioeconomic Data, 1975–2000]*, Hanoi: Statistical Publishing House.

Giebel, Christoph J.F. (1996) 'Ton Duc Thang and the imagined ancestries of Vietnamese communism', unpublished PhD dissertation, Ithaca NY: Cornell University.

Gill, Graeme J. (2000) *The Dynamics of Democratization: Elites, Civil Society and the Transition Process*, New York: St Martin's Press.

Glassner, Martin I. (1993) *Political Geography*, New York: John Wiley.

Glewwe, Paul, Michele Gragnolati and Hasan Zaman (eds) (2000) *Who Gained from Vietnam's Boom in the 1990's? An Analysis of Poverty and Inequality Trends*, Washington, DC: Development Research Group, The World Bank.

Goscha, Christopher (2000) 'Le contexte asiatique de la guerre franco-vietnamienne: Réseaux, relations et économie, d'aôut 1945 à mai 1954', Thèse de doctorat, Paris: Ecole Pratique des Hautes Etudes (Ive section).

Government Committee for Organisation and Personnel (2000) *Training Material for Members of the People's Council at all Levels (Term of 1999–2004)*, Hanoi: National Political Publishing House.

Government-Donor-NGO Working Group (1999) *Vietnam Development Report 2000, Vietnam – Attacking Poverty*, Hanoi: World Bank.

Government of the Socialist Republic of Vietnam (1998) *On the Exercise of Democracy in Communes*, Decree No. 29/1998/ND-CP, Hanoi: Official Gazette, 11 May.

Government of Vietnam (2001) 'Strategy for socio-economic development 2001–2010', presented by the Central Committee, Eight Tenure to the Ninth National Congress, Government of Vietnam.

Gray, Michael L. (1999) 'Creating civil society? The emergence of NGOs in Vietnam', *Development and Change*, 30: 693–713.

Griffin, Keith (1998) 'The role of the state in the new economy', in Keith Griffin (ed.) *Economic Reform in Vietnam*, Basingstoke: Macmillan, 37–56.

Grossheim, Martin and Vincent J.H. Houben (eds) (2001) *Vietnam, Regional Integration and the Asian Financial Crisis*, Passau: University of Passau, Institute for Southeast Asian Studies.

Gutmann, Amy (1993) 'Democracy', in Robert E. Goodin and Philip Pettit (eds) *A Companion to Contemporary Political Philosophy*, Oxford: Blackwell, 411–21.

Haggard, Stephan (1990) *Pathways From The Periphery: The Politics of Growth in the Newly Industrialising Countries*, Ithaca, NY: Cornell University Press.

Hang Chuc Nguyen (1989) 'Vien Phi: Noi Oan Nghiet Cua Nguoi Ngheo' [Hospital bills: the poor's heavy burden], *Dai Doan Ket*, 10 July.

Hardy, Andrew (2001) 'Rules and resources: negotiating the household registration system in Vietnam under reform', *Sojourn*, 16: 187–212.

Harris, Nigel and David Lockwood (1997) 'The war-making state and privatisation', *Journal of Development Studies*, 33, 5: 597–634.

Held, David (2001) 'Democracy', in Joel Krieger (ed.) *The Oxford Companion to Politics of the World* (second edition), Oxford and New York: Oxford University Press, 196–200.

Heng, Russell Hiang-Khng (2001) 'Media negotiating the state: in the name of the law in anticipation', *Sojourn*, 16, 2: 213–37.

HEPR (1999) *First Forum on the National Target Programme on Hunger Eradication and Poverty Reduction*, unpublished report: UNDP and GTZ.

Hiebert, Murray (1991) 'The rise of Saigon', *Far Eastern Economic Review*, 5 September: 62–5.

Hiebert, Murray (1996) *Chasing the Tigers: A Portrait of the New Vietnam*, Tokyo: Kodansha International.

Hiebert, Murray and S. Awanohara (1994) 'Lukewarm welcome', *Far Eastern Economic Review*, 17 February: 14–17.

Higgott, Richard (1999) 'The political economy of globalisation in East Asia: the salience of 'region-building', in Kris Olds, Philip F. Kelly and Peter Dicken (eds) *Globalisation and the Asia-Pacific: Contested Territories*, London and New York: Routledge, 91–106.

Hoang Quoc Viet (1965) *A Heroic People*, Hanoi: Foreign Languages Publishing House.

Hoang Van Chi (1964) *From Colonialism to Communism – A Case Study of North Vietnam*, New York: Frederick Praeger.

Hoang Van Hoan (1988) *A Drop in the Ocean*, Beijing: Foreign Languages Press.

IMF (1993) *Balance of Payments Manual* (fifth edition), Washington, DC: IMF.

IMF (1996) 'Vietnam: recent economic developments', *IMF Staff Country Report no. 96/145*, Washington, DC: IMF.

IMF (1999) 'Vietnam: selected issues', *IMF Staff Country Report No. 99/55*, Washington, DC: IMF.

IMF (2000) 'Vietnam: statistical appendix and background notes', *IMF Staff Country Report No. 00/116*, Washington, DC: IMF.

IMF (2002) 'Vietnam: selected issues and statistical appendix', *IMF Country Report No. 02/5*, Washington, DC: IMF.

International Youth Co-operation Development Center (2000) *Youth in Vietnam*, Hanoi: Youth Publishing House.

Irvin, George (1995) 'Vietnam: assessing the achievements of Doi Moi', *Journal of Development Studies*, 31, 5: 725–50.

Jamal, Vali and Karel Jansen (1998) *Agrarian Transition in Vietnam*, Working Paper, International Labour Organisation, SAP 2.74/WP.128 (http://www.ilo.org/public/english/dialogue/sector/papers/agrtrans/).

Jamieson, Neil L. (1993) *Understanding Vietnam*, Berkeley, CA: University of California Press.

Jamieson, Neil L., Le Trong Cuc and A. Terry Rambo (eds) (1998) *The Development Crisis in Vietnam's Mountains*, Honolulu: East-West Center.

Jamison, A. and Baark, E. (1995) 'From market reforms to sustainable development: the cultural dimensions of science and technology policy in Vietnam and China', in Irene Norlund, Carolyn Gates and Vu Cao Dam (eds) *Vietnam in a Changing World*, Richmond: Curzon, 269–92.

Japan External Trade Organization (1999) *JETRO White Paper on Foreign Direct Investment 1999*, Tokyo: JETRO.

Jerneck, Anne (1997) *The Role of the State in a Newly Transitionary Economy: The Case of Vietnam's General Corporations*, report prepared as part of a collaboration between SIDA Stockholm, the Department of Economic History at Lund University, and the Embassy of Sweden in Hanoi, Vietnam, September.

Keenan, Faith (1998) 'No rubber stamp: legislature reverses party bid for land reform', *Far Eastern Economic Review*, 10 December.

Kelly, P. Mick, Tran Viet Lien and Hoang Minh (2001) 'Responding to El Niño and La Niña – averting tropical cyclone impacts', in W. Neil Adger, P. Mick Kelly and Nguyen Huu Ninh (eds) *Living with Environmental Change and Social Vulnerability in Vietnam*, London: Routledge, 154–81.

Kerkvliet, Benedict J. Tria (1993) *State–Village Relations in Vietnam: Contested Co-operatives and Collectivization*, Working Paper 85, Monash University.

Kerkvliet, Benedict J. Tria (2001a) 'Introduction: analysing the state in Vietnam', *Sojourn*, 16: 179–86.

Kerkvliet, Benedict J. Tria (2001b) 'An approach to analysing state-society relations in Vietnam', *Sojourn*, 16: 238–78.

Kerkvliet, Benedict J. Tria and Doug J. Porter (1995) 'Rural Vietnam in rural Asia', in Benedict J. Tria Kerkvliet and Doug J. Porter (eds) *Vietnam's Rural Transformation*, Boulder, CO: Westview Press, 65–96.

Kerkvliet, Benedict J. Tria and Mark Selden (1998) 'Agrarian transformations in China and Vietnam', *The China Journal* (Special Issue: *Transforming Asian Socialism – China and Vietnam Compared*), July, 40: 37–58.

Khrushchev, Nikita S. (1990) *Khrushchev Remembers: The Glasnost Tapes*, Jerrold Schechter (trans.), Boston: Little, Brown and Co.

Kilgour, Andrea (2000) 'A study of low-income households and perceptions of environment problems during rapid urbanisation in Hanoi, Vietnam', unpublished PhD thesis, University of Liverpool.

Kleinen, John (1999a) 'Is there a "Village Vietnam"?', in Bernard Dahm and Vincent J.H. Houben (eds) *Vietnamese Villages in Transition. Background and Consequences of Reform Policies in Rural Vietnam*, Passau: Department of Southeast Asian Studies, 1–27.

Kleinen, John (1999b) *Facing the Future, Reviving the Past: A Study of Social Change in a Northern Vietnamese Village*, Singapore: Institute of Southeast Asian Studies.

Koch, Stephanie and Nguyen Bui Linh (2001) 'Child malnutrition', in Dominique Haughton, Jonathan Haughton and Nguyen Phuong (eds) *Living Standards During an Economic Boom: The Case of Vietnam*, Hanoi: Statistical Publishing House and UNDP.

Koh, David (2001a) 'The politics of a divided party and Parkinson's state in Vietnam', *Contemporary Southeast Asia*, 23: 533–51.

Koh, David (2001b) 'Negotiating the socialist state in Vietnam through local administration: the case of *karaoke* shops', *Sojourn*, 16: 279–305.

Kokko, Ari (1997) *Managing the Transition to Free Trade: Vietnamese Trade Policy for the 21st Century*, Stockholm: Stockholm School of Economics, Working Paper no. 34, May.

Kokko, Ari (2000) 'Structure, performance and reform requirements in the Vietnamese private sector', *Studies on Private Sector Development*, Stockholm: Swedish International Development Co-operation Agency.

Kokko, Ari and Fredrik Sjöholm (1997) *Small, Medium or Large? Some Scenarios for the Role of the State in the Era of Industrialisation and Modernisation in Vietnam*, Stockholm: Swedish International Development Co-operation Agency.

Kokko, Ari and Fredrik Sjöholm (2000) 'Some alternative scenarios for the role of the state in Vietnam', *The Pacific Review*, 13, 2: 257–77.

Kokko, Ari and Mario Zejan (1996) 'Vietnam 1996: approaching the next stage of reforms', *Macroeconomic Reports*, Stockholm: Swedish International Development Co-operation Agency.

Kolko, Gabriel (1997) *Vietnam: Anatomy of a Peace*, London: Routledge.

Laasko, Liisa (1995) 'Whose democracy? Whose decentralisation?', in Jochen Hippler (ed.) *The Democratisation of Disempowerment: The Problem of Democracy in the Third World*, East Haven: Pluto Press, 210–19.

Ladinsky, Judith and Ruth Levine (1985) 'The organization of health care in Vietnam', *Journal of Public Health Policy*, 6: 255–66.

Lall, Sanjaya (1993) 'India', in Daniel Chudnovsky (ed.) *Transnational Corporations and Industrialization* (United Nations Library on Transnational Corporations, vol. 11), London: Routledge, 217–42.

Lamb, David (2000) 'Vietnam ready to admit "free thinking" into its curriculum', *Learning English, Guardian Supplement*, 24 May.

Larmer, Brook (2001) 'Two girls and a shoe', *Newsweek* (special edition: *Issues Asia*), July–September.

Le Dang Doanh (1996) 'State-owned enterprise reform and its implications for industrialization in Vietnam', paper presented at Senior Policy Seminar on Industrialization and Integration: Vietnam and the World Economy, Hanoi, November.

Le Kha Phieu (2000) 'Phat Bieu Trong Le Khai Mac Ngay Viet Nam Tai Thuong Vien Phap' [Speech at the inauguration ceremony of Vietnam Day at the French Senate], in Hoc Vien Quan He Quoc Te [Institute for International Relations], *Tinh Hinh Quoc Te Va Chinh Sach Doi Ngoai Cua Viet Nam [International Affairs and Vietnam's Foreign Policy]*, Hanoi, 1: 20–6.

Liddell, Zunetta (1999) 'No room to move: legal constraints on civil society in Burma', in Burma Center Netherlands and Transnational Institute (ed.) *Strengthening Civil Society in Burma: Possibilities and Dilemmas for International NGOs*, Chiang Mai: Silkworm Books, 54–68.

Litvack, Jennie I. (1999) 'The dilemmas of change: revitalising social services in a period of transition', in Dennis A. Rondinelli and Jennie I. Litvack (eds) *Market Reform in Vietnam: Building Institutions for Development*, Westport, CT: Quorum, 47–69.

Ljunggren, Börje (1993) 'Market economies under Communist regimes: reform in Vietnam, Laos and Cambodia', in Börje Ljunggren (ed.) *The Challenge of Reform in Indochina*, Cambridge, MA: Harvard Institute for International Development, Harvard University Press.

Ljunggren, Börje (1996) '*Doi moi* in the year of the Eighth Party Congress: emerging contradictions in the reform process', mimeo, Hanoi, January.

Long, Lynellyn D., Le Ngoc Hung, Allison Truitt, Le Thi Phuong Mai and Dang Nguyen Anh (eds) (2000) 'Changing gender relations in Vietnam's post *Doi Moi* Era', *Policy Research Report on Gender and Development*, Working Paper Series no. 14, Washington, DC: World Bank.

Lowie, Robert H. (1921) 'Associations' and 'Theory of associations', *Primitive Society*, London: Routledge, 243-323.

Luhulima, C.P.F. (2000) 'Scope of ASEAN's security framework for the 21st century', *Trends in Southeast Asia No. 6*, Singapore: Institute of Southeast Asian Studies, April.

McAlister, John T. Jr (1971) *Vietnam: The Origins of Revolution*, Garden City, NY: Doubleday.

McCargo, Duncan (2001) 'Democratic consolidation in Pacific Asia', in Jeff Haynes (ed.) *Towards Sustainable Democracy in the Third World*, Basingstoke: Palgrave, 141–62.

McCormick, Barrett L. (1998) 'Political change in China and Vietnam: coping with the consequences of economic reform', *China Journal*, 40: 121–43.

MacLean, Ken (2001) *A Failure to Communicate: Socio-Cultural Obstacles to Translation and their Impact on Program Implementation*, Hanoi: Helvetas Vietnam.

McLeod, Mark W. (1999) 'Indigenous peoples and the Vietnamese revolution, 1930–1975', *Journal of World History*, 10: 353–89.

McNicoll, A. and P.B. Durst (1995) *Reform of the Forestry Sector: Towards a Market Orientation in China, Laos, Mongolia, Myanmar, and Vietnam, Fuzhou, Fujian Province, China, 21–26 March 1994*, Bangkok: FAO, Regional Office for Asia and the Pacific.

Mallon, Ray (1993) 'Vietnam: image and reality', in John Health (ed.) *Revitalising Socialist Enterprise: A Race against Time*, London: Routledge, 204–21.

Mallon, Ray (1996) 'State enterprise reform in Viet Nam: policy developments, achievements and remaining constraints', report prepared for the Asian Development Bank, Hanoi.

Mallon, Ray (1997) 'Mapping the playing field: options for reducing private sector disincentives in Viet Nam', paper prepared for the Swedish Embassy in Hanoi, mimeo, Hanoi, November.

Marr, David (1988) 'Tertiary education, research and the information sciences in Vietnam', in David G. Marr and Christine P. White (eds) *Postwar Vietnam: Dilemmas in Socialist Development*, Ithaca, NY: Cornell University Southeast Asia Program, 15–44.

Marr, David (1995) *Vietnam: The Quest for Power*, Berkeley, CA: University of California.

Marshall, Samantha (1998) 'Initial investors in Vietnam pack it in', *The Asian Wall Street Journal*, 26 June.

Merli, Giovanna and Jonathan London (2002) 'The decline of mortality in Northern Vietnam following independence', paper presented at the annual meeting of the Association of Asian Studies, Washington, DC.

Miller, Robert F. (1992) 'Civil society in communist systems: an introduction', in Robert F. Miller (ed.) *The Development of Civil Society in Communist Society*, Sydney: Allen and Unwin, 1–10.

Ministry of Agriculture and Rural Development (1999) *Guiding the Elaboration of the Convention on Protecting and Developing Forests in the Population Communities in the Hamlets and Villages in the Plains and Mountain Areas*, Circular No. 56/1999/TT-BNN-KL, Hanoi: Official Gazette, 30 March.

Ministry of Forestry (1991) *Vietnam: Forestry Sector Review Tropical Forestry Action Programme*, Hanoi.

MoET (1997) *Tong Ket va Danh Gia Muoi Nam Doi Moi Giao Duc va Dao Tao [Evaluation on Educational Reforms 1986-1996]*, Hanoi: MoET.

MoET (1999) *Tai Lieu Hoi Nghi Dao Tao Sau Dai Hoc – 3/1999 [Proceedings of the Conference on Vietnamese Postgraduate Education – March 1999]*, Hanoi: MoET.

MoET (2000a) *Du Thao De An: Quy Hoach Tong The Mang Luoi Cac Truong Dai Hoc, Cao Dang Va Trung Hoc Chuyen Nghiep Viet Nam Den Nam 2001 [The Draft Master Development Plan for the Higher Education and Vocational Education System up to 2010]*, Hanoi: MoET.

MoET (2000b) *Bao Cao: Chuyen De Giao Duc [Report on Education]*, unpublished report, Hanoi: MoET.

MoET (2001) *Du thao de an Quy hoach tong the mang luoi cac truong dai hoc, cao dang, va trung hoc chuyen nghiep Viet Nam giai doan den nam 2010 [A Proposed Master Plan for Reorganizing Universities, Colleges and Vocational Training centers in Vietnam, 2000–10]*, 5 January, Hanoi: MoET.

MoH (1991) *Health Statistics of Vietnam, 1986–1990*, Hanoi: MoH, Department of Health Statistics and Informatics.

Mol, Arthur P. and Frijns, J. (1997) 'Ecological restructuring in industrial Vietnam: the Ho Chi Minh City region', paper presented at EUROVIET III, University of Amsterdam, 6–10 July.

MoLISA (1999) *Tinh Hinh Thuc Hien Chuong Trinh Xoa Doi Giam Ngheo Cac Tinh Khu Vuc Mien Trung Va Tay Nguyen 6 Thang Dau Nam 1999 [Assessment of Hunger Elimination and Poverty Reduction Programmes in Central Highland Provinces in the First Six Months of 1999]*, unpublished report, Hanoi: MoLISA.

Möller, Kay (1999) 'Löst die ASEAN das vietnamesische Sicherheitsdilemma?' [Can ASEAN solve the Vietnamese security dilemma?], in Duy Tu Vu and Gerhard Will (eds) *Vietnams neue Position in Südostasien [Vietnam's New Position in Southeast Asia]*, Hamburg: Institut für Asienkunde, 265–86.

Mommsen, Wolfgang J. (1989) *The Political and Social Theory of Max Weber*, Cambridge: Polity Press.

MPI (1996) *Danh muc cac du an da duoc cap giay phep trong nam 1995 – List of Licensed Projects in 1995* [bilingual], Ho Chi Minh City: MPI, Tre Publishers.

MPI (1996–2000) *Danh muc cac du an da duoc cap giay phep – List of Licensed Projects* [bilingual, issued every quarter from 1996], Ho Chi Minh City: MPI, Tre Publishers.

National Assembly, Session 3 (1993) *Land Law*, 14 July (http://coombs.anu.edu.au/~vern/avsl.html)

Nattapong Thongpakde (2001) 'ASEAN free trade area: progress and challenges', in Mya Than (ed.) *ASEAN beyond the Regional Crisis*, Singapore: Institute of Southeast Asian Studies, 48–79.

Nestor, Curt (1997) 'Foreign investment and the spatial pattern of growth in Vietnam', in Chris Dixon and David Drakakis-Smith (eds) *Uneven Development in South East Asia*, Aldershot: Ashgate, 166–95.

Nestor, Curt (forthcoming) 'Foreign direct investment and regional economic development in Vietnam, 1988–2000', PhD thesis, Department of Human and Economic Geography, School of Economics and Commercial Law, Goteborg University.

Nevitt, Christopher Earle (1996) 'Private business associations in China: evidence of civil society or local state power?' *The China Journal*, 36, July: 25–43.

Ngo Vinh Long (1993) 'Reform and rural development in Vietnam: impact on class, sectoral and regional inequalities', in William S. Turley and Mark Selden (eds) *Reinventing Vietnamese Socialism*, Boulder, CO: Westview Press, 165–207.

Ngo Vinh Long (2002) 'Vietnam today', interview with Daniel C. Tsang, *Critical Asian Studies*, 34, 3: 459–64.

Nguyen Duy Quy (2000) 'Vietnam: contributions and initial results after five years of integration into ASEAN', *Vietnam Social Sciences*, 4: 3–17.

Nguyen Dy Nien (2000) 'We will successfully fulfil this responsibility', interview with H.E. the Minister for Foreign Affairs, *Quoc Te [International Affairs Review, Vietnam]*, August: 7–9.

Nguyen Hoang Anh (2000) 'Xay Dung Mo Hinh Cung Cap Tai Chinh Phu Hop De Phat Trien Nen Y Te Viet Nam' [Building an appropriate model for financing Vietnam's healthcare system], *Nghien Cuu Phap Luat [Journal of Legal Studies]*, 6: 68–77.

Nguyen Khac Vien (1974) *Tradition and Revolution in Vietnam*, Berkeley, CA: The Indochina Resource Center.

Nguyen Khac Vien (1993) *Vietnam: A Long History*, Hanoi: The Gioi Publisher.

Nguyen Manh Cam (1991) 'Phong Van Bo Truong Ngoai Giao Nguyen Manh Cam' [Interview with the Minister of Foreign Affairs, Nguyen Manh Cam], *Quan He Quoc Te*, October: 2.

Nguyen Phuong An (2002) 'Looking beyond *Bien Che*: the considerations of Vietnamese young graduates when seeking employment in the *Doi Moi* era', *Sojourn*, 17, 2: 221–48.

Nguyen Phuong An (2003) 'Between "still society" and "moving society": life choices and value orientations of Hanoi university graduates in post-reform Vietnam', unpublished PhD thesis, University of Hull.

Nguyen Thi Oanh (1998) 'Cac Hoat dong Xa hoi va Cong tac Xa hoi Chuyen nghiep' [Social activities and professional social work], *Sai Gon – Tp. Ho Chi Minh 300 nam hinh thanh va phat trien (1698–1998)[in Saigon – Ho Chi Minh City 300 Years of Formation and Development (1698–1998)]*, Trung Tam Khoa Hoc Xa Hoi va Nhan Van TP. Ho Chi Minh [Social Sciences and Humanities Centre of Ho Chi Minh City], So Van Hoa – Thong Tin Thanh Pho Ho Chi Minh [Culture and Information Committee of *Ho Chi Minh* City], 541–98.

Nguyen Thuong Luu, Vu Van Me and Nguyen Tuong Van (1995) 'Land classification and land allocation of forest land in Vietnam – a meeting of the national and local perspective', *Forest, Trees and People Newsletter*: 31–6.

Nguyen Tu Chi (1993) 'Le làng traditionnel au Bac Bo …' in *Le Village Traditionnel au Vietnam*, Hanoi: The Gioi, Edition en langues étrangères.

Nguyen Tuan Dung (1996) 'Foreign direct investment in Vietnam', in Suiwah Leung (ed.) *Vietnam Assessment: Creating a Sound Investment Climate*, Singapore: Institute of Southeast Asian Studies, 69–89.

Nguyen Van Chinh (2001) *Some Issues in the Estimation of Some Integrated Indicators and Compilation Main Accounts in Viet Nam*, Hanoi: General Statistical Office.

Nguyen Van Huyen (1994) *La civilisation ancienne du Vietnam*, Hanoi: Editions The Gioi.

Nguyen Van Phiet, Major-General (1992) 'Applying results of study on democracy-discipline measures in air defence service', *Quan Doi Nhan Dan*, 17 March.

Nguyen Van Tran (1995) *Viet Cho Me va Quoc Hoi [Writing for Mother and the National Assembly]*, California: Van Nghe.

Nguyen Van Trung (1996) *Chinh Sach Doi Voi Thanh Nien: Ly Luan Va Thuc Tien [Youth Policy: Theory and Practice]*, Hanoi: Chinh Tri Quoc Gia Publishers.

Nguyen Van Truong (1992) *An Approach to the Ecology of Vietnam*, Hanoi: Institute of Ecological Economy.

Nguyen Vu Tung (2002) 'Vietnam–ASEAN co-operation after the Cold War and the continued search for a theoretical framework', *Contemporary Southeast Asia*, 24, 1: 106–20.

Nhung Nguoi Cong San (1976) *[The Communists]*, Ho Chi Minh City: Thanh Nien.

Nilan, Pam (1999) 'Young people and globalizing trends in Vietnam', *Journal of Youth Studies*, 2, 3: 353–70.

Noordin Sopiee (1991) 'ASEAN and Indochina after a Cambodian settlement', in Dora Alves (ed.) *Change, Interdependence and Security in the Pacific Basin: The 190 Pacific Symposium*, Washington, DC: National Defense University Press, 315–36.

Nuscheler, Franz (1995) 'Democracy: a fragile export', in Jochen Hippeler (ed.) *The Democratisation of Disempowerment: The Problem of Democracy in the Third World*, East Haven: Pluto Press, 220–32.

OECD (1996) *Benchmark Definition of Foreign Direct Investment* (third edition), Paris: Organisation for Economic Co-operation and Development.

Pahl, Ray (1995) *After Success: Fin-de-Siècle Anxiety and Identity*, Cambridge: Polity Press.

Painter, M. (2003) 'The politics of economic restructuring in Vietnam: the case of state-owned enterprise "reform"', *Contemporary Southeast Asia*, 25, 1: 20–43.

Papin, Philippe (2000) 'Vietnam: party versus state', *Le Monde Diplomatique*, 12–13.

PFP (1996) 'Vietnam policy framework paper, 1996–1998', paper prepared by the Vietnamese authorities in collaboration with the staffs of the IMF and the World Bank, mimeo, Hanoi, January.

Pham Cao Phong (2002) 'Vietnam's new security perception: the role of economic security, paper prepared for the 43rd Annual ISA Convention, New Orleans, 24–27 March, 2002.

Pham Minh Hac (1998) *Vietnam's Education the Current Position and Future Prospects*, Hanoi: The Gioi Publishers.

Pham Minh Hac (1999) *Giao Duc Vietnam truoc Nguong Cua The Ky XXI* [Vietnam's Education at the Threshold of the Twenty-First Century], Hanoi: The Gioi Publishers.

Philippe Cao Van, Bourdeaut, J., Nguyen Minh Chau (1997) 'Les cultures fruitières au Vietnam, exemple des agrumes et du litchi dans la diversification agricole' [Fruit trees cultivation, the example of citrus and lychee in agricultural diversification], *Agriculture* and *Agriculture et Développement* (Vietnam Special, Joint Issue) September–October: 119–25.

Phillips, Herbert (1979) 'Some premises of American scholarship on Thailand', in Clark Neher (ed.) *Modern Thai Politics: From Village to Nation*, Cambridge, MA: Shenkman, 436–56.

Phong thong ke [General Statistics Office] (1996) *Nien Giam Thong Ke 1995 [Statistical Yearbook 1995]*, Hanoi: Nha Xuat Ban Thong Ke (Statistical Publishing House).

Phong thong ke [General Statistics Office] (1998) *Nien Giam Thong Ke Thanh Pho Ho Chi Minh 1997 [Ho Chi Minh City Statistical Yearbook 1997]*, Ho Chi Minh City: Ho Chi Minh City Statistical Office.

Phong thong ke [General Statistics Office] (1999) *Nien Giam Thong Ke Thanh Pho Ho Chi Minh 1998 [Ho Chi Minh City Statistical Yearbook 1998]*, Ho Chi Minh City: Ho Chi Minh City Statistical Office.

Phong thong ke [General Statistics Office] (2001) *Nien Giam Thong Ke 2000 [Statistical Yearbook 2000]*, Hanoi: Nha Xuat Ban Thong Ke (Statistical Publishing House).

Pike, Douglas (1994) 'Vietnam in 1993: uncertainty closes in', *Asian Survey*, 32, 1: 64–71

Pike, Douglas (2000) 'Informal politics in Vietnam', in Lowell Ditter, Haruhiro Fukui and Peter N.S. Lee (eds) *Informal Politics in East Asia*, Cambridge: Cambridge University Press, 269–89.

Politburo of the Communist Party of Vietnam (1998) *On Establishing and Implementing the Democracy Regulation in Localities*, Instruction No. 30/CT-TU, Hanoi: Official Gazette, 18 February.

Pool, M.M. (1999) 'Industrialization and modernization of the private sector in Vietnam 1991–1998', mimeo, Amsterdam.

Porter, Doug J. (1995) 'Economic liberalization, marginality and the local state', in Benedict J. Tria Kerkvliet and Doug J. Porter (eds) *Vietnam's Rural Transformation*, Boulder, CO: Westview Press, 215–46.

Porter, Gareth (1993) *Vietnam: The Politics of Bureaucratic Socialism*, Ithaca, NY: Cornell University Press.

Probert, Jocelyn and David S. Young (1995) 'The Vietnamese road to capitalism: decentralisation, *de facto* privatisation and the limits to piecemeal reform', *Communist Economies and Economic Transformation*, 7: 499–526.

Quan Xuan Dinh (2000) 'The political economy of Vietnam's transition process', *Contemporary Southeast Asia*, 22: 360–88.

Quinn-Judge, Paul (1982) *Far Eastern Economic Review*, 26 February.

Quinn-Judge, Sophie (2003) *Ho Chi Minh: The Missing Years*, London: Hurst.

Ramamurthy, Bhargavi (2001) 'The non-state manufacturing sector in Vietnam 1991–97: an analysis of the winners', in Per Ronnås and Bhargavi Ramamurthy (eds) *Entrepreneurship in Vietnam: Transformation and Dynamics*, Copenhagen: Nordic Institute of Asian Studies, 221–76.

Rivard, Richard J. and Khanh Hoang Ta (2000) 'Investing in Vietnam', *Business and Economic Review*, January–March: 8–13.

Robertson, David (1993) *A Dictionary of Modern Politics* (second edition), London: Europa Publishers.

Rondinelli, Dennis A. and Jennie I. Litvack (1999) 'Economic reform, social progress and institutional development: a framework for assessing Vietnam's transition', in Dennis A. Rondinelli and Jennie I. Litvack (eds) *Market Reform in Vietnam: Building Institutions for Development*, Westport, CT: Quorum, 1–30.

Rubin, Suzanne (1988) 'Learning for life? Glimpses from a Vietnamese school', in David G. Marr and Christine P. White (eds) *Postwar Vietnam: Dilemmas in Socialist Development*, Ithaca, NY: Cornell University Southeast Asia Program, 45–60.

Rüland, Jürgen (1999) 'Der Beitritt Vietnams zur ASEAN – Chance oder Hemmnis für die Vertiefung der regionalen Kooperation?' [Vietnam's accession into ASEAN: opportunity or obstacle for deepening of regional co-operation?], in Duy Tu Vu and Gerhard Will (eds) *Vietnams neue Position in Südostasien [Vietnam's New Position in Southeast Asia]*, Hamburg: Institut für Asienkunde, 333–62.

Sandhu K.S. (1992) 'ASEAN: achievements and prospects', paper presented to the ASEAN Seminar/Roundtable Conference, jointly organised by ASEAN Paris Committee (APC) and Institut Français des Relations Internationales (IFRI), Paris, 19–20 October.

Scholtes, Phillipe R. (1998) 'Business services and institutional support for industrial development in Vietnam', *ASEAN Economic Bulletin*, 15: 184–205.

Schraner, Ingrid (2001) 'A glimpse at the reality of a state farm and some theoretical consequences', in John Kleinen (ed.) *Vietnamese Society in Transition: The Daily Politics of Reform and Change*, Amsterdam: Het Spinhuis, 23–41.

Sidel, Mark (1996) 'The emergence of a non-profit sector and philanthropy in the Socialist Republic of Vietnam', in Tadashi Yamamoto (ed.) *Emerging Civil Society in the Asia Pacific Community*, Singapore: Japan Centre for International Exchange, Institute of Southeast Asian Studies, 293–304.

Sikor, Thomas and Dao Minh Truong (2000) *Sticky Rice and Collective Fields: Community-Based Development among the Black Thai*, Hanoi: Agricultural Publishing House.

Son Tung (1980) *Tran Phu*, Hanoi: Thanh Nien Publishers.

SRV (1994) *Report of the Government of the Socialist Republic of Vietnam to the Consultative Group Meeting*, Hanoi: SRV.

SRV (2002) *The Comprehensive Poverty Reduction and Growth Strategy*, Hanoi: SRV.

St John, Ronald Bruce (1997) 'End of the beginning: economic reform in Cambodia, Laos and Vietnam', *Contemporary Southeast Asia*, 19: 172–89.

Stowe, Judy (1997) 'Revisionism in Vietnam', paper presented at AAS conference, Washington, DC.

Sutton, Rebecca (1999) *The Policy Process: an Overview*, ODI Working Paper 118, London: ODI.

Tan Teng Lang (1985) *Economic Debates in Vietnam: Issues and Problems in Reconstruction and Development*, Singapore: Institute of Southeast Asian Studies.

Taylor, Peter J. (1993) *Political Geography: World-Economy, Nation-State and Locality* (third edition), Harlow: Longman.

Templer, Robert (1999) *Shadows and Wind: A View of Modern Vietnam*, New York: Penguin.

Tesoro, Jose Manuel (2000) 'Free to dream', *Asiaweek*, 24 November: 34–38.

Thai Duy Tuyen (ed.) (1995) *Nghien cuu Con Nguoi Viet Nam: Cac Quan diem va Phuong phap Tiep can* [Studying the Vietnamese people: perspectives and approaches], Hanoi: National Science and Technology Programme KX-07, Project KX-7-10.

Thai Quang Trung (1985) *Collective Leadership and Factionalism*, Singapore: Institute of Southeast Asian Studies.

Thanh Pho Ho Chi Minh Hai Muoi Nam (1975–95) (1996) *[Ho Chi Minh City: Twenty Years: 1975–95]*, Ho Chi Minh City: Ho Chi Minh City Publishing House.

Thanh Vu (2000) 'Chang le long nhan Hung Yen ton dong loi o chinh phu?' [Is the saturation of dry longan in Hung Yen due to the government?], *Nong Nghiep Viet Nam [Vietnamese Agriculture]*, 189 (1079), 19 December: 3.

Thaveeporn Vasavakul (1996) 'Politics of the reform of state institutions in the post-socialist era', in Suiwah Leung (ed.) *Vietnam Assessment: Creating a Sound Investment Climate*, Singapore: Institute of Southeast Asian Studies, 42–68.

Thaveeporn Vasavakul (1999) 'Rethinking the philosophy of central–local relations in post-communist Vietnam', in Mark Turner (ed.) *Central–Local Relations in Asia Pacific*, Basingstoke: Macmillan, 166–95.

Thayer, Carlyle A. (1992) 'Political reform in Vietnam: *doi moi* and the emergence of civil society', in Robert F. Miller (ed.) *The Development of Civil Society in Communist Systems*, Sydney: Allen and Unwin, 110–29.

Thayer, Carlyle A. (1995) 'Mono-organizational socialism and the state', in Benedict J. Tria Kerkvliet and Doug J. Porter (eds) *Vietnam's Rural Transformation*, Boulder, CO: Westview Press, 39–64.

Thayer, Carlyle A. (1997a) 'Force modernization: the case of the Vietnam People's Army', *Contemporary Southeast Asia*, 19, 1: 1–28.

Thayer, Carlyle A. (1997b) 'Vietnam and ASEAN: a first anniversary assessment', *Southeast Asian Affairs*, Singapore: Institute of Southeast Asian Studies, 364–74.

Thayer, Carlyle A. (1997c) 'The regularisation of politics revisited: continuity and change in the Party's Central Committee, 1976–96', paper presented at 49th Annual Meeting, Association for Asian Studies, Chicago, 13–16 March.

Thayer, Carlyle A. (2000) 'Review of authority relations and economic decision making in Vietnam: an historical perspective', *Contemporary Southeast Asia*, 22: 425–42.

Thayer, Carlyle A. (2001) 'The Vietnam People's Army as a constituency in the political system of the Socialist Republic of Vietnam', paper delivered at Catholic University of America, Washington, DC, to a Conference on 'Prospects for the constituencies of Vietnam in changing times', November.

Thayer, Carlyle A. and Ramses Amer (1999) 'Conclusion', in Carlyle A. Thayer and Ramses Amer (eds) *Vietnamese Foreign Policy in Transition*, Singapore: Institute of Southeast Asian Studies, 215–32.

Thomas, Mandy (2001) 'Public spaces/public disgraces: crowds and the state in contemporary Vietnam', *Sojourn*, 16: 306–30.

Thornton, Emily (1995) 'Yield to traffic', *Far Eastern Economic Review*, 19 October: 82–5.

Thrift, Nigel J. and Dean K. Forbes (1985) 'Cities, socialism and war: Hanoi, Saigon and the Vietnamese experience of urbanization', *Environment and Planning D: Society and Space*, 3: 279–308.

Toan Anh (1999) *Nep Cu Lang Xom Viet Nam [Old Customs of Vietnamese Villages and Hamlets]*, Ho Chi Minh City: Ho Chi Minh City Publishing.

Tonneson, Stein (1993) *Democracy in Vietnam?*, Copenhagen: Nordic Institute of Asian Studies.

Tosel, André (1995) 'Sur quelques distinctions gramsciennes. Economie et politique: société civile et état', *La Pensée*, n°301, 69–80.

Tran Bach Dang (2000) 'Vai suy nghi ve ngoai giao Viet Nam buoc vao the ky moi' [Some thoughts about Vietnamese diplomacy entering a new millennium], *Quoc Te*, 28 August: 8.

Tran Dinh Thanh Lam (2002) 'Education – Vietnam: college reforms off to a clunky start', Inter Press Service, 13 February.

Tran Le (2000) 'Cong nghe bao quan xa voi' [The long road to processing technologies], *Thoi Bao Kinh Te Viet Nam [Viet Nam Economic Times]*, 8, 19 January: 5.

Tran Ngoc Danh (1949) *Tieu-su Ho Chu-tich [Biography of Chairman Ho]*, France: Chi Hoi Lien-Viet Tai Phap.

Tran Quang Co (1995) 'Tuong lai cua cac quan he giua Viet Nam va cac nuoc chau A-Thai Binh Duong: tac dong den phat trien cua Viet Nam' [Future of the relationships between Vietnam and Asia-Pacific countries: impact on economic development of

Vietnam], in Bo Ngoai Giao [Ministry of Foreign Affairs] (ed.) *Hoi Nhap Quoc te Va Giu Vung Ban Sac [International Integration and National Identity Preservation]*, Ha Noi: Chinh Tri Quoc Gia Publishing, 103–14.

Tran Thi Que, Nguyen Thi Hong Phan and Tran Dang Tuan (1996) *Population Data of Sparsely Populated Areas in Vietnam*, Hanoi: Statistical Publishing House.

Tran Tu (1996) *Nguoi Muong o Hoa Binh* [The Muong in Hoa Binh], Hanoi: Vietnamese Historical Association.

Trinh Duy Luan (2000) 'Su Phan tang Xa hoi trong Qua trinh Phat trien Kinh te theo Co che Thi truong' [Social stratification in the process of economic development in the market mechanism], in Ha Huy Thanh (ed.) *Nhung tac dong tieu cuc cua co che kinh te thi truong o Viet Nam [Negative Impacts of the Market Economic Mechanism in Vietnam]*, Hanoi: Khoa Hoc Xa Hoi Publishers, 39–75.

Truong Chinh (1963) 'The August revolution' (facsimile edition) in Bernard Fall (ed.) *Primer for Revolt: The Communist Takeover in Viet-Nam*, London: Frederick A. Praeger, 1–80.

Truong, David H.D. (1998) 'Striving towards *doi moi* II', *Southeast Asian Affairs 1998*, Singapore: Institute of Southeast Asian Studies, 328–39.

Turley, William S. (1980) 'Political participation and the Vietnamese Communist Party', in William S. Turley (ed.) *Vietnamese Communism in Comparative Perspective*, Boulder, CO: Westview Press, 171–98.

Turley, William S. (1993a) 'Introduction', in William S. Turley and Mark Selden (eds) *Reinventing Vietnamese Socialism*, Boulder, CO: Westview Press, 1–15.

Turley, William S. (1993b) 'Political renovation in Vietnam: renewal and adaptation', in Borje Ljunggren (ed.) *The Challenge of Reform in Indochina*, Cambridge, MA: Harvard Institute for International Development, Harvard University Press, 327–48.

Turner, Robert (1975) *Vietnamese Communism: Its Origins and Development*, Stanford, CA: Hoover Institution Press.

Umbach, Frank (2000) 'ASEAN and major powers: Japan and China – a changing balance of power?', in Jörn Dosch and Manfred Mols (eds) *International Relations of the Asia-Pacific: New Patterns of Power, Interest and Cooperation*, Münster and New York: Lit and St Martin's Press, 171–214.

UNCTAD (1998) *World Investment Report 1998: Trends and Determinants*, New York: UN.

UNCTAD (2000a) *World Investment Report 2000*, New York: UN.

UNCTAD (2000b) *World Investment Directory, Vol. 7, Asia and the Pacific*, New York: UN.

UNCTAD (2000c) *Vietnamese Economy Boosted by FDI*, note to correspondents, 15 November.

UNDP (1996) *Catching Up: Capacity Development for Poverty Elimination in Viet Nam*, Hanoi: UNDP and UNICEF.

UNDP (2000a) 'Vietnam Disasters Management Unit' (http://www.undp.org.vn/dmu.dm-invietnam/en/institutional_framework.htm).

UNDP (2000b) *Human Development Report 2000*, New York: UNDP and Oxford University Press.

UNDP (2001a) *Modernizing Governance in Viet Nam*, Hanoi: UNDP.

UNDP (2001b) *Vietnam in ASEAN: Regional Integration Process and Challenges*, Hanoi: UNDP.

UNDP (2003) *Human Development Report*, New York: Oxford University Press.

UNESCO, MoET and UNDP (1992) *Education and Human Resources Sector Analysis*, Hanoi: MoET.

Unger, E.S. (1991) 'Media and society: social change in Vietnam since 1986', in Dean Forbes, T.H. Hull, D.G. Marr and B. Brogan (eds) *Doi Moi: Vietnam's Renovation Policy and Performance*, Canberra: Department of Political and Social Change Monographs, ANU, 46–53.

UN (2002) *Human Development Report* (http://hdr.undp.org/reports/global/2002/en/indicator/indicator.cfm?file=index.html).

UN and MoLISA (1999) *Basic Social Services in Vietnam: An Analysis of State and ODA Expenditures*, Hanoi: UN in Vietnam.

United States Pacific Command (2002) 'Volume 2: connecting economics to security', *Asia-Pacific Economic Update*, Honolulu: USPACOM.

Uy Ban Cong Tac Ve Cac To Chuc Phi Chinh Phu Nuoc Ngoai (2002) 'Bao Cao Tong Ket Muoi Nam Cong Tac Vien Tro Cua Cac To Chuc Phi Chinh Phu Nuoc Ngoai Tai Viet Nam' [Evaluation of aid activities of foreign NGOs in Vietnam], Hanoi.

Van Anh, Tran Thi and Hung, Le Ngoc Hung (1997) *Women and Doi Moi in Vietnam*, Hanoi: Woman's Publishing House.

Vandermeersch, Léon (1986) *Le nouveau Monde sinisé*, Paris: Perspectives Internationales coll., Presses Universitaires de France, 224.

Vietnam 1998–1999 (1999), Hanoi: The Goi Publishers.

Vietnam Corporate Philanthropy Workshop (1998) Co-sponsored by the US-Indochina Reconciliation Project, the American Express Foundation, and The Vietnam Union of Friendship Organizations, January 13, 18.

Vietnam Economic Times (2001) 'Government's overseas education scholarships offered to elite employees', published on *Vietnam Forum* (http://groups.yahoo.com/group/vnforum" —http://groups.yahoo.com/group/vnforum), 10 May.

Vietnam News (1999) 'Young scientists will get state funds to study in the world's advanced countries', *Vietnam Forum* (http://groups.yahoo.com/group/vnforum; http://groups.yahoo.com/group/vnforum), 1 September.

Vietnam Trade Information Center (1998) *Directory of Foreign Investment Projects in Vietnam by National Economic Activities 1996–1997* (bilingual), Hanoi: VTIC, Statistical Publishing House.

Vo Nguyen Giap (1995) *Chien dau trong Vong vay, Hoi uc [Fighting in the Encircled Zone: Memoirs]*, Hanoi: Quan Doi Nhan Dan.

Vo Nhan Tri (1992) *Vietnam's Economic Policy since 1975*, Singapore: Institute of Southeast Asian Studies.

Vo Than Son, Truong Thi Kim Nguyen Doan Thuan Hoa Nguyen Thi Thuy (2001) 'School enrollments and drop outs', in Dominique Haughton, Jonathan Haughton and Nguyen Phuong (eds) *Living Standards During an Economic Boom: The Case of Vietnam*, Hanoi: General Statistics Office and UNDP.

Vo Thanh Thu and Ngo Thi Ngoc Huyen (2000) *Ky thuat Dau tu Truc tiep Nuoc Ngoai tai Viet Nam* [Manual of Foreign Direct Investment in Vietnam], Hanoi: Thong Ke Publishing.

Vu Thu Hien (1997) *Dem Giua ban ngay [Darkness at Noon]*, Germany: Thien Chi Publishing.

Vu Trieu Minh (1997) 'Nhung Yeu To Anh Huong den Muc Chi Tieu trong Ho Gia Dinh Vietnam' [The factors affecting expense rates among Vietnamese families], *Xa Hoi Hoc [Sociology]*, January 1997, Hanoi: Institute of Sociology, 54–63.

Vu Tuan Anh (1995) 'Economic policy reform: an introductory overview', in Irene Norlund, Carolyn Gates and Vu Cao Dam (eds) *Vietnam in a Changing World*, Richmond: Curzon Press, 17–30.

Wain, Barry (1990) 'Vietnamese find political taboos fading', *Asian Wall Street Journal*, 13 June.

Wank, David L. (1995) 'Civil society in communist society: private business and political alliances, 1989', in J.A. Hall (ed.) *Civil Society, Theory, History, Comparison*, Cambridge: Polity Press, 56–79.

Watts, Michael J. (1998) 'Recombinant capitalism: state, de-collectivisation and the agrarian question in Vietnam', in Adrian Smith and John Pickles (eds) *Theorising Transition*, London: Routledge, 451–505.

Weber, Max (1930/1995) *The Protestant Ethic and the Spirit of Capitalism*, Talcott Parsons (trans.), introduction by Anthony Giddens, London and New York: Routledge.

Webster, Leila (1999) 'SMEs in Vietnam: on the road to prosperity', *Private Sector Discussion Paper No. 10*, Hanoi: MPDF.

Webster, Leila and Markus Taussig (1999) 'Vietnam's undersized engine: a survey of 95 larger private manufacturers', *Private Sector Discussion Paper No. 8*, Hanoi: MPDF.

Werner, Jayne (1988) 'The problem of the district in Vietnam development policy', in David G. Marr and Christine P. White (eds) *Postwar Vietnam: Dilemmas in Socialist Development*, Ithaca, NY: SEAP, Cornell University, 147–62.

Wilczynski, Jozef (1981) *An Encyclopedic Dictionary of Marxism, Socialism and Communism*, Basingstoke: Macmillan.

Will, Gerhard (1999) 'China und Vietnam – Chancen und Grenzen einer bilateralen Kooperation' [China and Vietnam – opportunities for and limits to bilateral co-operation], in Duy Tu Vu and Gerhard Will (eds) *Vietnams neue Position in Südostasien [Vietnam's New Position in Southeast Asia]*, Hamburg: Institut für Asienkunde, 287–308.

Wischermann, Joerg, Bui The Cuong and Nguyen Quang Vinh (2002) 'The relationship between societal organizations and governmental organizations in Viet Nam – selected findings of an empirical survey', paper presented to the workshop The Relationship between Societal Organizations and Governmental Organizations in Vietnam, Institute of Sociology, National Center for Social Sciences and Humanities, Hanoi, 14, 24.

Womack, Brantley (1992) 'Reform in Vietnam: backwards towards the future', *Government and Opposition*, 27: 177–89.

World Bank (1993) *Viet Nam: Transition to Market*, Washington, DC: World Bank.

World Bank (1994) *Vietnam Public Sector Management and Private Sector Initiatives: An Economic Report*, Report No. 13143-VN, Washington, DC: World Bank.

World Bank (1995) *Vietnam: Economic Report on Industrialization and Industrial Policy*, Report No. 14645-VN, Washington, DC: World Bank.

World Bank (1996) *Vietnam Fiscal Decentralisation and the Delivery of Rural Services*, Washington, DC: World Bank.

World Bank (1997a) *Foreign Capital Flows in Vietnam: Trend, Impact, and Policy Implications*, background paper, Hanoi: World Bank.

World Bank (1997b) *Vietnam: Deepening Reform for Growth: An Economic Report*. Report No. 17031-VN, 31 October, Washington, DC: World Bank.

World Bank (1999a) *Attacking Poverty: Vietnam Development Report 2000*, Hanoi: Government-Donor-NGO Working Group.

World Bank (1999b) *Preparing for Take-off? How Vietnam can Participate Fully in the East Asian Recovery*, Hanoi: World Bank.

World Bank (2000) *Vietnam: Macro-Economic Update*, Hanoi: World Bank.

World Bank (2001a) *Vietnam Development Report 2002: Implementing Reforms for Faster Growth and Poverty Reduction*, Hanoi: World Bank.

World Bank (2001b) *Putting Partnerships to Work in Vietnam*, Hanoi: World Bank.

World Bank (2001c) *Vietnam: Growing Healthy*, Hanoi: World Bank.

World Bank (2002) *Vietnam Economic Monitor: Spring 2002*, Hanoi: World Bank.

World Bank and ADB (2002) *Vietnam Development Report 2003: Vietnam delivering on its promises*, Hanoi: World Bank and ADB.

World Bank, ADB and UNDP (2000a) 'Volume 1: pillars of development', *Vietnam 2010 Entering the 21st Century: Vietnam Development Report 2001*, Hanoi: World Bank, ADB and UNDP.

World Bank, ADB and UNDP (2000b) 'Volume 2: partnerships for development', *Vietnam 2010 Entering the 21st Century: Vietnam Development Report 2001*, Hanoi: World Bank, ADB and UNDP.

World Bank, ADB and UNDP (2000c) 'Volume 3: overview', *Vietnam 2010 Entering the 21st Century: Vietnam Development Report 2001*, Hanoi: World Bank, ADB and UNDP.

World Bank, ADB and UNDP (2000d) *Vietnam 2010 Entering the 21st Century: Vietnam Development Report 2001*, Hanoi: World Bank, ADB and UNDP.

Wylie, Raymond (1980) *The Emergence of Maoism*, Stanford, CA: Stanford University.

Yeonsik Jeong (1997) 'The rise of state corporatism in Vietnam', *Contemporary Southeast Asia*, 19: 153–71.

Youth in Vietnam (2000) Hanoi: Youth Publishing House.

Zinoman, Peter (2001) *The Colonial Bastille*, Berkeley, CA: University of California Press.

Periodicals

Vietnam Economic Times (various issues, as indicated in the text).

Vietnam Investment Review (various issues, as indicated in the text).

Newspapers

Dien Dan [Vietnam Forum], monthly newspaper, Paris.

Far Eastern Economic Review.

Primary sources

Centre d'Archives d'Outre-Mer (CAOM).

Collection: Service de Protection du Corps expéditionnaire (SPCE).

Russian State Archive for Modern History (RGANI) formerly the Russian Center for the Study of Documents of Contemporary History.

Russian State Archive for Social-Political History (RGASPI) Moscow, formerly the Russian Center for the Preservation and Study of Documents of Modern History Collection: 495, The Comintern 542, The Anti-Imperialist League.

Service Historique de l'Armée de Terre, Vincennes (SHAT).

Service de liaison avec des originaires des Territoires d'Outre-Mer (SLOTFOM).

Index